Napoleon's Second Empress

Also by Patrick Turnbull

ONE BULLET FOR THE GENERAL
THE FOREIGN LEGION

MARIE LOUISE

Archiduchesse d'Autriche, Impératrice des Français,

Née à Vienne, le 12 Décembre 1791.

Marie Louise Archduchess of Austria

Napoleon's Second Empress

PATRICK TURNBULL

WALKER AND COMPANY ● New York

First published in the United States of America in 1972 by the Walker Publishing Company, Inc.

ISBN: 0-8027-0376-3

Library of Congress Catalog Card Number: 77-183925

Printed in the United States of America from type set in the United Kingdom.

Illustrations

Acknowledgements

My thanks are due to the following for permission to quote from works in which they hold the copyright: George Allen & Unwin Ltd, for *Marie Louise* by E. M. Oddie, and *Daily Life in France under Napoleon* (*La Vie Quotidienne au Temps de Napoléon*) by Jean Robiquet; La Bibliothèque Nationale de France, for *Lettres Inédites de Napoléon À Marie Louise* (1810–1814) by Louis Madelin; Flammarion et cie, for *Napoléon* by Octave Aubry; Hachette, for *La Vie Privée de Marie Louise* by Raymonde Bessard, and *Napoléon En Campagne* by Marcel Dupont; Hamish Hamilton Ltd, for *Napoleon's Son* (*L'Aiglon*) by André Castelot; and John Murray (Publishers) Ltd, for *The Private Diaries of Marie Louise* edited by Lady Thompson.

Introduction

A study of any contemporary portrait of the emperor Francis II*
of Austria gives the impression of a sad, deeply thoughtful man,
whose long aquiline nose, high forehead, large vaguely almond-
shaped yet sunken eyes, and highly-pronounced cheekbones
projecting through pallid tightly-drawn skin, suggest the humourless intellectual. Only one feature is out of keeping with this
picture of general asceticism: the typical Habsburg mouth,
sensuously overfull with the weak, drooping underlip.

Direct descendant of seventeen generations of Habsburgs,
beginning with Rudolph I who, in 1273, was elected German
king and Holy Roman Emperor Francis, on acceding to the
Austrian throne in 1792 at the age of twenty-four, could lay
claim to one of the longest family trees of any European monarch.

From so long a line of imperial ancestors he inherited an almost
terrifying mental rigidity. He believed in the divine right of
kings, in the principle of blind obedience to the emperor from
the humblest citizen to the highest of the royal family – including
the empress. When one of his brothers mentioned 'the people',
he said, 'People? I only have subjects.' His catholicism was
equally rigid and direct, not admitting of the least deviation in
practice. Loathing the idea of change, it was natural that from
the very first he looked upon the French revolution and its
principles as scourges sent by God to punish mankind for its sins.
Nor was it surprising that his hatred of France and the French
became personal as well as theoretical from the day the guillotine
fell on the slender neck of his aunt, Marie Antoinette, and her
head was bloodily displayed to the Paris mob.

* Francis succeeded his father, Leopold II, as Roman Germanic emperor,
Francis II. After the defeat of Austerlitz and the subsequent Peace of
Presburg when the Holy Roman Empire, as such, was abolished, he became
Francis I of Austria.

However, this pillar of traditionalism and rectitude possessed one human frailty to an exaggerated degree. 'This pious man, full of religious scruples, is a terrible husband. He wants his wife with him constantly, he never leaves her, he obsesses her and, morally, tortures her. Not that he is a bad man. It is simply that the idea of a mistress shocks him when, in actual fact, he needs many. Indeed, he is such a faithful husband that he is a wife killer . . .'*

Over-sexed but never realising for one moment, even in the reminiscent wisdom of old age, that his over-attention killed his first three wives as effectively as if he had poisoned them, he believed implicitly that 'marriage was ordained for the procreation of children', and considered that the larger the family the more firmly were the Habsburg roots dug into the throne not only of Austria but, tentacle-like, into those of contemporary Europe.

He certainly had excellent examples to imitate. Both his famous grandmother, Maria Theresa, and the Emperor Leopold II had families of sixteen and, thanks to diplomatic marriages, Habsburg blood ran in the veins of the royal houses of France, Naples, Parma, Saxony, Modena and Bavaria.

Imbued with this worship of fecundity, allied to his natural desires and intensely uxorious character, Francis embarked on matrimony at the age of twenty with Elizabeth of Würtemburg. She was not able to resist his amorous assaults for more than two years. Though Francis appeared weighed down with sorrow by Elizabeth's death, he was quite unable to do without a bed companion. Within six months of finding himself a widower he married his cousin, Maria Theresa of Bourbon Sicily, on September 19th 1790.

Maria Theresa was more robust physically than her predecessor. She came of a tough family, especially through her mother, Maria Carolina, daughter of the great Empress Maria Theresa. When Maria Theresa produced her first child, a daughter, Maria Carolina wrote congratulating her on being 'so sensible and brave when your time came upon you, for uncontrolled groans do not help pain and cause those present sorrow and disgust. One must put up with the evil for the pleasure of being a mother.'

The daughter to whose birth on December 12th 1791, the queen of Naples was referring was christened Maria-Luisa

* Frédéric Masson, *Marie Louise Impératrice de France*. Société d'éditions Littéraires et Artistiques, Paris, 1910.

Leopoldine Caroline Lucie who, just over eighteen years later, was to become the second wife of Napoleon and reign for four brief years in Paris as the empress Marie Louise.

As for Maria Theresa, she was to have plenty of experience of the 'evil' and 'pleasure' quoted by her mother. She died, in childbirth, on April 13th 1807, but not before she had filled the imperial nursery with thirteen children. In fact, but for several miscarriages, she might have equalled the record of the great empress after whom she had been named.

Once more, on the death of his second wife, Francis was prostrate with grief but, again, not many months had passed before the impossibility of celibacy was making him determined to embark on a third matrimonial venture.

In 1807 members of a number of ruling families had been chased out of their possessions by Napoleon. Most of those dispossessed took refuge in Vienna much as, one hundred and thirty-three years later, those driven from thrones or presidencies by Hitler fled to London. Amongst these refugees were the duke and duchess of Modena with their youngest and unmarried daughter, Maria Ludovica Beatrix.

When Maria Theresa died, Maria Ludovica was only just twenty, seventeen years younger than Francis and only five years older than Marie Louise. She was small, darkly pretty, brilliantly clever and ambitious, but fragile. Furthermore, her fragility was not a semi-fashionable pose. It was genuine, and she herself was perfectly aware of the fact. She was also fully aware of Francis' reputation as a wife-killer, and the reason for it. She should have known, and probably did, that for any girl or woman in her state of health, marriage with such a man was the equivalent of a protracted death sentence. But as soon as Francis shed a fraction of his profound melancholy and, in July, a bare three months after Maria Theresa's death, began to show an interest in her, she was determined that she and nobody else would be the third empress, for her ambition rode higher than self-preservation.

The marriage took place on January 8th 1808. The emperor's spell as a widower had not lasted nine months. Although, in principle, 'the King could do no wrong', Viennese society was profoundly shocked.

One of the few who was not was Maria Ludovica's eldest stepchild, delighted at the thought of a new *liebe mama* to enliven the Hofburg's none too cheerful apartments. It was a case of innate understanding. Marie Louise, though she was not to realise the fact for some years – indeed may never have done so since the individual of her time was stranger to the doctrines of psycho-analysis – had inherited her father's craving for the conjugal aspect of life.

Chapter I

Not even the sternest Victorian parent believed so firmly in the axiom 'Children should be seen but not heard' as did the Habsburgs. They carrried the principle still further. Not only were the imperial children never heard, they were seldom seen. From the moment of their birth, little archdukes were handed over to the care of tutors, the infant archduchesses to an *ayah* or governess. These almost foster parents played such an important role in the lives of the imperial children that Marie Louise always referred to her third *ayah*, Madame de Poutet,* who took over the post in 1799 when Marie Louise was eight years old and who, the same year, had married Count Colloredo (who had recommended her appointment),† as 'Mummy', while her own mother (and later her stepmother) were addressed and thought of as 'dear Mama'.

This 'Mummy' who played such an important role in Marie Louise's formative years was, strangely enough, French; a Folliot de Crenneville, a family of the minor aristocracy. Her first husband, Baron de Poutet, was colonel of a Walloon regiment. When he died, Madame de Poutet moved to Vienna with her daughter Victoria, born in 1789, who later became Marie Louise's life-long friend.

As Frédéric Masson says: 'Madame de Poutet, a widow, lacking neither the power to intrigue nor *savoir faire*, managed to become the legitimate wife of H.E. Count Colloredo-Walsee.' Her pre-marital relations with the count must have been intimate, as Masson seems to suggest, for it was before the marriage that she became an integral member of the imperial household.

It is quite possible that Countess Colloredo was a schemer. A widow's lot, especially that of a widow of minor aristocracy, was

* The previous *ayahs* were the Countess Maria-Anna of Wrbna (1791–1794), born Countess of Auersberg; and Countess Josepha de Chanclos (1794–1799).

† Colloredo's full titles were, His Excellency Count von Colloredo-Walsee, Minister of State, Head of Chancery, Grand Master of the emperor's Court. In spite of his autocratic nature, Francis was notoriously weak and hated making decisions. It was generally considered at the time that Colloredo was Austria's real ruler.

not altogether enviable. It was unlikely that the colonel was able to leave her much in the way of a fortune. She found herself, therefore, a sort of poor relation to all the world, exposed to snubs and humiliations particularly galling to a woman of her intelligence and initiative, and if, under the circumstances, she was able to persuade the count to change her status from mistress to legitimate wife, she is to be congratulated. In addition, she proved herself to be an almost perfect choice for the role of educating and forming the young archduchess.

Marie Louise adored both her and Victoria. And even when the countess was forced to resign her position as *ayah* and when, later, Marie Louise became empress of France, it was always to 'Mummy' or Victoria she poured out her thoughts in long letters.

The secret was that already, at the age of eight, Marie Louise was filled with a surfeit of affection which she had to lavish on someone. Because of prevailing etiquette it was not possible to be demonstrative with her parents. Had he not been emperor, Francis could have been a responsive father. He was being genuine when he said he 'adored children'. Later, in middle and old age, and when his children were grown up, he unbent, becoming more of a friend, especially to Marie Louise. But in the early years of his reign he was obsessed, dominated, by his position as emperor and the need to maintain the strictest near-feudal traditions throughout every facet of life, both public and private, while Maria Theresa's entire existence was so occupied by the trials of an unbroken series of pregnancies that she had no time to spare – even had she wished for it – to devote to the offspring she had already produced.

However, even if Marie Louise saw very little of her father and mother – almost godlike figures in her eyes – except on official occasions and rare formal visits to the nurseries, she was not allowed to forget that she was an archduchess, a person of considerable importance in her own right. Apart from her *ayah*, she had her own household: a lady-in-waiting, two ladies-of-the-wardrobe, a personal maid, five lackeys and her own personal washerwoman. She herself, though, was not allowed any contact with these 'servants'. All communications had to be addressed via the countess. She was not, because of her rank, allowed any friends other than Victoria, and, because of a dormant maturity, her brothers and sisters were too young to provide any real companionship.

The result was that her affection for Victoria, two years her senior, was a passion which lasted to the time of her first marriage, resolving itself then into an unbreakable, genuine friendship which today, when sexual aberrations are diagnosed so freely, might have been labelled lesbian; and which contemporary writers, and particularly those to whom she was anathema, described as 'unhealthy', *maladif*.

Whenever she was given a present – which was not often as the Austrian court was one of the poorest in Europe – she insisted on passing it on to Victoria. If Victoria went away, Marie Louise wrote to her every day: 'Is there anything you want? I'd like to give you everything I possess . . .' This excess of affection was also shown towards the countess herself, and the few occasions when Madame de Colloredo was allowed a brief holiday she was besieged by adoring letters in much the same vein – 'I wish I were your daughter, because you are such a good mother. I want to be just like Victoria, your real daughter . . .'

Although the countess was not displeased by her success or Marie Louise's passion for her daughter, she never let it go to her head and was astute enough not to try to exploit it, contenting herself trying to pass on some of her own erudition to a willing pupil.

Modern languages occupied the first place in the order of the young archduchess's studies. Francis insisted that his children be fluent in English, French, Spanish, Italian, Hungarian and Czech. Unlike most of his generation, he did not consider the classics as important. In addition, from the age of eight, general history – especially that of the Holy Roman Empire and the Habsburgs – geography, German literature, philosophy and a basic knowledge of the law were added to the syllabus. 'Her (Marie Louise) head,' comments Frédéric Masson, 'was stuffed with a mass of dates, facts, statistics, names and words, but not a single idea.'

When it came to literature, supervision was abnormally strict. It was taken for granted that the archduchesses would marry and present their husbands with the maximum number of children. But at the same time it was considered essential that they should go virgin not only in body but in mind to their husbands; that, in other words, they should be totally ignorant on their wedding day of what are known euphemistically as 'the facts of life'. So important was this considered that, to avoid even visual contamination, brothers and sisters were largely segregated.

There was no question, therefore, of Marie Louise having any say in the books which came into her hands. The countess was held personally responsible in this matter, and so as to make absolutely certain that she carried out her duties as censor with total efficiency it was not the proverbial blue pencil that she employed, but a pair of scissors. Any male figure, even the reproduction of a male statue protected by a miraculously stable fig leaf, any textual reference to male physiology, the physical side of love and human relationships, was ruthlessly cut out and the book, thus emasculated, passed to the empress herself for a final check. This concern over 'innocence' was carried to even further extremes. Marie Louise was a great animal lover. She was far happier in the summer palace, Schoenbrunn, set in its huge park, than in the city residence, the dark and gloomy Hofburg. Her greatest joy was to be allowed to play in her toy farm stocked with live creatures – rabbits, geese, ducks, chickens – and her own little bitch. These pets were, naturally enough, loved and pampered, and it is doubtful whether any of them met with the normal end of their species by appearing on the nursery dining table. On the other hand they had to pay for their security by leading frustrating, unnatural lives for, the reverse of Mount Athos, no male bird or animal was permitted to disturb the farm's zenana-like atmosphere.

Under normal circumstances, Marie Louise's childhood could have been totally untroubled. She was a very happy little girl. From her earliest days she showed a marked streak of naivety in her psychological make-up. The simpler pleasures delighted her: walks in the Schoenbrunn park, drives in the Prater's – the forest almost in Vienna's heart reserved for imperial hunts – alleys, her toy farm, the occasions when ceremoniously she was allowed to go through the gestures, under strict supervision, of baking a cake later to be shared with Victoria. This easy contentment was further helped by her natural piety. From the time she could think, she believed implicitly that life was directed by God's will setting a path from which there could be no deviation. This 'will', to which blind obedience was owed, was made known on earth by God's representative: His Most Catholic Majesty, her father, the emperor Francis II. It was all very simple. And such was her piety that after her first communion in 1803 she asked very sadly – as it would have been such a treat – if she could be excused from staying up for Christmas midnight mass as she was afraid she was too tired to pray with true understanding.

The veil of unreality surrounding the imperial children did not, however, cover the political scene. At an early age, soon after being taught about God, Marie Louise also learnt about the Devil. It was impressed on her that the Power of Evil, too, had a representative on earth, that his name was Bonaparte and his disciples the people of a country called France. Countess Colloredo, virulent anti-republican, thoroughly enjoyed imparting this knowledge and driving home the facts. She delighted in horrifying Marie Louise with lurid details of great-aunt Marie Antoinette's execution, and the horrors of her imprisonment before mounting the scaffold's steps. The creature Bonaparte, she was told, had a marked physical resemblance to the Devil of old masters. Undoubtedly she pictured him sprouting a forked tail and disclosing cloven hoofs when he removed his boots.

No attempt was made to hide the 'temporary' triumphs gained in recent years by the Forces of Evil. She was told of the Peace of Campo Formio and the Congress of Rastatt, both in 1797, entailing the loss of Lombardy, the Netherlands and the left bank of the Rhine, how her grandmother Maria Carolina, chased from her throne now occupied by one of Bonaparte's sisters, was a refugee in Vienna, of the duke of Enghien's murder. Even more horrifying were the tales of 'the Corsican's' godlessness; the banning of the Church in France, the massacre of priests and nuns, the sacking of cathedrals and monasteries by Bonaparte's soldiers. She loved quoting a story, told her by the countess, of Bonaparte's cynicism in Egypt and how '. . . he saved himself after his army had been destroyed with only two or three others by becoming a Turk, that is to say he said to them (the Egyptians), "I'm a Moslem and I recognise Mahomet as the great Prophet," but when he got back to France he pretended he was a Catholic and it was only then he was made First Consul . . .'

In 1805, when Marie Louise was fourteen, this theoretical evil – theoretical, that is, as far as she was concerned – assumed suddenly a terrifying reality.

Abandoning the idea of invading England, Napoleon, by then ten months an emperor, decided to turn against the Austro-Russian coalition. The subsequent campaign was, in many ways, his most brilliant.

Having concentrated round Strasbourg, the French army crossed the Rhine on September 27th and advanced so rapidly that General Mack with his 80,000 Austrians was forced back to, and besieged in, Ulm. On October 20th, after offering only a feeble resistance, Mack surrendered. Leaving a handful of men to guard the prisoners, Napoleon covered the distance from Ulm to Vienna in just under three weeks. The Austrian imperial family, not setting a very inspiring example, fled from the threatened capital which surrendered in turn on November 13th. What was left of the Austrian army fled north to join forces with the Russians. First enjoying the luxury of a couple of nights in Schoenbrunn palace, Napoleon then rode north on the Austrians' heels. Though outnumbered, he met and totally defeated the combined Austro-Russian army at Austerlitz on December 2nd. The allied losses were disastrous: 23,000 killed and wounded, 20,000 prisoners. A peace treaty was signed on Boxing Day at Presburg. By this treaty Francis lost all his Italian lands and another four million subjects and was obliged to bleed his country to pay a forty-million war indemnity.

Throughout the late summer and early autumn, Marie Louise had known that war was inevitable. Not having the least idea of the meaning of war, she was delighted. This time, she was quite convinced, the Almighty would be on Papa's side. Countess Colloredo, well informed by her husband who, indeed, was the leader of the pro-war clique, added that from the practical side victory was a certainty since the combined Austro-Russian army would outnumber the French by three to one.

In August, when Vienna was in the grip of a war fever induced by hysterical optimism, so often the prelude to a campaign, the teen-age archduchess was taken for a drive in an open carriage sitting opposite her father, resplendent in the white uniform of an Austrian field-marshal, to see the streamer-hung streets and listen to the crowds' wild cheers. Francis, always convinced that his subjects adored him and deeply touched – despite his belief that an unbridgeable abyss separated him from the ordinary run of mortals – by manifestations of their loyal affection, had tears in his eyes when he unbent to the extent of raising his hand in acknowledgement.

'There is no doubt,' Marie Louise wrote in her diary, 'that papa will win in the end, and at last the moment will come when the "Usurper" will be discomfited. Perhaps God has allowed him

(Napoleon) to get so far that when He abandons him, all will be lost . . .'

Vienna's belligerent enthusiasm did not long survive the outbreak of hostilities, although once it was known that the French were across the Rhine the usual 'victory' bulletins were published. The Viennese, however, are and always have been able to think for themselves and it was not long before it was realised that there was something abnormal about these victories, for a glance at the map showed that each place name mentioned brought the 'defeated' French so many leagues nearer the capital.

Francis, of course, who unlike most monarchs of the day had not taken command of his army, was not duped by these bulletins. Any slight illusions he might have entertained as regards the situation's gravity were finally shattered by the arrival of one of his younger brothers, the archduke Ferdinand who, disgusted by Mack's feebleness, had placed himself at the head of a picked cavalry force and literally hacked his way through the French lines. Ferdinand argued that now Austria's one hope of salvation lay in a rapid link-up with the slow-moving Russians, and that meant giving up Vienna.

Francis agreed with his brother's summing-up. For once he took an independent decision. With all available troops, abandoning the capital to its fate, he would move north to Moravia to meet the czar and Kutusov then, turning about, the Austro-Russians would fall on Napoleon's tired army with overwhelming force.

The royal family in its entirety must, of course, leave Vienna. Francis did not fear that falling into Napoleon's hands would endanger their lives – the early nineteenth century had not reached that state of civilisation epitomised by the mid-twentieth and the wholesale massacre of leaders of defeated nations; on the other hand he did not relish the idea of their being used as bargaining handles in any future peace negotiations.

Young as she was, Marie Louise had sensed the sudden change from wild optimism to mute pessimism. Even a *Te Deum* in the Hofburg Chapel to thank God for Nelson's victory at Trafalgar could not attenuate the fact that defeat at sea was having no effect on the rapidity of Napoleon's advance on land. Countess Colloredo was doubly perturbed. She knew that if, by chance she became a prisoner, she would not be judged kindly as the wife of a Frenchman who had sold himself completely to the 'enemy'. She probably thought a great deal of the duke of Enghien and of the fact that it was her husband who had been largely instrumental in persuading Francis to embark on this war of revenge which had started off so inauspiciously.

Early one late November morning, there was an unusual bustle in the Hofburg. The quiet corridors were filled with movement. Footsteps echoed. Running to her window, Marie Louise saw a string of heavy Berlins crowding the courtyard. Under Countess Colloredo's instructions maids were packing, not in the leisurely manner preceding a move to the Schoenbrunn but with a speed that carried a suggestion of panic. When asked what was afoot, the countess did not mince her words. The 'Corsican ogre' was approaching Vienna. His armies were, apparently, invincible. The only answer was flight from a city already doomed. Where? Anywhere! To Moscow if necessary.

Before midday they were on the road.

It was flight: an ignominious flight and, for the first time, Marie Louise was confronted by life's terrors combined with acute physical discomfort.

The great Berlins were not built for speed, even though drawn by a team of six horses. And since the refugees, as they could be called, were haunted by the thought of Murat's famous and dreaded light cavalry screen operating far ahead of the main body of the French army, distances had to be covered entailing hour after hour of lumbering, jolting progress, whatever the weather, over bone-shaking tracks. Not only had the extreme fatigue of each daily stage to be endured, but the fact that this was no pre-arranged imperial tour meant that nightly accommodation had to be taken as it was found. There was no question of a succession of castles, eager hosts, swarms of servants. Often the imperial cortège was forced to halt for the night at some wayside inn completely ungeared to such high-ranking guests. The meals would be of a stark simplicity, inferior in quality, the beds primitive and not in the least conducive to dreamless sleep. Frequently the young archdukes and duchesses found themselves sharing their mattresses with bugs and fleas who were no respecters of protocol.

It was during this flight, however, that Marie Louise displayed an unexpected and, it must be admitted, short-lived toughness. For the first time, she and her brothers and sisters were gaining practical knowledge of a world beyond the confines of palaces and royal parks, of the existence of dirt, poor food, weariness, latent physical danger. There was nothing gradual about this process; no stages of transition. It would not have been surprising if these misadventures had reduced them all to a pitiable helplessness. Marie Louise, however, accepted her role as eldest child with a complete natural dignity and herself assumed the task of keeping them all in good heart. She revealed a physical and moral toughness as well as a most unexpected sense of humour, announcing triumphantly, when a flea hunt had been successful, that she had killed a Napoleon.

The early days of 1806 saw a dispirited return to Vienna. True, normal existence was renewed, but Marie Louise was acutely aware of the humiliation imposed by the treaty of Presburg and worse of a deep sense of personal loss since one of the defeat's many victims was the countess of Colloredo.

Undoubtedly the count had strongly advocated war, but the ultimate decision was, after all, Francis's. But since the Austrian monarch ruled by divine right he could do no wrong and, since scapegoat there must be, Count Colloredo was the obvious designate. Deprived of his court functions, he was 'invited' to retire to his country estates. At the same time the countess was tactfully informed that, under the circumstances, it might be better if she asked to be relieved of her post as *ayah* to the archduchess and, with her daughter, join her husband in the country.

Marie Louise's distress was pathetic. She was losing not only her 'Mummy' but her only friend whom she adored. There was only one consolation. Francis was never vindictive. It is more than likely that the political necessity of dismissing the count was distasteful to him. He raised no objections to Marie Louise keeping up a correspondence with the exiles. She clung to this link. From then on every event in her life formed the subject of letters of almost novella length. The habit remained with her till her death, through triumph and vicissitude. Almost her last letter before her final brief illness, forty-two years later, was addressed to Victoria, then countess of Crenneville, and it was to Victoria that Albertine, Marie Louise's daughter, wrote immediately after her mother's death – '*Providence has struck us a cruel blow* . . .'

Sympathetically believing that hard work was the best antidote for Marie Louise's grief, the empress, though pregnant as usual, decided to take her education in hand personally. From then on, for the next eighteen months, the young archduchess's life stretched in a vista of remorseless study, relieved by a bare minimum of recreation. The new *ayah*, Madame Faber, was governess in name only, and it was not until 1807, when the empress seemed to have a premonition that her next labour would be her last, that this imperial supervision was relaxed and Madame Faber replaced by Countess Lazanski, née (in her own right) Countess Falkenhayn.

Sadly enough, Marie Louise never felt really at ease in her mother's presence, and the empress herself, more conjugal than maternal, never unbent with her children. 'I am going to ask my mother today for her blessing,' Marie Louise wrote to Victoria. 'It will make me very happy. I would be happier still if she would embrace me, but I don't dare to expect such a favour . . .'

Describing the long working days, Masson says: 'Lessons were no longer brightened by amusing observations; the day, strictly regulated, consisted of silent hour after hour of needlework, embroidery, knitting, of history and literature, of drawing and music . . . It was a merciful release when Madame Lazanski took over from the failing empress, and when she (the empress) died. If Marie Louise grieved, as a well brought up daughter should under the circumstances, it was not because of loss of an affection, a tenderness she had never known, but because of the sombre apanage of death itself . . .'

One thing, however, remained ingrained in Marie Louise's heart: hatred of France and her emperor. This hate had plenty to feed on.

After Austerlitz, rulers of vast territories nominally under Francis's domination, were kicked off their thrones to make way for Napoleon's relations in an unrestrained access of nepotism. The elector of Bavaria was raised to the dignity of king, and obliged to marry his daughter to Napoleon's stepson, Eugène de Beauharnais, while the prince of Baden was ordered to marry Stephanie, Eugène's cousin. Murat, husband of Caroline Bonaparte, was made grand duke of Burg. Jerome – the Benjamin of the Bonaparte family – was forced to repudiate his American wife in order to marry Catherine of Würtemburg, eventually becoming king of Westphalia; while Louis, married to Hortense de Beauharnais, was forced unwillingly to accept the throne of Holland. For the next few years the only good news, as far as

Marie Louise was concerned, came from Spain, and from the Russo-Polish frontiers when it was put about that the terrible battles of Eylau and Friedland, though trumpeted by French propaganda as crushing victories, had, in fact, fringed disaster and at best could be termed Pyrrhic.

This hatred was still further fanned by the arrival of a step-mother in the Hofburg, whose detestation of the Bonapartes approached mania. Maria Ludovica, the new empress and Francis's third wife, was Marie Louise's cousin, and only five years older than her stepdaughter. Few individuals had more reason to hate Napoleon. Her father, Archduke Ferdinand, one of the great Maria Theresa's later children, had been governor of Milan and, married to Maria Beatrix Riccarda of Este-Modena, had been about to take over the duchy of Modena when he was chased out of his possessions by the French and obliged to settle with a sort of poor-relation status in Neustadt. In addition, Maria Ludovica's eldest sister, Maria Theresa – there were nine children in the family – had married Victor Emmanuel, King of Sardinia. She, too, victim of French aggression, was living in comparative poverty in Cagliari while another sister, the dowager electress of the Palatinate, had been deprived of her possessions by the Treaty of Lunéville. On top of all this her father, who eventually moved to Vienna, had died so everyone said, and as he himself affirmed on his death-bed, of grief attributable to the depredations of the 'abominable Corsican'.

Yet, in spite of this spiritual link, Maria Ludovica had little time for the eldest of her thirteen stepchildren. She was intensely vivacious, alert, overwhelmingly ambitious – it was the only reason she accepted Francis's offer of marriage – and basically independent, by nature the antithesis of Marie Louise, whose somewhat ovine qualities and total submissiveness were a constant irritation. Even physically, the contrast was jarring, the one small and dark, the other large, unhealthily blonde.

Furthermore, Maria Ludovica was gnawingly jealous. Even if she did not love her husband, she resented the fact that he could bestow affection elsewhere. And it was not long before she realised that in his strange melancholy way Francis was as deeply attached to his eldest daughter as she was to him.

In her genuine simplicity, on the other hand, Marie Louise was totally unaware of this existing antipathy. She felt no resentment that 'my mother' had been replaced within nine months of her death and took it for granted that she owed love and obedience to the new empress to whom she was soon referring, with a touching naivety, as '*liebe mama*'.

Seven months after Francis's third marriage, a wave of optimism swept the anti-Bonaparte world. On July 22nd 1808, at Baylen in southern Spain, the French general Dupont, at the head of twenty thousand veterans, surrendered to a force of inferior Spanish troops backed up by a group of ragged, ill-armed partisans. For the very first time since the revolution and Napoleon's truly meteoric rise to power, a French army had been defeated. The excitement caused by this news can be compared with that which electrified the free world when, in the winter of 1942, a Russian counter-attack recaptured Rostov, inflicting the first setback on land known by Hitler's Germany.

Napoleon himself was the first to realise its gravity. The fact that he himself had been over a thousand miles from the scene of the action was immaterial. The invincible French army had been humiliated. 'Since the beginning of time no greater disaster has been known,' he stormed. 'Dupont has sullied our standards! What inefficiency! What despicable cowardice!' Nor was he mistaken about its far-reaching effects. Almost immediately the war party in Vienna was resuscitated, this time headed by Francis's younger brother and, by far Austria's most talented general, the archduke Charles.

Not having a very high opinion of Austria's military potential, Napoleon's one anxiety was to make sure of Russia's friendly attitude. So long as the czar remained an ally there was nothing to fear, he was convinced, from Europe's other powers. For this reason the fabulous meeting at Erfurt in Saxony with Alexander and the kings of Bavaria, Saxony and Westphalia was planned, and took place on September 27th. For eighteen days the emperors of France and Russia fêted each other. Together they attended performances by the leading artistes of the *Comédie Francaise*, dined together, hunted together, attended innumerable reviews and, in private – or so Napoleon imagined – agreed on a partition of Europe and what is known today as the 'Middle East' into two 'zones of influence'.

On leaving Erfurt, Napoleon felt himself free to turn on Spain. Once again he had proved that his brilliance as a soldier was only equalled by his naivety as a diplomat. The czar had not the slightest intention of honouring a single one of his many promises.

In fact, his first move on his return to Moscow was to inform London and Vienna of the terms of the 'secret' treaty drawn up by Napoleon and himself, and to assure the British and Austrian governments that he had no intention of honouring them. This dispatch was received with particular interest in Vienna, since one of the clauses ran – 'If Austria attacks France, Russia will come to her (France's) aid . . .'

Immediately, Austria started to re-arm in earnest, to such an extent that Napoleon came racing back, in January 1809, from Spain where he had temporarily restored the military situation and his brother Joseph to the Spanish throne.

Still unwilling to embark on another invasion of central Europe, he sent the following warning to Francis via the Austrian ambassador in Paris, a comparatively unknown diplomat by the name of Count Clement Metternich: 'It seems to me that it is the waters of Lethe and not those of the Danube which flow through Vienna. Have the lessons of the past been forgotten? If more lessons are needed they will be administered, and they will be terrible. All my attention was directed to the battlefield of England's choosing, that is to say, Spain. Austria saved England in 1805 just as I was about to cross the Channel. She has saved England again by stopping me just as I was on the point of pursuing her armies to Corunna; she will pay dearly for this second interference. Either she demobilises immediately, or I will destroy her.'

The Austrians ignored the warning. Already their commander-in-chief, Archduke Charles, was at the head of an army of half a million men.

Hostilities began on April 13th and once more Marie Louise was overjoyed, convinced as she had been four years previously that God would be with 'Papa' and the great army commanded by 'Uncle Charles' marching west to destroy the 'anti-Christ', as she was now in the habit of describing 'the Corsican'.

As in 1805, despatches proclaiming Austrian successes poured into Vienna, but once again a glance at the map showed that the defeated French were drawing steadily nearer. After Eckmühl, at first reported as a great victory, Marie Louise wrote excitedly: 'I was overjoyed to hear that Napoleon was present in person at the great battle he has just lost. I only wish he would lose his head!'

But a few days later, when it became obvious that the first reports had been more than over-optimistic, she confided in

Victoria: 'I still believe that God will grant us victory over the abhorred Napoleon. When we heard of the victory (Eckmühl) I was so happy, but now comes the sad news that the report was a false one, and I find myself plunged into the depths of despair and sadness.'

By May 5th, the French were so near that Maria Ludovica decided on flight to Buda, and so for the second time in less than four years Marie Louise and her brothers and sisters found themselves fugitives, bumping along the appalling roads to the east. On arrival at Buda, the empress collapsed from physical and nervous exhaustion. She was no stoic. There was, however, a glimmer of hope when news came through of the momentary setback suffered by the French at Essling. Once again Marie Louise hurried to write her impressions to the faithful Victoria: 'The morning of the 22nd (May) Napoleon led his cavalry in a charge and pushed us back, but at that moment the Archduke Charles dismounted, seized the Grenadiers' standard and led them against the French who ran leaving Napoleon behind screaming after them that he'd burn the bridge with them on it and kill their two generals. It's the first time that Napoleon himself has been defeated, and we must thank God for it . . . but we mustn't be too puffed up with pride because of this victory, and I must confess that I'm so accustomed to disappointments, that I daren't hope for too much . . .'

She was quite right.

Not only was Essling the briefest of setbacks but, at the same time, Eugène de Beauharnais, advancing from the south, was steadily driving back the archduke John's army. Soon Buda was judged unsafe. Once more the royal family piled into coaches and fled, this time to Erlau. Here conditions were – for them – appalling. Marie Louise had to put up with: '. . . a miserably uncomfortable room with a bed, two battered and torn sofas and four chairs, all swarming with the most horrible bugs. You can imagine that neither mother's (Maria Ludovica) health nor mine are any the better for these continual miseries. She (Maria Ludovica) is in a very poor state and the other day had herself bled and made us be with her at the time. It made me feel very ill and I felt ill for the rest of the morning. But please don't mention this to anyone. I feel so ashamed of myself . . .'

At Erlau came the news, authentic this time, of the Austrian defeat at Wagram in July, the second French occupation of

Vienna and the establishment of Napoleon's headquarters in Schoenbrunn palace. A little later arrived details of the peace of Schoenbrunn signed on October 14th, by far the most ruinous of those imposed on the defeated Francis, by which Illyria and part of Galicia were to be handed over, the Austrian armed forces cut to a half of their normal peace strength, and an indemnity of forty-five millions paid.

Even when the victorious French army departed, Marie Louise did not return immediately to Vienna. Maria Ludovica was in such a state of nervous exhaustion that she insisted on staying in Buda for a rest cure before returning to public life and her husband's over-enthusiastic embraces, keeping her numerous stepchildren with her, purely from jealousy. And it was in Buda that Marie Louise celebrated Christmas and saw in the year 1810.

By then, Napoleon's name was again on everybody's lips but, for once, war and conquest played no part in the interminable conversations involving him. The 'Corsican' had divorced the beautiful, though by now rather faded, creole, Josephine, and was looking round for a second wife!

Chapter II

Though she did not realise it at the time, the Wagram disaster was to have a decisive influence on Marie Louise's future. As an archduchess, she had no say whatever in her own destiny. Nor did it occur to her that she might have a right to make decisions for herself. So, like a dust atom in a whirlwind, her fate was interwoven with that of Europe's protagonists and buffeted in the turbulence of political intrigue.

Again without her knowledge, her future had assumed embryonic form in the closing days of the year 1806. Having defeated Prussia at Iena in October, Napoleon was advancing east to cross swords with the Russians and heading for Warsaw, knowing that in Poland he would be received with open arms as a potential liberator from czarist oppression. At a state ball given in his honour shortly after his arrival in the capital, he noticed a very young, slender, blonde girl among the crowd of guests. Always interested in attractive women, Napoleon told his grand marshal, Duroc, to ask the young blonde for the pleasure of the next dance. To his amazement, a rather embarrassed Duroc returned with the reply that as the lady did not dance she begged to be excused the honour. Not to be outdone, Napoleon then asked to be introduced to every woman present so as to be assured of making her acquaintance.

The blonde young woman in question was the countess Maria Walewice-Walewska who, on leaving school two years previously at the age of sixteen, had been married to Count Anastase Colonna de Walewice-Walewski who had just celebrated his seventieth birthday. Despite this almost criminal discrepancy in ages, and the fact that Polish society of the day was far from prudish, Maria took her marriage very seriously, entering upon it with every intention of being faithful to a man who could at a stretch have been her great-grandfather. The Polish notables, however, were not in the least interested in personal scruples. For the Liberation Party, headed by Prince Poniatowski, here was a unique and unexpected chance of securing Napoleon's support for Poland's cause. As a result, from the very moment of their meeting, the eighteen-year-old Maria's virtue was submitted to a double attack – from Napoleon himself and from the united forces of the Polish nobility, the former pleading the cause of his heart, the latter that of duty to the Fatherland. It is hardly surprising that in the end she succumbed.

What does lift this affair above the level of Napoleon's many previous facile conquests is the fact that it developed into a mutual passion. When the emperor returned to Paris after the victory of Friedland and his famous meeting with the czar on a raft in the middle of the Niemen river, he could find no consolation in his own capital. In reply to his pressing appeal, Maria left her aged husband and, arriving unobtrusively in Paris, was installed in No. 48 rue de la Victoire, where her imperial lover visited her every day. There she remained until war with Austria broke out in 1809 when, still unable to bear the thought of too long a separation, Napoleon begged her to accompany him, as an aristocratic camp follower. And it was while, for the second time, he was using Schoenbrunn palace as his headquarters, that Maria Walewska announced the fact that she was pregnant.

Seldom has such a very normal statement had such far-reaching effects.

Ever since his coronation, Napoleon had been tormented by the fact that he had no heir. He knew that if circumstances obliged him to be absent for any length of time from Paris, plots sprouted like weeds in an ill-kept garden. He was only too well aware that he was not immortal and suspected that his health was on the decline. Again, during the advance on Vienna, he had received a slight wound in the foot. After Wagram, he narrowly escaped an attempt on his life by a young Austrian fanatic. The thought that with his death his empire would collapse was his constant nightmare. Only an heir, he was convinced, could perpetuate his present, all-too-hollow glory.

For years Josephine had been insisting – it was after all her only hope of remaining empress – that he was sterile, and so forcibly that he was almost inclined to believe her. And although one of his mistresses, Eleanore Denuelle, had recently given birth to a son, not only Josephine but Caroline Murat, with the disturbing frankness of the time, assured him that the child was Murat's.

With Maria Walewska, however, there could be no doubts.

29

The hideous nightmare of sterility was banished. Perhaps with a tinge of regret – for a faint glow of sentimental passion for the once-lovely creole still lingered – Napoleon made up his mind to divorce, and select a new empress from the ranks of Europe's many unmarried princesses and archduchesses.

Once the decision was reached, he passed to action.

Returning to Paris, he broke the news to Josephine. Though shaken by her tears and a dramatic fainting fit – probably simulated – he was not to be deterred. A 'family council' was summoned for December 15th (1809) at which both husband and wife read a statement to the effect that they were separating and would be divorced by 'mutual consent'.

To begin with, Napoleon hoped to strengthen the ties between France and Russia by marrying the czar's younger sister, the grand duchess Anne. In this he was to be disappointed. The czar was his usual charming self when he discussed the matter with Caulaincourt, duke of Vicenza, French ambassador to Moscow. He repeated his feelings of amity for his great ally, the French emperor. But in spite of the many concessions Napoleon was prepared to make – a big loan needed by Russia was agreed upon in advance, all French interest in Poland would be shelved, the young princess could remain a member of the Orthodox Church, anything, in fact – Alexander hedged, always falling back on the excuse that, as his sister was only just fifteen, he could not make a move without his mother's assent. This was tantamount to a refusal for the old empress, widow of the czar Paul, made no bones about her detestation of the 'Corsican usurper'.

It was a great blow, and since Napoleon considered his own position far too exalted even to contemplate marrying into one of the minor German royal families, the only solution of this matrimonial problem seemed to be an alliance with his old enemy Austria.

The defeat at Wagram had also had a profound, and cumulative, effect on the emperor Francis. This naturally melancholy, introspective man who basically hated the imperial panoply – he was not even, like most Austrians, enthralled by the arts; his only relaxation was gardening – never, on the other hand, thought of laying down his imperial role. He believed and practised what he preached: blind obedience to God's will. And since it was by

God's will that he had mounted the throne, it was inconceivable that he should even contemplate abdication.

Yet he was profoundly distressed by his failure; by his unworthiness and ineptitude as the instrument of this calling. At the same time, his brain was both lucid and honest. He made no attempt to deceive himself, or close his eyes to Austria's tragedies since his accession. And the balance sheet was really horrifying. In the seventeenth year of his reign Austria had fallen from the position of the leading to the least of European powers, from richest to most impoverished, result of a succession of catastrophes due to the evil – from the Austrian point of view – genius of the man who called himself Napoleon I, emperor of the French.

Pondering this melancholy state of affairs, once more – by Napoleon's permission – established in his capital of Vienna, Francis came to the conclusion that he was incapable of directing his country's affairs. He had never had any hankering after military glory, and so had never had a genuine hand in any campaign. In this he might have found a loophole but, again, honesty compelled him to admit that, had he done so, the defeats suffered might well have been even more crushing. Count Colloredo had been dismissed for his untimely advice to defy Napoleon in 1805, yet his own attempt to direct foreign policy had resulted in the culminating humiliations of Wagram and the peace of Schoenbrunn. What more overwhelming proof of his own incompetence could he ask?

There was only one possible solution, he concluded after most bitter heart-searching. While retaining nominal leadership of his people, the real power, albeit exercised behind the official scene, must be entrusted to someone capable of succeeding where he, Francis, had failed.

Most obvious choice for this delicate role seemed to be his younger brother, the archduke Charles who, already, had shown himself to be Austria's most outstanding military figure. It was he who had gained the semi-victory of Essling, who at one moment had almost been victor on Wagram's field. Yet the archduke was a pure soldier. The army was his only love. He had a horror of politics and politicians, of diplomats and diplomacy's wiles. He was not prepared to sheath his sword and engage in a battle of wits. Yet with the lamentable state of the country's finances, and the inferiority complex from which, after an unbroken series of defeats, the ordinary soldier was suffering, this was no time for a dream of a war of revenge.

At last Francis's choice fell on the Austrian ambassador in Paris, Count Clement Metternich. From Austria's point of view, he could not have made a better one. For Marie Louise, the beginning of Metternich's underground reign marked the beginning of the constraint, frustration, often humiliation, over-shadowing her life, almost to the day of her death.

Clement Lothar Wenceslas Metternich, who was to prove – thanks to Francis's self-submission – to be Austria's greatest statesman, was not in fact Austrian but a Rhinelander, born at Coblenz in 1773. In 1794, however, just as he had started on a diplomatic career, he was forced to make a hurried flight with his father as French republican armies approached Coblenz, choosing Vienna as their land of exile.

It was to Francis's credit that he judged the young Clement Metternich to be a man of exceptional talent, helping him to such an extent that, by 1806, he was appointed Austrian ambassador to Paris, a post considered as the pinnacle of all diplomatic posts. For three most difficult years, Metternich carried out his functions brilliantly, earning even Napoleon's grudging admiration.

History is full of stories of lost opportunities, but few people have profited by fortune's least smile to the same extent as Metternich. Shortly after Wagram, Francis stated: 'We shall have a great deal to do to repair the mischief.' And when he had decided that Metternich was the only man capable of repairing this 'mischief', and that he should replace Count Stadion as foreign minister, he stressed: 'I count upon the feeling you have of the gravity of the situation and upon your patriotism . . .' Slightly hesitant at first, Metternich obeyed, thus assuming a power which he was to hold for the next forty years.

Though only thirty-six years of age when he became Austria's virtual master, Count Metternich's character, his beliefs, were already formed, his path set.

It should not be imagined that he had jumped to conclusions. After a careful study of principles and results, he had acquired a hatred of both the spirit and practice of the French revolution and, as a result, for the best part of half a century became the supreme defender of the 'old order'. To begin with, the personal element of this hatred converged on Napoleon as the revolution's embodiment. The fact that in 1804 General Bonaparte, surrounding himself with the most glittering apanages of imperial power, had proclaimed himself 'emperor' made no difference; he remained 'the revolutionary', the spirit of the 'new order', the 'upstart'.

Three years as ambassador in Paris, constant personal contact with the emperor, were an invaluable preparation for the great task which Metternich set himself with outward calm, but with an inner, burning fever. These years, these contacts, convinced him that despite all appearances Napoleon was intensely vulnerable, that his empire was built on sand and that, in the foreseeable future, its collapse was inevitable.

He was equally convinced, though, in those early days of 1810 that the time had not yet come for offensive action. In his own words, 'Our system must be exclusively one of accommodating ourselves to the victor. In this way alone we may perhaps extend our existence till the day of general deliverance . . . We have but one course open to us; we must reserve our strength for better times and work out our salvation by softer means without regard to the road we have followed hitherto . . .'

It was lucky for Metternich that, almost immediately after taking over the reins, the divorce which set all Europe talking played straight into his hands.

There was an old saying: 'Others wage war. You, happy Austria, marry (*Bella gerant alii, tu felix Austria nube*)'. For the moment, Metternich decided that this old adage must serve as his guide. On November 30th 1809, Prince Schwarzenberg, who had succeeded Metternich as Austria's ambassador in Paris, received a secret message that everything possible should be done, with the utmost discretion needless to say, to advance the cause of the archduchess Marie Louise where the emperor Napoleon's future matrimonial projects were concerned. A few weeks later Francis, acting on his foreign minister's advice, dropped a hint to his eldest daughter that she might be called upon to make certain sacrifices for the good of her country.

When she learned what these sacrifices might entail, Marie Louise's dismay can be imagined. On the other hand, such was her upbringing that it never occurred to her to suggest that she might *not* be prepared to make them. Oppressed, however, by this latent menace, she poured out her fears to Victoria and the countess of Colloredo: 'Kozeluch' (her piano professor) 'has been talking about Napoleon's separation from his wife and hinted that I might replace her. But he's badly mistaken, for Napoleon is too afraid of being snubbed and too anxious to go on harming us to put forward such a request, and I know Papa is too kind to force me over such a matter . . .'

Seldom, perhaps, has there been a more pathetic example of wishful thinking. At the same time, her letter to Victoria's mother was infinitely more realistic and tinged with most sombre foreboding. 'Since Napoleon's divorce, I scan each Frankfurt Gazette anxiously, hoping to read of the nomination of a new wife, and I confess this delay is worrying me greatly. I put my fate in the hands of Divine Providence who, alone, knows what is best for our happiness. But if by supreme misfortune I am the one, I am ready to sacrifice my happiness for the good of the State, persuaded as I am that true happiness is only to be found in the accomplishment of one's duties even at the expense of one's own feelings. I don't want to think about it, but my mind is made up although for me it would be a double and very painful sacrifice. Pray that it may not come about . . .'

Unfortunately for them, when it came to politics, archduchesses received less consideration than the daughters of the humblest peasants.* When, during the semi-secret negotiations taking place in both Paris and Vienna, Prince Schwarzenberg suggested with considerable frankness that, in view of the bitter hostility latent between France and Austria – to say nothing of memories of Marie Antoinette – the archduchess might not take kindly to the idea of a French husband, it was Metternich who replied: 'Our princesses are not accustomed to choose their husbands according to the dictates of their hearts, and the respect that a good, well-brought-up child like the archduchess has for her father's wishes leads me to hope that she will not create any difficulties . . .'

For some weeks, however, the bargaining for the physical person of the emperor Francis's eldest child, having in it as little

* Six years later, Marie Louise's younger sister, Leopoldine, was shipped off like a prize filly to marry the Emperor of Brazil. She lamented, 'I admit that the sacrifice of leaving my family, perhaps for ever, is more than painful, but this alliance makes my father happy, and I have the consolation of knowing that I have bowed to his will, being persuaded that God has a particular way of ruling the destinies of us princesses, and that submitting to our parents is to submit to His will . . .'

humanity as if a plot of desert land had been at stake, remained strictly unofficial while Napoleon waited, though with declining optimism, for a favourable reply from the czar. Metternich himself was unperturbed. Already he had established a personal liaison with Alexander, and was well aware that the dowager empress's prejudices would be respected.

On February 5th, Napoleon received a long despatch from his Moscow ambassador, the duke of Vicenza, which was another repeat of the czar's eternal prevarications. He could not be fooled any longer. This much-hoped-for Russian marriage was a chimera. He had no choice in the matter. Baffled in his hope of an alliance with Europe's most powerful reigning family, he must return to the oldest. Having made up his mind, he acted with typical precipitation.

Eugène de Beauharnais was charged with the task of informing the ambassador Prince Schwarzenberg that the emperor Napoleon had decided to marry the archduchess Marie Louise. Since Eugène was Josephine's son, the choice of messenger seems unfortunate, but Eugène, devoted to his stepfather, raised no objection. Schwarzenberg, much to Napoleon's annoyance, was away from Paris on a shooting expedition but on his return, about six o'clock that evening, he found himself faced with a crisis. In addition to announcing his decision to marry the archduchess Marie Louise, Napoleon insisted that the marriage contract be drawn up and signed that same evening.

It could hardly have been a more difficult moment for an ambassador. Although Schwarzenberg was well aware that Vienna had been plotting for months to obtain just this decision on the part of the French emperor, he was not legally in a position to pledge his sovereign's word and, again, the extreme haste aroused his suspicions. Nevertheless, he was able to judge for himself that Napoleon was in a highly excitable frame of mind and liable to break off negotiations on the least sign of pro-crastination. Acting on his own initiative, therefore, he signed on behalf of His Majesty Francis II of Austria a marriage contract which was a replica of that which had been drawn up for Marie Antoinette and Louis XVI.

As soon as Eugène had rushed off to wave the precious document before his stepfather's eyes, Schwarzenberg hastened to pen his own apologia – not to the emperor, but to Metternich: 'Knowing the Emperor Napoleon's character, I don't think there is any doubt that had I shown the least sign of prevaricating, he would have dropped the project and pursued another . . . You will agree, I am sure, that unless I was prepared to compromise everything, it was impossible for me to take any other course of action; if I had insisted that I was not authorised to sign, he would have broken matters off . . .'

Schwarzenberg's understandable agitation was without cause. For Metternich the contract's signature marked the first victory over the enemy.

The next step – purely conventional since the contract was already signed – was to inform Marie Louise that her future had been settled and then, also a matter of form, to ask whether she consented to the decision taken on her behalf.

Though nothing definite had been said Marie Louise was, as has been seen, becoming daily more afraid that she might well be the destined victim. In a moment of panic it occurred to her that there might be a slight chance of escaping this horrible fate if she could become engaged – or, better still, married – before the 'Corsican ogre' finally made up his mind. One of the few men she had been allowed to meet was the archduke Ferdinand, her stepmother's brother. It is unlikely that they had indulged even in the mildest of supervised flirtations, but this did not deter her from writing to her father a letter wholly engendered, one can see reading between the lines, by fear. After a frank confession that she was terrified by the thought that Napoleon would be considering her as his future bride, she went on: 'You have always assured me with your customary goodness that you would never force me to marry against my will, and since I have been at Ofen I have met the archduke Ferdinand. I am sure he possesses all the qualities needed to make me happy. I have confided in my dear mother (Maria Ludovica) and she shares my confidence in this young man and has suggested that I write to you about my sentiments concerning him. Knowing that I cannot place my future happiness in better hands than yours, I await your decision, remaining always your loving and obedient daughter.'

This letter was never even answered.

The blow fell shortly before the return to Vienna.

On receiving Schwarzenberg's despatch that the marriage contract was already signed, Metternich immediately informed the emperor Francis – to whom he referred invariably, with an almost perverted sense of humour, as 'My Master' – and suggested that he should break the news straightaway to his daughter that it was indeed she who was now destined to occupy the throne Josephine had been obliged to vacate.

Francis did not receive the news as enthusiastically as his foreign minister. His misgivings, however, were human rather than political. He was only too well aware of his daughter's carefully-fostered horror of the 'Corsican'. As a father he grieved at the thought of her certain distress, despite the fact that, as he saw it, the step was inevitable and as such met with his full approval from the point of view of Austria's destiny. He said, one suspects with a touch of hypocrisy, 'My daughter must, of course, make the ultimate decision, and before I can consider my duty as a sovereign, I must know her views. Go and speak to the arch-duchess and let me know what she says . . .'

Metternich was willing to continue with this farce.

Received in Marie Louise's apartments and in the presence of Madame Lazanski, he delivered a long lecture on an imperial daughter's duty not only to her father, but also to her country, before asking her to state her views. Her reply was worthy of one of Corneille's heroines. 'Where the interests of my father and the empire are at stake, it is they and not my personal sentiments which must decide. Tell my father to consider his duty as a sovereign, and in no way to consider me as an individual.' Stilted and pompous as was this little speech, there is not the slightest doubt that she meant every word of it.

Returning to Vienna a few days later, Marie Louise was surprised to find herself the object of a tremendous ovation from crowds lining her route to the Hofburg and swarming in the Heldenplatz. News of the impending wedding was now the only subject of conversation in the city.

The Viennese were not warlike, yet they had been forced by circumstances to live in an atmosphere of war for the last twenty years. Young men, hankering after more peaceful trades, were constantly drafted into the army. Too many of them had left their bones rotting on the battlefield. Nor had the civilian population been spared. Vienna had been bombarded by the French artillery. Twice within five years they had watched the flight of their own royal family and the triumphal parades of the *grognards* and Murat's horsemen striking sparks from the cobbles of the Ringstrasse and the Kärntnerstrasse.

37

Now, unexpectedly, the nightmare of the past was dissipated. This was no uneasy truce between successive and progressively more disastrous peace treaties. Suddenly the enemy had become the friend; the ties between them the indissoluble bonds of marriage. And because they were so happy, the gay, life-loving Viennese wallowed in a *gemütlich*-hazed sentimentality. Their blonde young archduchess they likened, tears of relief filling their eyes, to the heroine of Gluck's *Iphigenia in Aulide*: a sacrifice to the Corsican Minotaur.

Only two people had the courage to voice their objections to this marriage of convenience. Though Maria Ludovica was quite pleased at the idea of marrying off her eldest stepchild, and of her subsequent departure from Vienna, she was revolted by the physical implications of an archduchess of Austria in the arms of a commoner. It needed Metternich's persuasive tongue and cold logic to persuade her that the marriage was a national necessity – and perhaps not more than temporary. More difficult to win over was the archbishop of Vienna. It was not at all easy to convince him that the annulment of Napoleon's marriage with Josephine was acceptable in the eyes of the Church. Finally, it was the French ambassador, Count Otto de Moslay, who came to the rescue by producing a document – which he insisted must be for the archbishop's eyes only and never, under any circumstances, made public – to the effect that he had 'seen and read the entries in the Paris diocesan registry concerning the marriage between the emperor Napoleon and the empress Josephine, and that in accordance with the Catholic ecclesiastical laws existing in the French empire, the marriage had been declared annulled since, when the marriage was concluded, the essential formalities demanded by the laws of the Church and recognised in France as necessary to ensure the validity of a marriage had been neglected.' 'Furthermore,' the count added, 'in accordance with existing civic laws regarding marriage, every conjugal union was founded on the principle that it could be dissolved by the mutual agreement of the parties concerned . . .'

Probably doubting, and certainly against his better judgment, the archbishop was obliged to accept this specious document as valid proof that Napoleon was, indeed, free to enter into a second marriage with the Church's blessing.

*   *   *

Marie Louise was agreeably surprised when she received her future husband's first letter, written from Rambouillet, and dated February 23rd 1810:

My Cousin,
The brilliant qualities which make you so outstanding have inspired us with the desire to serve and honour you, and we have addressed ourselves, therefore, to the Emperor your father, begging him to entrust us with the happiness of your Imperial highness. Can we hope that Your Highness will be in agreement with the sentiments that have inspired us to act thus? Can we flatter ourselves that Your Highness will not be dominated uniquely by the spirit of filial obedience? If Your Highness has but the least of amical sentiments towards ourselves, we wish to cherish them, and set ourselves the task of being agreeable in all things so that we may presume to succeed one day in winning Your Highness's affection; this indeed is our aim and object, and we pray that Your Highness may regard it with favour.
In which we pray that God, may keep you my cousin, always in His holy and worthy care,
Your good cousin,
Napoleon

Used to the ludicrously formal style of the day, such a letter, even though the writer was her predestined husband, must have seemed almost frivolous, yet not at all displeasing. What was more, it managed to convey the flattering impression that she, as a person, did have a role to play in what till then Marie Louise – like everyone else in the Austrian court – had looked upon as a purely politico-business arrangement.

Meanwhile, Napoleon was showing the same precipitate haste in his desire to see the wedding celebrated, and consummated, as he had regarding the contract's signing. Marshal Berthier was sent to Vienna to present his master's formal demand for the archduchess's hand, and to arrange a proxy wedding, also in Vienna, before the second of Napoleon's empresses set out for Paris. While, at the same time as the marshal, the first of the great convoys carrying Napoleon's fabulous wedding gifts for his bride-to-be headed east.

Berthier, Prince of Neufchâtel – conveniently forgetting his second, recently-acquired title, Prince of Wagram – arrived in Vienna accompanied by Prince Paul Esterhazy who, with a guard of honour, had been waiting to greet him at the Austrian frontier and escort him to the capital. Three days before the final ceremony in the great hall of the Hofburg were spent by the envoy extra-ordinary on official visits and conferences, during one of which, rather unwillingly, the archduke Charles agreed to stand in for his old enemy at the proxy wedding.

The ceremony in the Hofburg was comparatively simple. The Austrian emperor, the empress Maria Ludovica on his right, Marie Louise accompanied by Madame Lazanski on his left, were seated on a raised dais at the far end of the hall, facing the doors. Detachments of the Hungarian guard of nobles, white-uniformed Bohemian dragoons, Austrian grenadiers and halberdiers formed a double hedge the length of either wall. When, on a sign from the emperor, the doors were thrown open, Berthier, dressed in the uniform of a marshal of the empire, his 'bicorne' pulled down firmly over his brow, followed by his aides-de-camp and a hussar escort, walked up to the dais and in a short but flowery speech, only uncovering his head when either of the two emperors concerned was mentioned by name, conveyed Napoleon's request for the hand of 'the most perfect archduchess, Marie Louise'.

Very pale, Francis replied, 'I grant my daughter's hand to the French emperor.'

Berthier then turned to speak directly to Marie Louise. 'It is above all the gift of your heart, Madame,' he said, 'that the Emperor, my master, wishes to receive from you.'

Marie Louise's answer, spoken clearly but softly, ignored the invitation to introduce a more personal note into the proceedings. 'With my father's permission, I give my consent to my union with the emperor Napoleon.'

The captain commanding the hussar escort then presented Marie Louise with a jewel-encrusted box which he handed her on a scarlet velvet cushion embellished with gold tassels. It was the first of the avalanche of Napoleon's presents, and contained his miniature in a frame set with twelve enormous diamonds. Because of Austria's parlous finances due to nearly twenty years of war, this was the first gift of any intrinsic value Marie Louise had been offered. But, it is recorded, it was not its very considerable value which most pleased her – in any case she was only vaguely aware of its worth – it was the fact that her husband-to-be, whose features she contemplated with fascination was not, as she confided to Madame Lazanski – physically at any rate – the monster she had been led to imagine.

The next day, March 9th, a second marriage contract, a duplicate of that drawn up in Paris, was signed by Berthier, Metternich, and Count Trautmannsdorff acting as Francis's personal representative. In addition, this second contract stated that Marie Louise should receive a dowry of 200,000 florins (equivalent of 400,000 francs), and that she renounced all rights of succession to the Austrian throne and to those of any of the states still left in the Austrian empire. That same evening – but apparently without a hint of *arrière-pensée* – the Vienna State Opera gave a performance of Gluck's *Iphigenia*.

The 10th was comparatively quiet, but the 11th, a Sunday, the proxy wedding took place – not, as some have suggested, in St Stephen's cathedral, but in the Augustin church – the archduke Charles speaking the responses in the place of his erstwhile enemy, in the presence of Berthier, the emperor Francis and the entire royal family. That evening, history was made at the royal banquet to celebrate the wedding: Berthier – who was to return to Paris the following day – was permitted to sit at the emperor's table, a privilege reserved exclusively, hitherto, for visitors of royal blood. Enchanted by the success of his mission, flattered by the emperor's attentions, Berthier was too thick-skinned to notice the frigidity of the Austrian nobility and their studious efforts – with the archduke Charles a notable exception – to avoid talking to him.

Time was now running short for Marie Louise. She was due to leave her home on March 13th – Napoleon was in a hurry and not prepared to let numerological superstitions act as a delay. As the hours slipped by, her apprehensions increased, but fortunately – and this thought must have been in Napoleon's mind – her fears were distracted by the non-stop arrival of the incredible wedding gifts which poured daily into Vienna.

A detailed list of these gifts would require a chapter in itself, for no fabled prince of the (then) mysterious East, no eager imperial bridegroom of any known European dynasty, nor yet in more modern times any oil baron or cinema king has ever heaped such a fortune, such a quantity and diversity of presents at his bride's feet.

The clothes alone cost the emperor 418,834 francs. They included eight *grand habits,* pearl-spangled dresses, embroidered with gold thread, each varying in price from eight to twelve thousand francs; six *robes de bal* of finest tulle, also embroidered with gold and silver thread. Janssen, Napoleon's shoemaker, had to produce forty-eight pairs of shoes. Fans were supplied by Friese and Devillers, the most elaborate being inlaid with emeralds and diamonds. Since Kashmir shawls were popular at the time, two whole cases of these shawls, costing the amazing sum of 39,860 francs, were also added. Bizarre indeed was the *necéssaire de toilette* consisting of no less than thirteen hundred articles. Not content with such normal objects as hand mirrors, brushes, combs – all of course in gold – the practical-minded Napoleon also included dinner services, tea and coffee pots, saucepans and even such intimate utensils as several sets of toothpicks, and gaily painted enamel *pots de chambre* and *bidets*. As for the jewellery, according to Masson, its value was estimated at close on 3,500,000 francs, the finest pieces being a tiara made up of 1,329 diamonds and a pearl necklace which cost the treasury 509,773 francs.

That stern old matriarch, Madame Mère, whose constant comment during the empire's days was *Pourvu que ça dure,** must have thought rather cynically, confronted with such uncontrolled extravagance, of the stark austerity of her own wedding and the continually grim struggle for existence at the times when she had brought her children into the world.

Yet, in spite of this munificence, Marie Louise was near to breaking down when the huge procession of hcavy coaches, herself in the heaviest and most lumbering, started off on the long journey to a foreign country, her ultimate destination the bed of a man she had never seen and who, from infancy, she had been taught to hate and fear. No doubt the memories of Countess Colloredo's horrific descriptions of Marie Antoinette's miseries and execution tormented her. In addition, it should be remembered that even at this stage, when she was already a bride by proxy, she was completely ignorant of marriage's physical aspects.

The morning of March 13th, Marie Louise said good-bye – as far as she knew it was farewell – to her stepmother, brothers and sisters and, accompanied by Countess Lazanski, took her place in her carriage. Dense crowds lined the streets to watch her procession go by. It is said that most of those who caught a glimpse of her tear-lined cheeks felt rather ashamed of themselves. And though, secretly, they were still delighted at the era of peace this

* It's all very well as long as it lasts.

sacrifice seemed to open up for them, wanting a scapegoat for their consciences and their own lack of courage, they were inclined to blame the emperor Francis for permitting it. Needless to say, this heart searching was of the shortest duration as prosperity returned to the city and business boomed.

The first stage was short, a halt being made at St Polten so that Marie Louise could spend the rest of the day with her father. There is no record of their conversation, but it must have been a sad occasion for them both, and especially for the remorse-torn Francis.

The following morning, after attending Mass together, there was a brief yet infinitely painful separation.

Two days later, March 16th, the bridal cortège arrived at Braunau, the frontier post between Austria and France's German states where – literally – Marie Louise was 'handed over' to her future subjects.

Chapter III

Although Napoleon had shown himself tactful and understanding in his few dealings with Marie Louise till that moment, he displayed an astonishing lack of sensitivity in his 'remote control' orders for the 'taking delivery' of his bride, as she was from a legal, if not a practical, point of view, since the Viennese proxy wedding. It was his wish that, once across the frontier at Braunau, everything Austrian be discarded and, with his usual impatience, he failed to consider the psychological effect of so brutal a metamorphosis.

For the purpose a large, pretentious, neo-classical building had been hastily thrown up by French military engineers, spanning the demarcation line, and divided into three compartments. To the east, just after the village of Altheim, the first compartment was Austrian territory; the central, neutral; the western, before reaching the village of Braunau itself, French.

Passing through the Austrian sector with her Viennese entourage, dressed in a heavy (Austrian) gold brocade robe, Marie Louise was led to a slightly raised cloth-of-gold-draped dais in the centre of the neutral compartment, on which she seated herself facing the French compartment's tightly-closed doors. Baron de Bausset, at that time *Préfet du Palais,* has recorded that as everyone was so anxious to get a glimpse of their empress before the beginning of the official ceremony, he hit on the brilliant idea of including a drill in his luggage and, so armed, set about making three peep-holes in the door.

As soon as Marie Louise entered the neutral ground there was an undignified rush, ladies and gentlemen of the court jostling each other with scant regard for rank or sex, to be first at the vantage points and make their uninhibited comments about the new empress, till Count von Seyssel, Austrian master of ceremonies, knocked on the door – he could scarcely have failed to notice the peep-holes – to announce that the official 'take-over' could begin.

The Austrians, most of them, men and women alike, in tears, then filed past their archduchess to kiss her hand in a gesture of farewell. After which Count von Trautmannsdorff gave his arm to Marie Louise and led her across to the prince of Neufchâtel (Berthier) who then presented her to the waiting members of her new household, headed by her first equerry Count Aldobrandini Borghese, her *dame d'honneur* the duchess of Montebello, widow of Marshal Lannes, and her lady of the wardrobe Countess de Luçay. These introductions ended, Caroline, queen of Naples, Napoleon's sister and wife of Marshal Murat, entered and embraced her young sister-in-law before leading her to a waiting carriage in which, escorted by a glittering escort of the 7th Hussars commanded by General Montbrun, they drove the short distance to the village of Braunau itself.

The choice of Caroline for-the delicate task of introducing his very young and very innocent wife to France and the French was not a very genial decision of Napoleon. To begin with, the Murats had mounted the throne of Naples as a result of Napoleon's eviction of Marie Louise's grandparents, Maria Carolina and her husband. At the same time, Caroline – despite the fact that she and her husband, the son of an innkeeper, owed everything to her brilliant and all-powerful brother – felt no gratitude, but only a consuming jealousy because her brother Joseph had been created king of Spain while she and her husband had been relegated to the minor – in her opinion – throne of Naples. And though, during the years that Metternich had been ambassador in Paris, Caroline who was as unfaithful as she was ambitious had forsaken her current lover General Junot to become the Austrian's accredited mistress, this did not prevent her from affecting an intense anti-Austrian complex. Furthermore, having learnt – probably from Metternich – of the closely guarded upbringing of the Habsburg children, she combined an instinctive social inferiority with a loose-living, woman-of-the-world's basic hatred of an irreproachably innocent girl. Nor was Marie Louise's preconceived dislike and mistrust of this *soi-disant* queen, as so often she had dubbed her, in any way alleviated by the process of gallicisation which, under Caroline's supervision, she was forced to undergo.

Arrived at Braunau, Marie Louise was taken to a house which had been prepared specially for the occasion. There she was stripped of every item of her clothing, bathed, perfumed, her hair re-modelled by a French coiffeur, before being re-dressed according to the latest Paris fashion. Altogether there was something inhuman, almost humiliating, about the whole procedure. It lingered at the back of her mind and, four years later, when Napoleon fell, she was to include this incident among the many reasons, both real and imaginary, advanced for her faithlessness.

During this time the two delegations mixed and exchanged presents and later, while Caroline and Marie Louise, accompanied only by Madame Lazanski, partook of a rather frigid dinner, the Austrians were entertained at a banquet presided over by Berthier and the duchess of Montebello. In spite of the lavishness of the gifts which had been distributed to the Austrians, this banquet, intended to symbolise the new-born Franco-Austrian friendship, was a fiasco from the social point of view; especially where the women were concerned. 'The ladies from Vienna were coldly critical of the peacock gorgeousness with which the ladies of the imperial court of France were adorned. Bad taste, they thought, while the men, bitterly resentful at the marriage of their emperor's daughter to the man who had beaten them in a thousand battles, made no attempt to be friendly . . .'

There is no record of the *diner-à-trois*, which could hardly have been very convivial either, but before going to bed Marie Louise wrote a long letter to her father highly indicative of the turmoil of doubts and fears besetting her, which she confided next morning to von Trautmannsdorff.

My very dear Papa,
　　Thanks to Prince (*sic*) Trautmannsdorff, I have the chance to write to you just once more completely openly, and I seize it joyfully so as to be able to tell you that I am always thinking of you and always will think of you. It is God who has given me the strength to bear the shock of separation from you and my Austrian friends. I put my trust in Him. He alone can console me in the accomplishment of my duty, in this sacrifice for you. I arrived at two o'clock today in the French camp, after having rested a little on Austrian territory. I really hardly knew what I was doing when all those bidding me farewell kissed my hand. I was shivering and so distressed that the Prince of Neufchatel shed tears of sympathy. I turned to him when all my friends had left me.
　　My God! What a contrast between the French and the Viennese women. The Queen of Naples embraced me and

seemed very friendly but I don't trust her; I don't think it was the desire to help me that prompted her to make this journey! She led me into the French camp where she took two hours re-dressing me. I can assure you I'm now scented like all the French women. The Emperor sent me a gold toilet set, but he didn't write. Since I've had to leave you, I'd rather be with him. I'd rather travel with him than all these women! Oh God! I can't stop thinking of all the happy days I passed at home. I'm really learning to appreciate them now. I can assure you, dear papa, that I'm uncontrollably sad . . .

It was perhaps significant that already this young girl who had never for a moment been allowed to be alone with a man should now express the desire to be with 'the ogre', to face the terrors of matrimony's dark secrets, rather than continue in the company of 'all these women'. Already those strong, conjugal instincts seemed to be awakening.

They formed, in fact, a strange couple of travelling companions, these two over-sexed women; the younger, still virgin, being thrust unwilling to the summit of temporal power; the older, with a formidable list of lovers, tormented by a lust for still more power and warped by jealousy.

The contrast in temperament, the difference in birth between these two royal personages, did not make for light conversation during the interminable hours they rocked and jolted over the ill-made roads. Caroline mistook Marie Louise's gaucherie for a deliberate snub inspired, she imagined, by the fact that she – Caroline – was a parvenue queen who had usurped the Habsburg grandmother's throne; while Marie Louise, for her part, had enough natural perspicacity to know that the ponderous compliments produced from time to time, as if learnt from a textbook, were completely lacking in sincerity, and to have the suspicion that the queen of Naples was seeking to impose a moral domination dragging her thus into one of those webs of intrigue which – with a neo-Borgian passion – she never ceased attempting to weave.

The evening of March 18th, the bridal cortège reached Munich where Marie Louise was the guest of the king and queen of Bavaria. A carnivalesque air reigned in the city. The crowded streets were hung with banners and lined by state troops in gala uniform as the procession drove up to the palace where the

Bavarian royal couple waited at the foot of the steps to receive their new sovereign, to the accompaniment of salvoes of artillery rivalling the frantic pealing of church and cathedral bells.

Very tired by the journey, Marie Louise dined alone but, before going to bed, she was handed a letter from Napoleon written from Paris and dated March 10th. According to Madame Lazanski, the letter charmed her. Once again it gave her the feeling that he would definitely not prove to be the monster who had haunted her childhood's dreams.

Madame, I hope Your Majesty will receive this letter at Bruneau (*sic*). I'm counting the moments; the days seem long; and so it will be till I have the happiness of meeting you. My people share my impatience. I have said that you will be a loving mother for the French people. You will find them, Madame, loving children who will cherish you. I hope by now you have no doubts as to the sincerity of my affection; you could not wish for it to be greater, but I am impatient to know that you reciprocate it. Believe me, there is no one on earth who loves, and wishes to love, you as I do.

Napoleon

The next day proved as exhausting for the young empress as any on the road: official receptions, a state banquet, a gala performance at the opera. Moreover, it was the first time that she was being honoured as a reigning monarch in her own right, and the Bavarians were tumbling over themselves in their anxiety to make a good impression, hoping by so doing to earn a metaphorical pat on the back from their master in Paris.

It was in many ways a fateful day for, that same evening, Caroline was guilty of a gross psychological error which gained her her sister-in-law's lifelong enmity.

Annoyed by Marie Louise's coldness, the queen of Naples determined to hurt her and, at the same time, give a practical demonstration of the power she was capable – or, rather, liked to fancy she was capable – of wielding, thus browbeating the young 'foreigner' from the very beginning into a recognition of the fact that 'the family', the Bonaparte clan, dominated court circles. It was an illusion to which Caroline clung but one which was, in fact, completely without foundation.

No one could attempt to deny Napoleon's deep-rooted sense

of family loyalty. He showered honours, position, wealth on his brothers and sisters – Joseph king of Spain, Caroline queen of Naples, Louis king of Holland, Jerome king of Westphalia. Yet at the same time, a shrewd judge of character, he had no false ideas as to their abilities; he did not even trust them. For this reason, though pandering to their greed and ambition, he paid no attention whatsoever to their too-frequently offered advice and insisted on their obedience to his dictates. Caroline, however, chose to forget this.

In the short time they had spent together since the arrival at Braunau, she had noticed that Marie Louise was only really at ease when talking with Madame Lazanski, sole survivor of her Austrian entourage. In Munich she formed a plan, after which she held a rapid consultation with the duchess of Montebello, Marie Louise's *dame d'honneur* – so soon to impose, detrimentally, the domination Caroline sought in vain. The two women agreed that Lazanski was hindering the gallicisation process and that they should pretend to have received instructions from Napoleon himself to the effect that, to eliminate 'anti-French' influence, the countess was to be sent straight back to Vienna.

Having reached this decision, Caroline sent for Countess Lazanski, informed her coldly that she would be returning to Vienna the following morning and that, 'to avoid unpleasantness', she should depart without taking her farewell. There was no question of disputing this order, but the countess refused to leave without first saying goodbye.

Marie Louise was bewildered and heartbroken. But so severe had been her upbringing, especially as regards the prime virtue of obedience that, though she was now empress, she never dreamt of countermanding the order and insisting on her old governess staying by her side, at least as far as Paris. This is all the more extraordinary when, from a letter she gave to the countess to deliver to her father, it can be seen that, naive as she still was, she was suspicious. 'My fiancé' (she still seemed unable to grasp the fact that she was married) 'could not have called on me to make a greater sacrifice, though I suspect he is not really the one to blame!'

From that moment on, sullen resentment was added to her natural shyness. Understandably, she never forgave the queen of Naples.

For the ordinary peasant and citizen, the cortège's procession across the German states was a triumph, visual proof of the success and popularity of this astounding marriage. At each stage – Augsburg, Ulm, Stuttgart – there were fêtes, banquets, processions, flowery discourses, gala theatre and opera performances, till the final pomp and ceremony of the entry on to French soil at Strasbourg on March 22nd. But behind this mask of general rejoicing, Marie Louise sulked. She had caught cold, complained continually of aches and pains, and scarcely bothered to be polite to her various royal and ducal hosts and hostesses whose duty it was to entertain her at vast cost to themselves which, in most cases, they could ill afford.

Caroline, probably realising that she had made a fatal mistake at Munich and although she had begged Napoleon to be entrusted with the 'privilege' of escorting his bride, was now equally loud in her lamentations – when Marie Louise was not present – at having been *forced* into such an ungrateful task, to such an extent that the king of Würtemburg, in all innocence, noted in his diary: 'The poor Queen of Naples is worn out. And I'm not surprised. What an appalling job! One cannot imagine a worse one . . .'

When the journey was resumed from Strasbourg, on March 24th, Marie Louise became more cheerful. The end was in sight. The emperor Napoleon was due to meet her at Compiègne on the 27th. 'I'm quite resigned to my fate,' she wrote to her father just before leaving Strasbourg, 'in fact I'm surprised to be able to say that I feel happy. I'd like you to see the letters the Emperor Napoleon writes me . . .'

When Napoleon had written that he was aglow with impatience to welcome his bride, he was not exaggerating.

To begin with, he had been bitterly disappointed with the breakdown over the negotiations with the czar, chiefly because of his deep-rooted respect for Russia's power and the fighting qualities of the Russian soldier. The murderous battles of Eylau and Friedland had been very close-run affairs; in both, for hours, victory – hanging by a thread – was gained in the end only by the narrowest of margins. As he saw it, France and Russia allied by marriage could divide the civilised world into two zones of influence, thus exercising a power no one would dare to challenge. The young grand duchess Anne, as a person, never entered into these dreams; she was merely the tangible expression of this power phantasmagoria.

But once the initial disappointment was overcome, Napoleon with his innate optimism and natural powers of self-persuasion was soon able to convince himself that the Austrian alliance was, in fact, preferable. Despite his dominant position in Europe as a conqueror, he was flattered. He, descendant of a family of comparatively impecunious Corsican notaries – in 1776 his father, Charles Bonaparte, had been granted a 'certificate of indigence' confirming that he had not the necessary means to educate his children – was to be the son-in-law of the ruler of one of Europe's longest-established thrones, husband of 'the first princess of the world'.

Having satisfied himself on the political plane, Napoleon's thoughts began to take on a more personal note as the day of Marie Louise's departure from Vienna approached, and by the time he arrived at Compiègne, their pre-arranged meeting-place, he was bubbling over with impatience, torn between excitement at the thought of an eighteen-year-old virgin bride and apprehensions born of whispered suggestions that the young Austrian was not exactly a beauty. Undoubtedly there was a certain malicious pleasure attached to needling the emperor into asking himself whether the act of procreating a tribe of sons was likely to be an agreeable or an irksome duty.

Napoleon was the traditionally hot-blooded Latin, violently attracted to women. Though still fond of Josephine, during the last few years of their married life he had boasted openly of an imposing array of beautiful mistresses, among them the actress Mademoiselle Georges, the *prima donna* La Grassini and, really loved, Maria Walewska. The idea of an ugly, unpleasingly-shapen woman – or girl – genuinely revolted him.

One contemporary description of Marie Louise portrays her as 'a charming girl, blonde, fresh pink-and-white complexion, wide but low forehead, very like her father in features, especially as regards the eyes – slightly wide apart – and the lower lip, heavy and pendulous, true lip of Philippe le Beau and Charles Quint . . .' Another states that her complexion was somewhat marred by faint scars of a mild attack of smallpox when only two years old, and a tendency to break out in red blotches. 'But,' the writer goes on to say, 'she had a magnificent and pronounced bust, small hips, legs inclined to be spindly, but the most exquisite little feet.'

Napoleon was not prepared to trust any of the descriptions supplied him at his insistent demand, and his anxiety became the most ready source of amusement, not only in court circles but among the people, and especially the Parisians. It was an anxiety which rose to a climax during the days of waiting at Compiègne.

Although the actual meeting between bride and bridegroom was not due to take place till March 28th, Napoleon insisted that everyone be *in situ* by the 23rd.

Arriving the evening of that day, he was greeted by news of the countess Lazanski's dismissal and of Marie Louise's distress, news supplied by Berthier who, jealous of Murat, also cordially disliked Caroline. Furious, but too tied by family loyalty to take drastic action, he immediately sent off a letter by the hand of a marshal of France: '. . . I am very sad about this. But Madame do not be angry with your husband. I am more than distressed at the thought of having displeased you . . . Caroline writes to me that you wish to know what to do to make me happy. I will let you into the secret, Madame. It may seem very simple, but it is none the less true; *be really happy yourself, at the thought of our union.* If you feel sorrowfully inclined, remind yourself; the Emperor will be very sad because he can only be happy when his Louise is happy too . . .'

Time, alternating between boredom and irritation, passed slowly for the vast company of kings, archdukes, dukes – both of the new and old orders – and palace notables, assembled to greet their new empress. The emperor's moods were unpredictable. Not even before a battle had he been known to be so on edge. The merest trifle enraged him. At meals he scarcely touched the dishes set before him, leaving the table before his unfortunate guests had swallowed a couple of hasty mouthfuls. No amusements were provided and no one really appreciated Compiègne's rural setting. To make matters worse, it rained almost continuously. The only permitted relaxation was the rehearsal, repeated *ad nauseam*, of the terrifyingly complicated welcoming ceremony, carried out under the careful and meticulous supervision of Baron de Menéval, Napoleon's private secretary, a devoted but humourless individual who, as might be imagined, was a stickler for detail and a perfectionist.

The morning of the 27th, the rain was torrential. Napoleon was in one of his most irritable moods, brooding over the fact that, since his arrival in Compiègne, he had been quite unable to master the rhythm and intricacies of the latest popular dance, the waltz. And this in spite of several hours' private tuition from his stepdaughter Hortense, queen of Holland, miserably unhappily married to Napoleon's brother Louis, who hummed the latest airs while he twisted and turned clumsily pushing a chair as a partner.

Worse, he had just questioned a despatch-rider who, the previous day, had actually seen Marie Louise: what was she like, was she pretty? Miserably embarrassed, the young cavalryman had blushed, stammered, contradicted himself. The emperor was in despair.

'You see,' he said to Murat, 'I can hardly get a word out of him. Obviously my wife is hideous as not one of these young rips has dared say the contrary.' He shrugged. 'Ah, well! As long as she presents me with fine big sons, I'll try to love her as if she were beautiful.' Another pause, and then the historic remark. '*Après tout, c'est un ventre que j'épouse.*'

To console himself, he pestered Dr Corvisart, the court physician.

'I know *I'm* only forty but if a man of sixty, say, marries a very young girl would he have children?'

'It's possible, sire.'

'And if he were seventy?'

'Then he certainly would.'

Like a caption from a pre-1914 copy of *Punch*, Constant, Napoleon's valet who recounts these scenes, adds, '. . . said the doctor smiling sardonically'.

Moodily, Napoleon had warned de Menéval that there must be a further welcoming ceremony rehearsal before midday, when another despatch-rider arrived with the news that Marie Louise had reached Vitry.

Shortly after this, Napoleon rang for Constant. The valet found his master a changed man. The ugly temper had vanished. The emperor was actually chuckling, his eyes sparkled: immediately, a hot bath and his clothes! He'd changed his mind, he said briskly. Instead of waiting for the empress, he was going to meet her *en route*.

After his bath, and while he was sousing himself with eau-de-Cologne, Constant came in staggering under the weight of the gold-braided brocade suit specially made for the occasion by the famous tailor, Leger. This produced a further burst of hilarity from the emperor. Not that nonsense, he said. What he wanted was his plain green *chasseur* uniform and, by what Constant describes as '*une coquetterie de gloire*', the plain grey frock coat he had worn at Wagram.

Once Napoleon was dressed, de Menéval and Murat were summoned and told of the new plan. De Menéval would be in charge while the emperor was absent, was to open all incoming despatches – even those marked *personal* and *secret* – and was not to enlighten the assembled guests regarding the radical change decided at the last moment. Murat was to order a light carriage, plain with no royal arms, no standards and no escort, which was to be ready to leave in exactly thirty minutes. Murat, himself, would have the privilege of accompanying his sovereign.

On the open road, the rain beat down mercilessly. It did not dampen Napoleon's spirits. Amused, he studied his brother-in-law. Murat was a superb cavalry leader, fearless on the battlefield, but he had a horror of what he termed 'unnecessary' discomfort and, seeing him huddled miserably in his corner, Napoleon said gaily: 'Don't look so put out, and cheer up. With any luck we'll both spend the night tucked up snugly in bed with our respective wives.'

Soissons was passed in record time, but as they reached the little village of Courcelles dusk was beginning to fall.

The road from Vitry ran through the middle of the village. Napoleon ordered a halt and, much to Murat's dismay, insisted on getting out into the pouring rain and walking over to the porch of the village church. There, more or less sheltered, they commanded an unbroken view of the road rising to a slight prominence, typical of the rolling champagne countryside.

A bare quarter of an hour passed. Suddenly, outriders appeared on the crest, followed by the leading troops of the escort, in turn closely followed by the cortège's first carriages slowing down as they approached the village, where the horses were to be changed.

Recognising the Berlin bearing his bride – it was the only one to be drawn by a team of eight (bay) horses – and forgetting Murat, Napoleon rushed out into the rain, bawling to the coachman to pull up immediately. Though nobody guessed the identity of the small, rain-dripping figure, the orders were given so peremptorily that they were obeyed automatically, while an equerry let down the flight of steps.

At that moment, the escort commander came galloping up angrily, sword drawn, wanting to know what the devil was going on, then, suddenly recognising the well-known silhouette, dismounted, rushed to hold open the door, and bellowed:

'The emperor!'

Like a small boy whose practical joke had been ruined, Napoleon turned furiously, on the over-zealous officer, hissed *'imbécile!'*, and then was in the coach.

Caroline gave a startled shriek. He paid no attention to her. Facing him was a young girl whose china-blue eyes were wide open with astonishment. Many years later, on St Helena, he confided that he had been most agreeably surprised by this first glimpse of his bride. He had been prepared for the worst. But, he told Marchand, he was straightaway fascinated by the peach-blossom complexion (evidently in the semi-darkness the slight smallpox scars and red blotches were invisible), the ampleness of her bosom and, above all, by her tiny feet, for he had a horror of women with large hands and feet which he was in the habit of describing as *'abats canailles'*.

A little out of breath, he said: 'Madame, I am delighted to see you.'

Then, before Marie Louise could reply, he had seized her in his arms, completely ignoring Caroline's presence, all dripping with rain as he was, and began kissing and caressing her with the enthusiasm of a callow youth alone for the first time with the object of his calf passion.

At last releasing Marie Louise – whose macaw-plumed toque had been knocked rakishly over one eye – only when he felt the need to draw breath, Napoleon made another spur-of-the-moment decision.

All he wanted was to get to Compiègne as quickly as possible and to be alone with his enchanting – as he now found her – young bride. He was fully aware of the fact that receptions had been arranged at every town – especially Soissons – and village *en route*. Too bad! To the bewildered escort commander, he gave the order to head for Compiègne as fast as possible within the limits of safety and *without a stop*. At this point Caroline murmured something about the Soissons reception and was told politely, but firmly, to mind her own business.

As the coachman whipped up the horses and the carriage swayed into motion, Marie Louise murmured, 'You are even nicer than in your portrait,' a remark which was the signal for another passionate embrace.

The distance between Courcelles and Soissons was covered in a time which may well have constituted a record for a heavy coach, and one can imagine the bewilderment, followed probably by resentment, of the drenched citizens after the trouble and money spent in preparing a welcome for their new empress, when the cavalcade charged through their town as if pursued by some Mongol horde, splashing them with mud from head to foot before they even had time to open their mouths, let alone cry '*Vive l'Empératrice!*'

A despatch-rider had galloped ahead to warn de Menéval that the emperor and empress were close on his heels. One of the Austrian diplomats present described the scene: 'Towards ten o'clock, a mud-spattered rider arrived to say that they were just down the road. Everybody started rushing round. The staircase was draped, kings and queens arranging themselves hastily at its foot. Orchestras everywhere, torchbearers more than you could count. Then a tremendous din, the rolling of drums. And here they come, marshals, generals, equerries, chamberlains, pages, at the gallop, two or three carriages drawn by six horses, steaming and foam-flecked, and then at last the coach with the eight-horse team in which were Their Majesties and the queen of Naples. A wind orchestra, beautiful but a little subdued, struck up. I saw the empress jump lightly from the coach, then go up the steps on the arm of her little husband. As she was a good half-head taller than he was, it was rather comic . . .'

'It wasn't a marriage,' says another historian, 'it was more like a kidnapping. Obviously beside himself with impatience, Napoleon cut short presentations, bows, curtsies, suggesting that the empress would like to be shown straightaway to her apartments, whereupon the duchess of Montebello and Madame de Luçay promptly led her upstairs. On the way, Marie Louise whispered, "The emperor is very charming. I think I'm going to love him very much." '

In the meantime Napoleon, ignoring a group of little girls waiting to bombard him with rose-petals, turning his back on the musicians, gave the harassed and scandalised de Menéval the order for supper for three – two pheasants and three bottles of champagne – to be served without delay in his private rooms and, without a word to the assembled guests, hurried upstairs after the women.

The original plan for that night had been that the emperor should sleep at the Hotel de la Chancellerie, while Marie Louise occupied the Château's royal apartment. But the sight of his young bride had so fired Napoleon's ardour that impatience proved stronger than protocol which, in any case, had been decreed by him.

As in the carriage, Napoleon completely ignored Caroline during supper, partaken cosily by a roaring log fire, subdued candlelight lending to the scene something of the charm of a clandestine rendezvous. Encouraged by Marie Louise's frankly approving glances and the flush on her cheeks – she was drinking champagne for the first time and enjoying it – he whispered: 'Madame, before leaving Vienna did you receive any particular instructions?'

With a disarming naivety, Marie Louise answered: 'I was told I must belong to you entirely, and obey you in all things.'

Napoleon's reactions were again as prompt as those he usually displayed on a battlefield. For the first time addressing himself to his sister, he said:

'Take the empress to her room and prepare her for bed.'

According to popular gossip: '. . . when, half an hour later, wearing only a dressing-gown and smothered, as usual, with eau-de-Cologne he' (Napoleon) 'was alone at last with his bride, he threw himself on her like an impatient soldier on a tart . . .'

One imagines that there were not, as at Braunau, any peep-holes and that this statement must, of a necessity, be pure hypothesis; but, whether or not it were true, the result was evidently highly satisfactory for both parties.

The following morning the emperor was radiant. To one of his A.D.C.s he remarked, beaming: 'My dear fellow, marry a German girl. They make the best wives in the world; sweet, good, naive and fresh as roses.'

Breakfast was served in the bedroom, Marie Louise in bed, the emperor sitting beside her. The amorous glances they exchanged, the empress's contented, almost smug look, amused everyone and was widely commented, especially when this first night was extended to a two-day, highly-concentrated honeymoon.

This rather unconventional behaviour shocked a good many

people, among them Lord Liverpool, who noted: 'Never was a young woman courted in so strange a fashion. Napoleon's conduct savoured more of a rape than a wooing . . .'

This, however, was not the opinion of the couple concerned. Napoleon, in lyrical vein, wrote to Francis:

Monsieur my Brother and Father-in-law,
  Your Majesty's daughter has now been here for two days. She has fulfilled all my expectations, and for two days I have never ceased offering her and receiving from her the proof of the tenderest feelings uniting us. We suit each other perfectly. I will make her very happy, and I owe my happiness to Your Majesty. Will he (Your Majesty) allow me to thank him for the perfect gift he has made me, and may his paternal heart rejoice in the certainty of the happiness of his child . . .

And Marie Louise, not to be outdone, writing by the same courier:

. . . I've been with him (the Emperor) the whole time since my arrival and he really loves me. I'm more than grateful and I reciprocate his love most sincerely. The more you get to know him, the more charming he is; there is something both endearing and exciting about him which is irresistible . . .

So, within a couple of days, a marriage, in its conception no more than a political manoeuvre, gave every indication of having blossomed into the perfect love match.

Although, looking perhaps to the future, Napoleon had never been anxious for the Church to legalise his civil wedding with Josephine de Beauharnais, he did not intend to leave the least loophole for the charge of illegality in this, his second matrimonial venture. Not content with the Viennese proxy wedding, he had ordered that its bonds be made all the more indissoluble – if that were possible – by a civil wedding according to French law, at Saint Cloud, to be followed by a second religious service in the Tuileries chapel.

The departure from Compiègne for Saint Cloud took place at midday on March 30th.

An elaborate welcoming ceremony, reminding one spectator of a race meeting at Longchamps, had been arranged for the royal couple's entry into the Seine province. There were at least four hundred carriages, apart from those of the official guests. Smart young men-about-town had ridden out from Paris on their most spirited horses. A triumphal arch, embossed with the imperial arms, spanned the road and, just beyond this, a flag-draped stage on which the prefect, the municipal council members and mayors of all the towns and villages of the province had taken up their stand, and were silently rehearsing their speeches.

The emperor's coach appeared at around four-thirty in the afternoon. Again he was in a tearing hurry. He interrupted the prefect's discourse and shouted to the escort commander to force the pace to the Porte Maillot. As Hortense, queen of Holland, put it: 'In military fashion, he' (the Emperor) 'cut short the speech of which he had not heard a syllable. In all, the carriages did not stop for more than three minutes before the horses were whipped up and the cortège departed at full speed . . .'

At the Porte Maillot, Napoleon was happier. It was a scene of martial splendour which greeted him – he always felt uncomfortable in the company of civilians. Two hundred dragoons and *chasseurs-à-cheval* joined the escort which, a bare three miles from Saint Cloud, was swelled by the entire cavalry of the guard while, as they crossed the Seine bridge, salvoes were fired by a hundred cannon.

Once again previous arrangements were changed. Instead of Marie Louise being lodged in the Trianon, Napoleon and his bride retired to bed in the Saint Cloud royal suite.

The crowd of courtiers who usually trailed after Napoleon were rather amused that April 1st – All Fools' Day – should have been chosen for the civil wedding, and there were a number of derogatory comments about the new empress's nose and underlip, giving rise to a mildly crude pun: *Elle est laide, mais elle sera beaucoup mieux quand elle aura un nouveau né (nez)*. However, as Berthier points out, there were no sniggers when Marie Louise and Napoleon agreed to 'take each other' in matrimony, and when Cambacères, the arch-chancellor recently created duke of Parma, announced: 'In the name of the Emperor and the Law, I declare that His Imperial and Royal Majesty Napoleon, Emperor of the French, and Her Imperial and Royal Highness the Archduchess Marie Louise are united in Marriage.'

The following day, it was the religious marriage which was celebrated with a pomp and splendour unique in Europe's history.

It is a long drive from Saint Cloud to the Tuileries, and Marie Louise wrote to her father that the crown Napoleon had himself placed on her head was so heavy that she had hardly been able to bear it. Furthermore, her robe, made by Leroy and costing 12,000 francs, lavishly embroidered with jewels, was also crushingly heavy. Many thought that it would have been more fitting if Napoleon had stuck to his role of warrior monarch and appeared at his wife's side in uniform; but, desperately anxious that everything should follow the most strictly conventional lines – fearing also that his over-ardent reception of his bride might have raised a few Viennese eyebrows – he seems to have lost his instinctive sense of humour and was dressed in 'a Spanish costume of white satin embroidered in gold, the mantle of which was covered with golden bees. On his head he wore a black velvet cap ornamented with eight rows of diamonds and three white feathers fastened together by a knot in the middle of which blazed the regent diamond. The cap did not fit, it had been altered a good twenty times and every possible way of wearing it had been tried out, but finally it was pronounced satisfactory . . .'

The royal coach, mostly of glass, heavily gilded and drawn by a team of eight horses, brought up the rear of a long procession headed by lancers, dragoons and *chasseurs-à-cheval* of the guard and preceded by thirty-six coaches carrying members of the Bonaparte family, kings and queens, marshals, ambassadors and foreign dignitaries, among the latter being Metternich on a short visit from Vienna to be eye-witness to the success of his Machiavellian policy.

There was a halt at the Arc de Triomphe, still uncompleted but effectively disguised by boards skilfully painted to give the impression of a finished building, where the prefect of the Seine was able to enjoy a mild revenge, and read, uninterrupted, his discourse: 'Madame the presence of Your Majesty reveals to all eyes those inimitable gifts from Heaven which have called you to the throne . . .' and so on, for the best part of half-an-hour.

Arrived at the Tuileries and before proceeding to the *Salon Carré* – converted into a chapel for the occasion – Marie Louise was obliged to support the extra burden of the cumbersome gold-embroidered cloak worn by Josephine in 1804, and whose weight had nearly toppled her physically from the throne. The huge train was carried by the queens, Julie of Spain and Catherine of Westphalia, and the two Bonaparte princesses, Elisa and Pauline. With the exception of the good-natured Catherine who was also the only one of the four with genuine royal blood in her veins, the other three were alternately petulant and sulky, feeling that their newly-acquired royal dignity was outraged at being obliged to carry out the menial task of train-bearer.

Napoleon himself was radiant but Marie Louise, as people were quick to note, looked exhausted. This was hardly surprising. To begin with, she had been worn out with the long journey from Braunau, hardly alleviated by the mental shock of Madame Lazanski's dismissal. There followed immediately the exciting but violent and uninhibited initiation into those facts of life so carefully withheld before her departure, in the bed of an exuberant husband she had known for only a few hours. Not a moment's repose had been possible after leaving Compiègne in the continual round of receptions and ceremonies, alternated by further proof of Napoleon's insatiable virility.

'She looks like a big doll who's been rather roughly handled,' it was murmured in the waiting crowd as she walked stiffly, leaning on her husband's arm, feeling every moment that 'I was going to collapse under the weight of the cloak and the robe which I found almost unbearable.'

In the circumstances, it was uncharitable that she should have been held up to almost universal denigration by all the court hangers-on, her 'unbending' demeanour compared so unfavourably with Josephine's 'natural charm'. But then, most of the official guests were also in a vile humour. They had been obliged to conform to the timetable laid down by the emperor, and, themselves dressed in the most cumbersome of garments – also dictated by the Master – had been made to wait eight hours before the royal couple appeared.

Captain Coignet, one of the officers on guard duty that day, and a methodical diary keeper, does not appear to have been impressed by the dazzling feminine *toilettes*: '. . . And the ladies' dresses! *Decolletées* at the back almost as far as the waist! And in front you could see at least half of their breasts; bare shoulders and bare arms. And what necklaces! What bracelets! What earrings! Nothing but pearls, rubies and diamonds. I'd never seen the great ladies of Paris at such close quarters and practically naked, before. Believe me, it wasn't a pretty sight.'

This marriage, the third binding Marie Louise to Napoleon, was celebrated by that highly political prelate, the Bonaparte uncle, Cardinal Fesch. It should have been the great day of Napoleon's life. But, as so often happens on such occasions even in the lives of humbler mortals than emperors, it was marred by an unforeseen incident. 'When the Emperor passed by,' wrote Denis Etienne Pasquier, also an inveterate diary keeper, 'we were struck by the triumphant aura with which he seemed to glow. His features, usually so serious, were transformed with happiness and joy. The marriage service celebrated by Cardinal Fesch didn't last very long, so imagine our amazement when we saw on the way back that those same features which such a short while ago had radiated contentment, were sombre and menacing. What could have happened in this brief interval?'

The answer was simple. Twenty-seven cardinals had been invited. Only twelve of the seats reserved for this imposing array of princes of the Church were occupied.

Napoleon was trembling with rage. 'I will never forget his look of fury at the sight of those empty places,' wrote Count von Lebzeltern, one of the Austrian diplomats present. 'He was hardly able to concentrate on the service. "I know what they want," he was heard to mutter. "They want to throw doubts on the legitimacy of my dynasty." '

His first reaction was to have the absent cardinals tried for sedition, at least to forbid them to wear the traditional scarlet. But like so many of his rages this, too, petered out and in the end no measures were taken against the recalcitrants. The incident upset him so much, however, that even the crowds' tremendous enthusiasm seemed at first lukewarm to his tortured mind.

'I've spoilt them' (the Parisians) 'so much,' he grumbled, 'that they'd be blasé even if I'd married the Madonna herself.'

Later, during the official banquet, he was slightly mollified when Metternich, one of the principal guests, suddenly leapt to his feet and, obviously taking the bride's fertility for granted, raised his glass, saying loudly, 'I drink to the king of Rome' – this being the title which Napoleon had already decreed should be conferred on his first (of many, he hoped) son – while outside the clamour of the public festivities redoubled. Understandably! For the city fountains were spouting wine, and for those who wished to temper their drinking with a little solid nourishment, 4,800 *patés*, 1,200 tongues, 1,000 legs of mutton and 3,000 sausages – among many other 'victuals' – had been provided free by the municipality.

'Thus,' says Jean Roubiquet, 'Marie Louise's wedding remained synonymous, for the man in the street, with a terrible attack of indigestion.'

Chapter IV

For the first time since he had assumed the imperial crown in 1804, Napoleon's empire was at peace. It was a peace which was to last for almost exactly two years. Yet in spite of all the appearances of stability, Napoleon knew, though he would not admit it, that it was what today might be described as a 'phoney' peace. There was the wretched Spanish affair, which he talked of ruefully as 'a running sore', where his marshals were proving singularly inept and unworthy of their great reputations, discovering to their discomfiture that the British soldier was just as tough and as redoubtable an opponent as the Russian. The British government was open in its statement that 'Bonaparte' must be kicked off his usurped throne. The continental blockade, meant to starve Britain, was not being enforced and was merely irritating the maritime powers. The Russian friendship on which Napoleon's whole European policy had been based now no longer had even a theoretical value.

Yet he shut his eyes resolutely to all danger signals. The modern Alexander was determined to forget war and devote himself, like any other respectable young bourgeois husband, to his wife. This he proceeded to do so thoroughly that Metternich was able to write with great satisfaction: 'He' (the Emperor) 'is so much in love with her' (Marie Louise) 'that he can't hide the fact even in public, and all his normal ways are changed so as to fall in with her least wish . . .'

This letter was largely inspired by the fact that Marie Louise, having temporarily overcome her dislike of the man whom she suspected of having manoeuvred her wedding for political ends and of exercising an influence fringing on disrespect over her adored 'papa', had confided in him: 'I'm not a bit afraid of the Emperor, but I begin to think he's afraid of *me*.'

The two greatest changes which so impressed contemporaries were the one political, the other domestic. Napoleon had always been profoundly sceptical of the abilities of those surrounding him and convinced that he, alone, was capable of taking a decision, great or small. Every despatch, every report, however apparently trivial, had to be submitted to him for his approval, whether incoming or outgoing. Every directive, whether it concerned the movement of vast armies, a new design for a belt, the re-alignment of a Paris thoroughfare, the details regulating a palace ceremony, the livery of the coachmen, the programme for the opera season, all had to bear the emperor's personal seal. But, fascinated by his teenage virgin bride – innocent yet temperamentally a true daughter of her father and inspired by a neophyte's enthusiasm for these new mysteries unveiled to her by an eager husband – Napoleon showed an incredible indifference to affairs of state, resenting every moment robbing him of her physical presence.

Equally astonishing was the way he was now prepared to linger over meals. All his life he had ignored gastronomic pleasures, preferring a snack served at a camp table, hastily swallowed and hastily washed down by a glass of neat brandy, to the most lovingly-prepared or rarest delicacies. His *'bonne Louise'* on the other hand was notoriously greedy, with a schoolgirl's passion for the rich cakes and pastries, specialities of Viennese *cuisine*. She adored really copious meals and liked to linger over them. To everybody's amazement Napoleon never showed the least impatience at being kept for hours rather than minutes at table. He would sit smiling patiently and complacently while she chattered, addressing him – much to the servants' amusement – rather kittenishly as 'Nana', 'Popo', or *'mon très méchant galant'*, while he in turn delighted in a form of horseplay not usually associated – in public at any rate – with court circles, slapping her behind, pinching her cheeks, nibbling her ears and calling her his *'grosse bête'*. For her sake he was even prepared to sleep in an unheated bedroom with the window open.

This extended honeymoon lasted till April 26th when, regretfully, they started off on a tour of the Low Countries.

Napoleon was so proud of his bride that he wished her to be seen by as many of his subjects as possible. At the same time, since he was anxiously awaiting Dr Corvisart's statement that the empress was pregnant, he thought it best to carry out the projected tour before her 'condition' was liable to make protracted journeys inadvisable.

The Netherlands, forced to accept Louis Bonaparte as their king since 1806, strongly resented the imposition of the continental blockade, since so much of their normal trade had been with Britain. Napoleon hoped, a little naively, that a display of imperial splendour and the sight of a former archduchess of Austria now empress of France might impress the stolid Dutch into forgetting their troubles, if only temporarily. Above all he was terrified of a second Spain developing on his northern frontiers.

There was, therefore, nothing savouring of informality about this official visit.

The imperial cortège, divided into three sections, comprised some thirty-three coaches and a cavalry escort of over a thousand picked troopers. Despite this ostentation, the tour was of no historic interest and achieved nothing. On the other hand, Marie Louise kept a very detailed diary of this her first official visit as empress, which affords a remarkable insight into the character of this eighteen-year-old girl plunged straight from the convent-like atmosphere of the Austrian royal family into the complex world of intrigue surrounding this parvenu giant, beneath whose shadow lay most of Europe, and who was now her husband. It shows that, despite being so cut off from the outside world in childhood and adolescence, she was remarkably shrewd – sometimes even to the extent of being spiteful – in her judgment of those with whom she was in daily contact, inclined to be peevish, showing signs of embryonic hypochondria and, already so confident, concerning her influence over her *très méchant galant*, that she does not hesitate to criticise, ridicule at times, and indulge in remarks of the 'just like a man' category. Within a month, the frightened, tearful girl who had set out so miserably from Vienna had undergone a complete mental metamorphosis.

To begin with she displayed the enthusiasm of a child being taken on its first holiday: 'I set out from Compiègne delighted with the idea of such a pleasant journey. I had never before travelled without sadness, but now felt it would be a most pleasant experience, and I'm certain I shall love travelling to distraction.

'We left Compiègne on April 27th at nine in the morning. The country as far as St Quentin is very pretty, even beautiful, also very fertile. There are many hamlets and villages, but what struck me most was the quantity of wind mills.

'In every place the Emperor was received with the ringing of bells and the firing of salutes, expressions of a devotion as simple as it was touching. Everywhere the young girls presented us with flowers and poems, most of the latter were very poor.

'We arrived at St Quentin at midday and were lodged in the Prefecture where everything was uncomfortable and dirty, and what was worse was the fact that I was a quarter of a league away from the Emperor . . . I went to bed with lumbago not being used to continuous travelling over paved roads . . .'

The same day, we get an example of waspishness: 'the Emperor was much amused while telling me of an incident which happened to Monsieur Jouan* who, while galloping without looking where he was going, was caught on the branch of a tree; the horse went on, and after a few minutes he fell to the ground without hurting himself in the least. Malicious tongues say that for more than an hour he thought himself dead. Which is very like him! . . .'

Next day there were more caustic comments after a visit to St Quentin–Cambrai canal. 'It is over 22 leagues in length and very deep. We went on board' (on what she described as a 'gondola') 'and continued on our way beneath a blazing sun which gave us terrible headaches. We reached the first tunnel into which water had not yet been run, and entered carriages in order to pass through it. The length is a quarter of a league, cut out of rock. The roof is very high and was illuminated by two rows of lamps which produced a most striking effect . . .'

The second tunnel was traversed by boat. 'We went through this tunnel in a rowing boat which was not very serviceable as it let water which wet my feet, but as there was nothing we could do about it we had to put up with it cheerfully which wasn't very difficult for me, as I'm not easily upset. In addition we nearly capsized several times because fat Prince Schwarzenberg† would keep leaning out of the boat making it heel over dangerously because of his weight . . . We saw the source of the Scheldt, here so narrow that one could easily jump over it. The bridge too was so narrow that we were obliged to get out of the carriages which were then lifted over. This delayed us more than an hour and put the Queen of Naples in such a bad temper that no one could say a word to her for the rest of the journey. I cannot understand how anyone can get upset by such trifling incidents. To me they were nothing compared with what I had put up with on other journeys without a word of complaint . . . On reaching the

* Chief surgeon of the Guards.
† Austrian ambassador in Paris.

Hotel de Ville (Cambrai) I went to bed for the sun had given me a shocking headache. I was, however, quite pleased with myself at not having grumbled once, unlike many of the ladies . . .'

Later there is a piece of gossip tinged, perhaps, with a hint of jealousy. 'The Queen of Naples left us here with her Metternich. So much the better. I shan't miss them. But it was very ungallant of the Grand Duke of Wurzburg to desert us to follow the Queen of Naples. It is only too true that when love and friendship are in the balance, poor tranquil friendship has to go by the board!'

On arrival at Brussels, and taking up residence in the palace at Laeken, there was a slight tiff. 'My first step was to take a bathe to get rid of the horrible black dust.* I don't know if the bath was bad for me because it was too hot, but I was seized with stomach cramps and colic. The Emperor must needs send for Monsieur Jouan who, after many pompous and florid phrases, informed the Emperor that I was going to have a child and should have a miscarriage if I continued the journey. The Emperor believed him, which annoyed me so much that I suffered still more. To get my revenge on Monsieur Jouan I pretended to be much more ill than I really was. He came hurrying into my room, felt for my pulse which he declared he could not find, and then rubbed my nose with vinegar. After about five minutes, I pretended to return to consciousness, for by this time he was talking of bleeding me. The next day (April 30th), the Emperor, instead of letting me rest, wakened me at seven in the morning just to have a look at the garden. Fortunately while sleeping he seemed to have forgotten Monsieur Jouan's portentous phrases, so there was no further question about my being left behind in Brussels . . .'

The next stage of the journey was Malines (Mechlin) where, for the first time in her life, Marie Louise boarded a man-of-war. 'We climbed on board the *Charlemagne*, but it required a lot of courage. The gangway was like a ladder with the steps so far apart that we mounted it on our knees. And the wind, I am sure, caused some very embarrassing incidents. I'm certain we exhibited our legs to the gentlemen, and I vowed that never again would I go on board a battleship unless I were wearing trousers. The Minister of the Navy' (Admiral Missiessy) 'really might have been gallant enough to have had another gangway constructed for us, but he is nothing after all but a rough sailor. Really one must be

* From the Mons coalmining area.

68

very agile in boarding a battleship for the first time to avoid laming oneself. I know I returned to Antwerp with a sprain, two lumps on my head, and a gown covered with tar . . .'

At Antwerp the unfortunate Monsieur Jouan once more incurred the empress's wrath. 'I was again annoyed with that tiresome Monsieur Jouan, who urged the Emperor not to take me to the Island of Walcheren, and also with the Emperor for listening to him. Doctors are real ignoramuses, they do not realise that far more harm is done to their patients, even when they are ill, by thwarting them, than by letting them do as they wish: but I can be obstinate when I want something, and we will see which of us will prevail . . .'

There follows a long description of Antwerp, a certain admiration for the Dutch style of architecture but, nevertheless, the comment: 'There are many charming country houses round Antwerp, but I should hate to live here, because the climate is very unhealthy. The neighbourhood is marshy and nasty smells come from the Scheldt, consequently three-quarters of the inhabitants have fever every year!'

To begin with, as we have seen, Marie Louise was sure she would love travelling, but obviously she had not reckoned with her husband's restless energy and, as the journey was prolonged, she began to display the same irritation at the slightest mishap that she had so castigated when shown by the queen of Naples. 'The hour for lunch had long passed; it was nearly two o'clock and the Emperor would never allow me to eat in a carriage. He had a fine reason for this, which was that a woman should never feel hungry. These precious arguments, added to the fact that I was famished, made me so angry that I had a terrible headache by the time we reached Breda. I thought that we would be allowed to stay there. However, the Emperor, who treated us like grenadiers, forced us to continue the journey after lunch! I was in such a bad temper that the Emperor was displeased but, feeling quite indifferent, I let him scold me as much as he liked without answering. There is nothing which quiets a man as quickly as this method. They are insufferable creatures, and should I ever return to this world in another incarnation, I wouldn't dream of getting married . . .' Her boast that 'she was not afraid of the emperor' does not seem to have been an exaggeration!

From Antwerp, the royal cortège moved on to Bergen-op-Zoom

where, according to the empress, the houses were 'dreadful' and were accorded pages of complaints; but, as Marie Louise tired, complaints about conditions rapidly deteriorated into squabbles with other ladies of the party, and notably with Catherine, queen of Westphalia – rather surprising in view of the latter's reputation of level-headed good humour. 'I resigned myself to the situation' (reportedly bad accommodation at Middleburg) 'but not so the Queen of Westphalia; her women arrived twenty-four hours after we did, so she made the unfortunate Countess von Liverstein stay up all night in the antechamber to make tea for her, and when it was brought she scolded her, would not drink it, and cried with rage. It requires an angel from Heaven to put up with her. I know very well what I would have done with the tea had I been the lady-in-waiting . . .'

Marie Louise does not in fact say what exactly she would have done with the tea, but it is more than likely that these gibes were prompted by her own ill-humour, proving that the prevalent art of accusing others of one's own misdeeds was not, after all, the invention – though perfected by – the late Adolf Hitler. Indeed, most historians are agreed that Catherine was not only good-tempered, but loyal and courageous. Like Marie Louise, she had been forced into marriage – with Jerome Bonaparte – for political expediency. In spite of this, she proved a devoted wife and one of the very few who later refused to desert the Bonapartes in their moments of irreparable disaster. But Marie Louise now had her knife into her complacent sister-in-law, and again we read: 'I find the Queen of Westphalia very much out of temper because I had not taken her with me' (to visit Middleburg) 'and she wearies me with her constant querying – "Are you still fond of the Duchess of Montebello?"

'I have only known the Duchess of Montebello two months, and am most attached to her, so could not help replying to the Queen – "My dear, I do not change my friends like my chemises." What she said to me is just the way a queen talks. People say that women of our rank do not know how to make friends. But I want to prove that there are exceptions. It is quite true that the poor queen is very unfortunate with her friends. Hardly has she made a friend before the King makes her his mistress, and that really is not the way to keep her attached to them . . .'

In relating one incident, Marie Louise shows a definite sense of humour, but once more ends up on a peevish note. Brought up in Vienna, she had never seen the sea, and this she did for the first time on a visit to Fort Haag. To do this, she had to climb over a series of steep sand dunes: 'Each step we took was equally troublesome, but the ascent was nothing to travellers as intrepid as ourselves, and we were well repaid by the fine view that greeted us when we reached the top of the hills' (dunes).

'We saw the ocean as an immense surface of water bounded only by the horizon; the sun was setting, colouring the sea like a rainbow. Far off, we could descry some fishing boats returning from their labours, protected by a sloop. They have to be protected from the English who take their fish and refuse to pay for it. The sea was very calm except on the shore where it was breaking angrily. The Queen of Westphalia and I amused ourselves by picking up some shells with which the beach was covered. Some were lovely, but I am told that those of the Mediterranean and the Indian Ocean are infinitely more so. These shells, combined with the unwholesome air and the mischievous trick of the King' (Jerome) 'were the cause of my having three attacks of fever!

'While we were enjoying ourselves, I saw that the Viceroy' (Eugène de Beauharnais) 'and the Duke of Istria were looking towards us and laughing in a very significant manner. There was no need to ask why before the tide, coming in with incredible speed, faster than we could run, had wet us up to the knees. Fortunately it receded just as quickly.

'These gentlemen then explained to us that this was quite normal, but they might have been gallant enough to have warned us. We gave up our search' (for shells) 'and asked the Emperor's permission to change. His reply was, "Stay as you are, ladies, this bath will do you good." So he made us wait till eight o'clock. The next day the weather was shocking, and I remained in bed with a high fever. I do not know what has happened to my iron constitution, it has just vanished. I am sure this is the doctor's fault. During the whole journey he has done nothing but dose me . . .'

The diary stops at Middleburg, though the tour continued for another eighteen days. The cortège returned to Laeken palace on May 14th, remained there three days, then set out on the homeward journey via Ghent, Bruges, Ostend, Lille, Boulogne, Dieppe and Rouen, finally arriving at Saint Cloud on June 1st.

*   *   *

Even more than a picture of the Netherlands in the year 1810, this diary gives an insight into the young Marie Louise's latent, expanding character, presaging the path she would adopt in later years.

There is the tendency to hypochondria, soon to become so pronounced that many of the cruel blows, both physical and psychological, she would be called upon to endure were absorbed by her obsession with her ailments, most of them imaginary, the real pain being dulled by this self-built armour. At the same time enjoying ill health, she was able to use with an infinite cunning this classical 'frail little woman' weapon in clashes with her dominant husband in moments of minor crisis. Yet the disobliging remarks about the emperor and men in general caused, perhaps, by a lingering resentment of a forced marriage, never occur again. Till the moment of their final separation her physical love for her husband, and her distress when affairs of state forced a temporary parting, were irrefutably genuine.

Significant also is the hint of the attachment which later developed – especially as a result of the emperor's increasingly forced absences – into a near-Lesbian passion, reminiscent of that which she had nourished in her childhood for Victoria de Poutet, countess de Crenneville, for the duchess of Montebello who during the journey had gained, subtly, the domination over the young empress which the tactless Caroline had so dismally failed to achieve.

For his part, Napoleon was not entirely satisfied by the tour. He could not persuade himself that the acclamations were entirely spontaneous. He suspected that his brother, Louis, who had not been happy about accepting the Netherlands' throne in the first place, was now at heart more pro-Dutch than pro-Bonaparte. Nor was he able to close his eyes to the fact that, though Marie Louise was the eldest child of one of Europe's oldest monarchies, the gaucherie she had displayed at her wedding and all other public occasions since her arrival in France was not due to fatigue and extreme youth but, rather, inherent.

This long tour completed, Marie Louise had looked forward to a little rest, a drift into the semi-bourgeois tranquillity for which she had so marked a predilection. She was sadly mistaken.

In his passion to show the world that this marriage was a success, Napoleon was determined that Paris must be the centre of European gaiety. Everybody must be happy, and make their happiness apparent, by indulging in a non-stop round of festivities. It was an order.

This imperial decree was the signal for a series of uninterrupted fêtes, dances, receptions, whose lavish extravagance have never before or since been rivalled in Europe's history. The vaster the expense, the greater the emperor's approval. The monster fête offered to their majesties by the city of Paris, and at which their majesties put in an appearance for a bare couple of hours, cost its citizens over two-and-a-half million francs. In addition, a 'toilette', presented during this fête to the empress and which she accepted without offering a word of thanks, had drained their purses of a further half million. It was hardly surprising that the comments of the average man – and especially woman – in the street were caustic in the extreme and the word *l'Autrichienne* used, as in the time of Marie Antoinette, in a pejorative sense, was on most people's lips.

One of the most memorable of these fêtes was given by Napoleon's highly immoral but equally beautiful youngest sister, Pauline, then married to Prince Borghese, a gangling homosexual.

'The proceedings opened with a musical comedy, *La Danse Interrompue*. At the end of this the emperor and the empress went into the park (Neuilly) illuminated with fairy lights. Suddenly, living statues leapt down from their pedestals and conducted the royal couple to the temple of Hymen. From there they were led through this fairyland to a miniature reproduction of the Schoenbrunn palace, Marie Louise's home outside Vienna. Then there was a firework display, and at midnight the ball opened. All this was noted and described by several of the guests who wrote memoirs of the occasion. Napoleon enjoyed the evening so much that he ordered Pauline to repeat the performance next week – to Pauline's dismay because of the expense . . .'*

Once again, however, Marie Louise's behaviour, her seeming indifference to all these superhuman efforts to amuse her, brought forth an outburst of adverse comment.

'She went through the evening in a state of imperturbable impassivity; a veritable statue as cold, as inanimate as marble,

* Pierson Dixon: *Pauline.*

and for all Pauline's pains, which had cost her 76,476 francs, not even a word of thanks.'*

The real trouble was that on these occasions Marie Louise's lack of manners was due almost entirely to intense shyness which caused her such acute misery that, according to one writer, her fingers contracted so violently when she was searching for some pertinent word or subtle compliment that, one after the other, she broke all the beautiful gold fans, part of her wedding trousseau, offered by Napoleon. Her only defender was the duke de Broglie who, in an attempted apologia, wrote to Marshal Marmont, duke of Ragusa (present-day Dubrovnik): '. . . the Empress danced at all these fêtes, and it is said that she is beginning to lose her Germanic habits; her feet, which are two of the smallest that ever trod the streets of Vienna, now turn outwards, and she curtsies with her head instead of her knees . . .'

There was one more fête to be held before the festive season was declared closed. It was given by Prince Schwarzenberg, in the old Hotel Montesson in the rue de la Chaussée d'Antin. Like its rivals, it was a most sumptuous affair, with the usual pseudo-classical temples so popular at the time, a subterranean grotto, a *ballet champêtre,* orchestras playing mixed German and French programmes, choirs and the inevitable trumpet fanfares to remind the guests of the French emperor's military renown.

For the actual dancing, Schwarzenberg had an enormous wooden ballroom built in the garden, which was connected with the main building by a wooden gallery. The ballroom ceiling, from the middle of which hung a vast chandelier, was covered by wax-paper-lined tarpaulin. The walls, sconced and hung with gold and silver brocades, projected the light of a thousand candelabra. The flowers alone had cost a fortune.

For once, Marie Louise seemed to be enjoying herself.

'The Emperor himself exuded the joy his new marriage had brought him. Never, men said, had they seen him so happy, so buoyant, so infectiously gay. His eyes followed the Empress wherever she went and she, flushed, excited and radiant, looked her best . . . And then suddenly, without any warning, a window curtain fluttering in the soft breeze bellied towards a sconce and, in a moment the scene was illuminated by a thousand leaping tongues of flame . . .'†

* Ibid.
† Oddie: *Marie Louise Empress of France, Duchess of Parma.* Matthews. 1931.

Fire precautions had been the very last of Schwarzenberg's preoccupations in the preparation of this fête. As a result, the wooden building was a death-trap. Within seconds this elaborate, ornate ballroom was a vast torch. To make matters worse, of the four small exits – for close on fifteen hundred guests – three were blocked almost immediately by flames.

Panic was as instantaneous and as violent as the fire. Two of the guests, however, remained absolutely calm: Napoleon himself and Eugène de Beauharnais. Napoleon took Marie Louise's arm, saying, 'Madame, a fire has broken out. We had better leave,' – it is doubtful if history records a more supreme example of the art of understatement – and led her out and across the already smouldering gallery into the house. Only a few seconds later it burst into flames and collapsed.

'. . . the confusion and the tumult were appalling,' Marie Louise wrote to her father. 'We couldn't find either the Grand Duke of Wurzburg or the Queen of Naples and thought at first they must be dead. My sister-in-law Catherine thought her husband had been caught in the flames, and fainted. I was separated from my ladies. General Lauriston, who was looking for his wife, was screaming like a madman and blocking our way. I was in an agony of fear when the Emperor left me to go back to help. Catherine stayed with me till he came back at four in the morning, literally soaked to the skin. The Duchess of Rovigo, one of the palace *dames d'honneur*, has serious burns, as have the Countesses Loewenstein and Bucholz, *dames d'honneur* of the Queen of Westphalia. The Duke of Istria burnt his feet and hands very badly saving General Thouzard's wife, herself in a very bad condition. Count Kourakine is also badly hurt with terrible burns; he was almost trampled to death while he lay unconscious. Prince Metternich has also been burnt, but not so badly; on the other hand Princess Schwarzenberg, who refused to leave before she was assured that everybody was safe, has been terribly burnt and her son too. They haven't yet found Princess Pauline Schwarzenberg . . . The Emperor has just arrived with the dreadful news; Pauline (Schwarzenberg) was in the garden separated from her two children and frightened that they had come to harm, she tore herself away from those who were trying to hold her back and rushed into the flames. Later searching in the debris, they found her body; face, feet and legs completely burnt. Beside her was a pendant inscribed with the names

Eleanore and Pauline; it was the only way they could identify her. She leaves nine children, the oldest twelve, and she was about to give birth to another. Her family is inconsolable, and I'm so upset by it all, I'm prostrate . . .'

After such a disaster, especially as there were rumours – false in this case – that the fire could be attributed to an attempt on the emperor's life, a scapegoat had to be found. Bernard, the architect responsible for the construction of the wooden ballroom, was arrested and Dubois, prefect of police, dismissed.

However, the gloom cast over the season of festivities by this tragic conclusion was soon dispersed.

The eagerly awaited news was broadcast a few days later, in early July. An official palace bulletin informed the world in general that the empress was pregnant. As usual, Marie Louise's first reaction was to write to her father: 'I'm doubly happy because the doctor has assured me that I've been pregnant for more than a month. God grant there is no mistake, for the Emperor is beside himself with joy. He's told me already that I mustn't ride or dance any more . . .'

To which Francis, who still believed that he had given his daughter to Napoleon in all good faith, replied: 'You can imagine my joy at hearing that you are pregnant, for your sake, for that of your husband, and for my own, because I have such a deep affection for you. You are quite right not to dance or ride, but try also always to be calm and never to be frightened, because my late wife, as a result of this, lost several of the children she was carrying . . .'

According to a Dr Ganiere, however, there might have been complications following this announcement: 'Corvisart was obliged to tell the Sovereign rather contritely that he had made a mistake over the date and that Her Majesty was only in the second month of her pregnancy in August, which meant that the birth of the Imperial Infant could not be expected to take place till the latter half of March the following year (1811). To excuse himself for this mistake he pleaded extenuating circumstances. To begin with, the young Empress's menstrual periods were so capricious that they engendered false interpretation; and second the veritable maternity psychosis existing at the Court had to be taken into consideration . . .'

Napoleon was not in the least annoyed with his favourite physician. All that mattered was the fact that Marie Louise was truly pregnant, and that at the end of the winter, or very early in the spring, his dynasty would be assured, for he had not the slightest doubt that the child would be a son.*

Though the war in Spain still raged and there were increasing reports of Russia's open defiance of the blockade, Napoleon never left his wife's side during the ensuing months. All problems, he was certain, would be settled automatically by the birth of his son. His one distraction was hunting, which he indulged in three times a week, Marie Louise following in a *calèche*. This devotion was considered all the more remarkable as, in the past, Napoleon had always been disgusted by the sight of a pregnant woman. It was an aversion which still hovered as from time to time he would be heard to remark that the empress was beginning to be *'déformée'*, and confided once to Constant, *'l'Imperatrice commence a être un peu monstrueuse . . .'*

For someone brought up less strictly than Marie Louise, Napoleon's intensely possessive love might have proved more than irksome, for she was kept almost as isolated from the outside world as if she had been the favourite of some jealous sultan, guarded within the zenana's walls.

It is more than likely that, despite his noted promiscuity, Napoleon was indeed jealous; that in his jealousy he trusted nobody, convinced as he was of woman's basic frailty and natural tendency to infidelity. He cannot be entirely blamed for such an outlook. During the early years of his marriage to Josephine, particularly during his absence in Egypt, she had been notoriously unfaithful. Caroline made no bones about her liaisons with Metternich and the grand duke of Wurzburg. Pauline, his favourite sister – and of whom he was so fond that vicious tongues have suggested, quite wrongly, that he had incestuous relations with her – drifted serenely through a succession of lovers. Even the shy Hortense, at the same time his stepdaughter and sister-in-law, could no longer disguise her pregnancy or pretend that the child waiting to be born was her husband's.

---

* This certainly was not shared by the Parisians. There was a popular verse:

> La sexe de l'enfant, espoir de la Patrie,
> Même pour l'Empereur est encore un secret.
> C'est la seule fois dans sa vie
> Qu'il n'a pas su ce qu'il faisait.

Marie Louise was young and naive, and Napoleon was determined to make sure that temptation never came her way. He contrived that a veritable bastion of protocol and etiquette separated her from all members of the male sex with the exception of her doctors, and it was for this reason that his choice for the all-important post of *dame d'honneur* fell upon the duchess of Montebello who, he was in the habit of stating quite openly, was the only virtuous young woman at court. This may well have been true. Nevertheless his choice was unfortunate, to the extent that it went as far as contributing to his own downfall.

The duchess, born Louise Scolastique Guehennec of a lower-middle-class Breton family, married Jean Lannes, son of a dyer risen to the rank of general, on September 15th 1800, when she was eighteen years old. Napoleon was fond of Lannes and admired his wife, not only for her beauty but for her fidelity and devotion to her five children born between 1800 and 1805. At the time of her appointment, a contemporary stated: 'In spite of being mother of five children, she was certainly one of the most beautiful women at the imperial Court; a serenely virginal face with slightly aquiline features, a majestic bearing with, however, a hint of aloofness . . . an unblemished reputation, and even the gossips admitted that she repulsed all advances, however advantageous they might have been . . .'

Lannes, promoted marshal of France, prided himself on being a man of the people, a staunch republican. He cultivated a gruffness of speech and a quasi-egalitarian manner when addressing the emperor. His Jacobin views, on the other hand, did not go so far as to oblige him to refuse the honours heaped on him by his master – marshal of France, commander of the 9th Cohort, colonel-general of the Swiss, grand Eagle, duke of Montebello and, with all this, a 'salary' of 327,820 francs a year, as well as many cash gifts from the emperor which, we are assured, ran into millions. In addition, he was an ardent looter, and treasures he saw fit to appropriate – one might be forgiven for saying stole – from Spanish churches are said to have added a further four-and-a-half millions to his capital.

Although Napoleon was fully aware of his friend's violently-expressed anti-royalist principles, Lannes could do no wrong in his eyes. When the marshal died, some twenty-four hours after wounds received at Essling, he was overwhelmed by grief. He was seen to tear the famous *bicorne* from his head, hurl it to the ground and burst into tears. With his typical loyalty to those who served him and which so few reciprocated, he made haste to promise Lannes' widow that she would never have any material cares. 'I have lost my finest general,' he wrote, 'my companion in arms for the last sixteen years, whom I looked upon as my best friend. His family and his children will always enjoy my protection.'

Words were followed by action: immediate confirmation of the eldest son's rights to the title, lands and revenue of the duchy, titles of count and baron for the next two sons, with suitable incomes, an immediate 50,000 francs pension for the widow.

There is no doubt that Louise Lannes mourned her husband's death but, young as she was, she was also intensely practical. Within a year, playing on the emperor's generosity, she had obtained for her brother-in-law, the engineer general Kirgener, the post of commander of the engineers of the guard – the guard did not include engineers but, to please her, Napoleon created the title. Her father, who was in the forestry department, soon found himself a senator and count of the empire; while her brother, then a *chef d'escadron* (roughly the equivalent of captain) was made A.D.C. to the emperor with the title of baron, the rank of brigadier general and an income of 16,000 francs.

One would have imagined that the tiniest spark of gratitude for these unique favours might have been lighted in the duchess's heart. Exactly the contrary. Her dislike of the emperor, instilled into her by her left-wing husband, even after her appointment as *dame d'honneur,* increased. Yet despite the fact that she made little attempt to hide this dislike, she retained her position and was adored by Marie Louise. One is amazed to read that, apart from political sentiments, the reason she gives for her dislike is the emperor's ingratitude! This avowedly ardent republican was, apparently, deeply wounded by the fact that her husband had only received a dukedom for his services whereas Marshals Davout, Berthier and Masséna were princes!

Many contemporary writers and historians lay the blame for Marie Louise's unpopularity on the duchess of Montebello and, to a certain extent, the stigma is justified. Although – if one can believe her – the duchess hated court life and would have preferred a quiet life, devoting herself to her children, she was, nevertheless, fully cognizant of its intricacies; she was on more or less intimate terms with the principal actors in the serio-comedy of imperial circles. For many years, from close quarters, she had observed the ex-empress Josephine and gauged the secret of the general affection she commanded.

This knowledge could have been invaluable when it came to advising the young and inexperienced empress Marie Louise who was only too anxious to look on her as a reincarnation of the beloved *ayah*, Madame de Poutet. Instead:

'. . . It soon became obvious that the Duchess of Montebello was singularly ill-placed at the head of the Empress's household . . . she took a delight in reminding the Empress of her imperial birth and made no effort-to help her to get to know, or love, France, or to have any friendly relations with the imperial' (Bonaparte) 'family. She recounted unpleasant anecdotes about each one of them, she sought to embitter petty disputes, and pushed Marie Louise into various little actions which caused great offence. She didn't like any of the ladies at Court either and about them, too, she had many a scurrilous tale to tell in private. Marie Louise, who hated any hint of scandal, then felt herself obliged to be off-hand with the persons in question.

'It was the same at the theatre. After three nods of the head, on arrival in the royal box, which always evoked applause if the Emperor were not present, she would retire to the back of the box and not move from there the whole evening. When somebody suggested that the people had gone to the theatre to see their Empress and were very disappointed, the Duchess replied, "What of it? Her Majesty isn't an exhibit in a fair! If she doesn't want to show herself, no one has the right to criticise."

'At presentations, it was still worse. It was the Duchess's duty to announce those being presented. Not only did she fail to give the Empress any information about the individuals concerned, she didn't even bother to pronounce their names clearly as she hadn't taken the trouble to cast a preliminary glance over the list. Holding the list in her hand, she would begin – "I have the honour to present to Your Royal and Imperial Majesty . . ." At this point she would hesitate, stammer and try to decipher the name. The Empress would lean forward, read the name for herself, then ask the individual – "Are you married? Have you any children?" And before even listening to the replies would dismiss him with a nod of the head.

'It soon became the fashion to repeat all the Empress's idiotic remarks, and to laugh over her childish mistakes over uniforms, families, relationships and the rest . . .'*

A detailed study of the empress's household, conceived by Napoleon himself with all his passion for the smallest detail, would fill a medium-sized volume. A number of the attendants and members of the household held posts based on the studies of former courts and royal establishments, but the sixteen women who made up *Le personnel de l'Appartement et des Atours* owed their positions largely to the emperor's fancy. Forming a little personal bodyguard, they were divided into three ranks known, in order of seniority, as *Les Femmes Rouges, Les Femmes Noires* and *Les Femmes Blanches.*

The *Femmes Rouges,* red-uniformed, were six in number. Four were constantly on duty, one at the entrance to the empress's apartments, another at the door of whichever room in which the empress happened to be. The other two had to attend the empress when she got up in the morning and when she went to bed, wait on her at table if she was eating in her apartments and, of these two, one had to sleep in the room adjoining the empress's bedroom. One of the *Femmes Rouges* was also responsible for the empress's jewellery which had to be checked once a month, another was responsible for the library, another the music room and studio, and each had to take it in turn to act as secretary when the empress dictated her letters. It was a hard job, but one much sought after. Hand-picked by the emperor, they were usually daughters, sisters, wives or widows of senior officers.

Again one may attribute this constant twenty-four-hours-a-day surveillance to Napoleon's jealousy and his complex over women's supposed inability to resist advances of the opposite sex. As one anonymous contemporary points out: 'Not only had he' (Napoleon) 'had too many facile successes himself, but he had also been Josephine's husband.' Even when Duplan, the hairdresser, who was paid 24,000 francs a year to act as coiffeur (he was forbidden other clients) to the empress, was at work on Marie Louise's blonde curls, he did so with two *Femmes Rouges* standing grimly one on either side of him.

The six *Femmes Noires,* who wore black aprons, were normally wives or relations of the emperor's *valets de chambre.* Their duties were directed largely by the countess de Luçay, the lady of the wardrobe. They had to be expert seamstresses and have a know-

* Frédéric Masson: *op cit.*

81

ledge of hairdressing. The upkeep of Marie Louise's vast wardrobe, all her personal belongings – with the exception of her jewellery – was their responsibility, to such an extent that they could be reprimanded for the loss of a single hairpin.

They were not allowed to forget their inferior grade and could not enter the empress's presence except on direct order of a *Femme Rouge*; and while one of the *Femmes Rouges* slept on a bed in the room adjoining that where the empress was sleeping, a *Femme Noire* had to sleep on a mattress across the foot of the empress's door.

The *Femmes Blanches*, at the bottom of this close-knit social scale, appear to have been anonymous, so lowly were they considered. Theirs were the humblest duties: cleaning, dusting, emptying *pots de chambre*, preparing baths, laying fires, trimming candles. They were not even allowed to set eyes on the empress, and their least movement was directed by the *Femmes Rouges*, one of them being obliged to sleep fully dressed in the room next to the duty *Femme Rouge* in case the latter should be in need of anything during the night.

In this state of semi-, though much-gilded, reclusion, perfectly happy with it all, Marie Louise passed the last months of 1810 and the cold winter of 1811. She had, she told herself, every reason to be supremely happy. She was proud of the fact that she was about to fulfil her duty as an empress by giving an heir to her adopted country. The emperor's attentions redoubled, her least whim was gratified instantly. Because of her condition, much to her delight the wearisome round of official sorties, banquets, receptions, was heavily curtailed and, somewhat disillusioned regarding the joys of travel, she was equally pleased that there would be no question of a further tour for many months.

Up to March 4th, she was in the habit of taking a short drive, usually with the emperor, and always accompanied by the duchess of Montebello. But from then on Corvisart considered the motion of a *calèche* as possibly harmful, and she was obliged to be satisfied with a brief walk, leaning heavily on her *dame d'honneur*'s arm. An anonymous writer who had seen her on one of these promenades wrote: 'She was enormous and not very impressive. One would have said a very ordinary housewife. Her face was quite expressionless . . .'

*   *   *

82

As with all the great events in Napoleon's life, the birth of the much-longed-for child was sharply tinged with melodrama.

With the approach of the predicted date of birth, both Napoleon and Marie Louise became markedly agitated. Dr Corvisart was a much-harassed man, bombarded by continually repeated questions. 'Is there not some way of divining a child's sex?' Marie Louise kept asking, while Napoleon, who had been fed maliciously with horrific stories of difficult deliveries, also pestered the doctor for assurances that these were exceptions rather than the rule, plying him at the same time with abstruse obstetrical enquiries, to such an extent that the exasperated doctor was heard to say, 'I can't think why a so-called warrior should be in such a panic over such a minor affair.'

The evening of March 19th, Napoleon had arranged for a play to be put on in the empress's apartments, hoping to take her mind off her anxieties. It was, however, a very different spectacle which was offered to the guests. Napoleon had decreed that, 'When the Empress feels the first pains announcing that she is on the point of giving birth, the *dame d'honneur* will immediately inform the Emperor. As soon as she has done this, she will receive H.M. the Emperor's orders and warn the princes and princesses of the Family, the prince grand dignitaries, the grand officers of the Crown, the ministers, the grand officers of the Empire, the ladies and officers of the Household. All these persons must then collect in Her Majesty's apartment, dressed as for Sunday Mass . . .'

Conveniently, most of the persons involved in this dictat were already in the audience, waiting patiently for the arrival of the royal couple before the rise of the curtain, when the duchess of Montebello suddenly burst in with the news that the empress was suffering from severe pains in the back.

The guests were then hustled into the billiard room. Dubois, the *accoucheur*, was already by the empress's bedside carefully arranging his instruments on a table within full view of his patient who was far from feeling comforted by the sight of them. Berthier and Cambacères, who would have to draw up the birth certificate, had arrived in the antechamber. The emperor, more agitated than at Marengo, paced up and down, hands clasped behind his back.

At odd intervals, the crowd assembled in the billiard room could hear Marie Louise's groans. Hours passed. Wine and chocolate were served. Then Corvisart suddenly appeared. Being a law unto himself he said that, as the pains had eased, there was no urgency and he was going home to bed. Leaving his subordinates, doctors Bourdier, Yvan and Dubois at the empress's side, he departed.

Meanwhile the guests were fidgeting, getting more and more bored and irritable and, finally, almost unbearably sleepy, cursing the empress for taking such an unwarranted long time to carry out a very natural function of womanhood, and so keeping them out of bed.

At five o'clock Marie Louise dropped off to sleep. The worried Napoleon tiptoed away to refresh himself with a little food and a few mouthfuls of brandy before seeking the consolation of a scalding bath. After wallowing in the near-boiling water, he was on the point of calling for Constant to dry him and massage him with eau-de-Cologne, when Dubois was shown into the room. The *accoucheur* was literally staggering. Napoleon, recounting the scene later, said that he was deathly pale, sweating and could hardly utter coherently.

'What is it?' Napoleon shouted. 'Is she dead?' and he added, 'If she is she must be buried.'*

Dubois pulled himself together and gasped:

'No, Sire. The empress is not dead, but the child has presented itself by the feet.'

'And what does that mean?'

'I shall have to operate.'

'My God! And does that imply there is danger?'

'It means it will be probably a question of saving either the mother or the child.'

Napoleon was already out of his bath, being helped into his clothes without drying himself properly.

'Save the mother,' he ordered, 'we can have more children.'

When Marie Louise saw her husband come into the bedroom with Dubois, her screams redoubled. Terror was now added to pain. She was convinced that Napoleon had decided that she must be sacrificed for the child. Frantically, Napoleon assured her that this was not the case, while Madame the countess of Montesquiou – who had been chosen for the post of governess

* At St Helena, Napoleon explained this apparently astonishingly callous remark. 'I was used to shattering events. Because of this I never felt anything when they happened. The reaction came later. . .'

for the coming child – tried to comfort her by saying that two of her own children had been helped into the world by 'the irons', and that there was no need to worry.

Dubois, who was so terrified that he was near to losing all self-control, then refused to operate without Dr Corvisart. Napoleon lost his temper.

'What can he' (Corvisart) 'tell you that you don't know already?' he shouted. 'If it's a witness you need, or justification, well here I am. I've had enough of this, Dubois. I order you to deliver the empress.'

Fortunately, Corvisart arrived at that moment. A nightmarish scene followed, reminiscent of a mediaeval torture chamber rather than a clinical procedure. Marie Louise was seized and held down on the bed by sheer force, by Corvisart and Bourdier, while Dubois applied his instruments. Unable to stand either this horrific spectacle or Marie Louise's tortured screams, Napoleon rushed from the room and took refuge in the nearest lavatory.

When at last, after twenty-six minutes of inhuman agony, the child was delivered and the emperor had emerged from his hiding-place, Marie Louise was unconscious.

Although the whole reason for this Austrian marriage had been to ensure his succession, the haggard Napoleon's first thought was for his wife as he came timidly, weakly, back to the bedroom. He bent over her and her eyes reopened. He seized her in his arms, kissing her and murmuring incoherently.

Suddenly the cause of all this drama, the baby, into whose mouth Corvisart had breathed a few drops of brandy, uttered his first cry. Napoleon turned, ran over to Madame de Montesquiou and snatched the child from her arms.

Holding him up, he said, 'My son!'

He had not much time, though, to enjoy these first moments of longed-for paternity. Etiquette's crushing rules had to be obeyed and it was he, after all, who had dictated them.

Madame de Montesquiou showed the baby to Berthier and Cambacérès who then dictated the terms of the birth certificate to Baron Regnault de Saint Jean-d'Angely, the family's secretary of state, after Napoleon himself had announced: 'It is my wish that my son should bear the names Napoleon, Francis, Joseph, Charles.'

The certificate was signed first by Napoleon, then by his mother (Madame Mére) and, in turn, by the grand duke of

Wurzburg, Prince Eugène de Beauharnais, Elisa, Caroline, Pauline, Hortense, Berthier and, finally – a strange choice one feels – Talleyrand.

This done, Napoleon was then able to issue the triumphant order: 'My pages, and the salute of a hundred and one guns!'

He was still so moved that Hortense noted: 'When I went to embrace him, he was so agitated that he pushed me away. "Ah," he said to me, "this happiness is almost more than I can bear. My poor wife has suffered so horribly." In fact, he was so shaken by the sight of his wife's agony that he was terribly nervous for the rest of the day . . .'

However, there were no counter emotions as far as the mass of Parisians was concerned, when the hundred and one reports split the cold morning air. The popular outburst had in it something of the delirium of a Greek Easter after the archbishop has pronounced the *Christos Aneste*!

'I rushed to the Tuileries with my friends,' said a medical student. 'Already the streets were thronged; workmen were abandoning their jobs, merchants closing their shops; it was a wild outburst of joy. By the time we arrived, the river banks, the Carrousel, the gardens were packed. People were singing, dancing, deafening one with their "hurrahs" . . .'

Only one old die-hard supporter of the exiled royal family, Baron de Freuilly, noted gloomily: 'It seemed to us to spell the death of the Bourbons . . .'

Not only Paris rejoiced. The visual telegraph system flashed the news so rapidly that the same day Brussels and Strasbourg learnt that the future Napoleon II had seen the light of day, and only forty-eight hours later – somewhat ironically – Parma was echoing to the shouts of *Vive le Roi de Rome*! From Vienna, Countess Lazanski wrote to her former charge: 'I can guess the joy the news must have caused in Paris by its effect here. Everybody is enchanted . . .'

And from Francis: 'I'm giving the courier these few lines of heartfelt congratulations. The birth of a son adds to my happiness . . .'

Napoleon, traditionally proud father, exclaimed: 'Lucky child! Glory is his, while I had to chase it. I am Philip; he will be Alexander. To seize the world, he has only to stretch out his arms . . .'

Even a very old soldier who had fought at Fontenoy, and who

one might have expected to be anti-Bonaparte, composed a touching form of *Nunc Dimittis*: *Roi de Rome et du monde, amour du genre humain, Mes yeux ont pu te voir, qu'ils se ferment demain.*

As for the real heroine of this drama, fussed over, spoiled, petted, her sentiments were admirably expressed in her first letter to her father, written after this more than 'happy event': 'You can imagine how happy I am. I would never have believed I could be so happy. Since the birth of my son, my love for my husband grows all the time, and when I think of his tenderness I can hardly prevent myself from crying. Even if I hadn't loved him before, nothing could stop me from loving him now. He begs me to remember him to you and is always asking after you. Every day he reminds me how happy you must be to have a grandson. I will send you the little one's portrait and you will see for yourself how like his father he is. He is astonishingly strong for only five weeks, and already can lift his head off the pillow. He weighed nine pounds at birth and was twenty inches long, and since then he has been growing rapidly. He is in perfect health and spends all day in the garden. The Emperor takes an astonishing interest in him. He carries him about in his arms, plays with him and has made him ill because he insisted on feeding him. My uncle' (the grand duke of Wurzburg) 'has told you how I suffered for twenty-four hours, but I have forgotten my pain in the joy of being a mother . . .'

Chapter V

With the birth of his son, the year 1811 marked the apogee of Napoleon's power.

By then, as a result of the emperor's conquests and policy, France numbered thirty-two departments. In 1810, northern Spain, the provinces of Catalonia, Aragon and Navarre, had been separated from the Spanish crown and were ruled direct from Paris. On the pretext that his brother Louis was becoming more Dutch than the Dutch themselves and deliberately thwarting the edicts of the blockade, Holland was also declared part of metropolitan France on July 9th 1811. By the end of the year, the Hanseatic cities of Hamburg, Lübeck and Bremen, and the grand duchy of Oldenburg, suffered the same fate. In addition, Napoleon was king of Italy, mediator of Switzerland, protector of the Rhine Confederation, while the kings of Spain, Westphalia, Würtemburg, Bavaria, Saxony and Naples were his vassals.

'Never had a man been so favoured by Fortune. Everything, even his mistakes, had been crowned with success. All trembled beneath his gaze. He was the visible master of Europe. Eighty million men were his subjects . . .'*

Yet this great edifice was creaking. More than ever could the Spanish question be called 'a running sore', draining his armies, sapping the morale of his marshals. Britain's total command of the seas was a constant threat to his hegemony. No illusions were left as to the Russian alliance so dear to his heart. Furthermore, discontent was rife in France itself. Again, according to Aubry:

'Agriculture, lacking men, was in a parlous state. Bread was often short. Industry and commerce, the merchant fleet, paralysed by the blockade, had lapsed into the deplorable state from which the Consulate had rescued them. Taxes soared. The bourgeoisie, deprived of political aspirations, turned its back on glory, regretting liberty . . .'

There is no doubt that the French people as a whole were sickened by the thought of further wars. There was a passionate

* Octave Aubry: *Napoléon—Le Soldat—L'Empéreur*.

88

desire for peace. It was a desire which was shared genuinely by the emperor – especially since the birth of his son – who now thought only of consolidating the dynasty created by his genius. The popular representation of him as a bloodthirsty monster seeking still further conquests is false. On the contrary, it was the representatives of the established order, the established dynasties, who were determined never to accept the upstart as one of them, even though Habsburg blood ran in his child's veins. Divided in most matters, they were united in their resolution never to rest till he was overthrown; their brain was Metternich, their sword Alexander, their purse Britain.

Though aware of these gathering clouds, Napoleon refused to admit them. He lived in a state of self-induced euphoria which was to prove to be all too brief. As for Marie Louise, she was at this moment blissfully ignorant of the brewing storm. Undoubtedly had she been told by some prophet that in less than three years she was to be kicked from her throne, to find herself a fugitive and semi-prisoner in the land of her birth, she would have suggested, in all sincerity, that the individual be certified as insane by Dr Corvisart.

Malicious tongues were soon wagging to point out the fact that though the empire had gained an heir, the ordeal of the child's birth had had a disastrous effect on the empress's appearance. She had lost the few good looks she had ever possessed, since these depended on her youthful freshness, her pink and white complexion and general aura of innocence, enhanced by an agreeable *embonpoint* which might be described, more plebeianly, as puppy fat. When she reappeared at court functions, everybody was quick to notice that her cheeks had turned muddy, she had lost her appetising plumpness, and generally aged greatly. This physical deterioration might have been avoided if she had not been so terrified at the thought of physical separation from her husband.

Shortly after the little king of Rome's birth, Napoleon planned a rapid inspection of coastal defences in the Cherbourg area. He had taken it for granted that he would be making this inspection alone. As the date of departure approached, however, Marie Louise became plaintive, accusing him of wanting to get away from her, indulged in fits of weeping and lamentations till Napoleon, genuinely moved and secretly flattered, agreed to let her accompany him. Yet, though he realised that such a journey was bound to have an ill effect on his wife's apparently fragile state of health, he made no attempt to modify the tour's exhausting rhythm.

Four in the morning was the normal hour to be on the road. The third day after leaving Paris, no less than nineteen hours were spent in the lurching, swaying carriage. As a result Marie Louise was, from start to finish, verging on collapse. Vis-à-vis her subjects, the tour was again a dismal failure, serving only to increase her unpopularity. Nobody was prepared to admit attenuating circumstances to explain why she was never seen to smile, could never relax, gave the impression of being almost dumb and quite incapable of making an amiable, or even a tactful, remark.

Only once was she reported as having shown some sign of human warmth; during a visit to the Cherbourg docks, Napoleon, in an access of that boisterous horseplay so dear to him, suddenly seized her in his arms and, holding her above the gurgling sea, called out, 'Now! Shall I let you go?', while she, clutching him round the neck and smiling, murmured, 'If you want to.'

The first major state function after the return from this unwisely undertaken journey was the young king of Rome's christening on June 9th, in the cathedral of Notre Dame, celebrated with the usual Napoleonic passion for pomp and ceremony.

The imperial escort, which included not only the entire cavalry of the guard but also Dutch dragoons, Mameluke light horse and Polish lancers, took two hours to cross the Place de la Concorde. The little king was alone in a carriage with his governess, Madame de Montesquiou. Seated on her knee, quite unperturbed by all the fuss, he was dressed in a long lace robe, across his small bosom the ribbon of the Grand Cross of the Legion of Honour. The members of the imperial family, the household and court dignitaries, occupied twenty-four carriages, each one drawn by six horses, while the emperor and Marie Louise, in the magnificent glass state carriage with its eight-horse team, brought up the rear. Napoleon was in purple velvet liberally gold-besprinkled; Marie Louise in white satin, weighed down with jewellery; around her neck the superb eight-string pearl necklace, her husband's gift to her on the evening of the child's birth.

The Bonaparte cardinal, Fesch, was officiating. Wrapped in a gold, ermine-lined cloak, the little king of Rome, escorted by his god-parents the grand duke of Wurzburg, Madame Mére and Hortense (standing in for Caroline, again pleading the excuse of ill health), was carried to the font by Madame de Montesquiou.

The baptismal service concluded, Madame de Montesquiou presented the child to his mother, while the herald – the sieur Duverdier – proclaimed three times: '*Vive le Roi de Rome!*'

The fact that they were in a cathedral did not stop the huge assembled crowd from applauding; and when Napoleon, eyes shining with excitement, obviously bubbling over with joy, snatched the little boy from Marie Louise's arms, kissed him, then held him up at arms' length above his head in a gesture of triumph, cheers drowned organ and choir.

Once more, though, he was disappointed by the lack of fervour greeting the procession's return from the cathedral; but this deception was short-lived and *Le Moniteur*, reporting the occasion, was careful to avoid any hint of half-heartedness: 'The happy event, about which we write at this moment, is the subject of general rejoicing throughout this vast Empire which this great people offers to the Divine Power, which causes hymns of joy to re-echo through our churches, our public places, our peaceful cities, our fertile countryside and the camps of our invincible warriors, which crowns at one and the same time the wishes of the people for the happiness of their sovereign and those of the sovereign himself for the consolidation of those institutions which he has devoted to his people's prosperity. More than anything else it should prove to be the inspiration for our poets to give of their noblest verse . . .'

It was not long before Marie Louise realised sadly that her normal day-to-day routine was changing.

Much to her distress, the comfortable honeymoon intimacy of the first year of married life was a thing of the past. Napoleon's empire was, indeed, too vast to allow him to turn aside permanently from the cares of its direction, trusting the great edifice's running to subordinates while he dallied in idleness with his young wife and son. Of his empire he was both architect and mason; he alone had planned, he alone had built. He was surrounded by kings, princes, grand dukes, marshals of his own creation, many of them brave, a few capable in their subordinate roles, yet not one of them could be relied upon to take the helm, even for a brief period, without inviting disaster; in fact, all too many were not even to be trusted. His was a position of immense, almost unbearable, loneliness.

Because of this, the crushing daily round slowly re-imposed itself. He was no longer able to spend hours at table. Kept up frequently till midnight was well past, he spent more and more of his nights in his office on a camp bed surrounded by maps. It was not only work, however, which kept him from his wife's arms. Dubois, the *accoucheur*, had been so terrified at the thought of what might have happened to him had the empress died, that he enlisted Corvisart's help – the over-privileged physician had been intensely bored and irritated by the imperial couple's badgering during Marie Louise's pregnancy – to impress on Napoleon that such was the delicate state of his wife's health that, unless an appreciable time were allowed to elapse, a second pregnancy might well prove fatal. As the emperor was firmly convinced that Corvisart was the world's best doctor, it never occurred to him to question this statement and, being devoted to his young wife, it seemed to him only logical that abstinence was the only sure way of preventing an accident.

This new phase of married life was far from pleasing Marie Louise, still completely the prisoner of etiquette and protocol in her semi-zenana-like existence. Now, all her congenital amorous instincts having been awakened by Napoleon's ardour, finding herself more or less deserted, she was spending many a sleepless night, prey to erotic frustration. She would never have thought of rebelling – and indeed she, too, was often haunted by the dread of another pregnancy – but she became increasingly hypochondriacal.

Other young mothers might have found consolation in their baby's company and maternal responsibilities. But once Marie Louise had successfully accomplished the physical act of bringing the infant into the world, to all intents and purposes the child no longer belonged to her.

A wet nurse, Marie Victorine Auchard, twenty-five years old, satisfied his voracious appetite, while all other details of his daily existence were supervised and regulated by his *gouvernante*, the countess of Montesquiou. This in every way admirable woman had also been hand-picked by Napoleon, and on this occasion he could not have made a happier choice. Countess in her own right, wife of the *President du Corps Legislatif*, stern, puritanical, deeply devout and, though a member of the old aristocracy, imbued with an admiration for Napoleon – not so much as a man but as a French hero dedicated to his country's glory – which, though undemonstrative, bordered on fanaticism, she was the only woman at court of whom the emperor was slightly in awe.

It was not surprising that the *gouvernante* was most cordially detested by the duchess of Montebello, jealous of her influence and maddened by her air of condescension. The three years that were to elapse before the empire's collapse witnessed a bitter, behind-the-scenes battle between these two women, both equally stubborn and determined, the one in the cause of self-interest, the other in that of duty.

The fact that she was not expected to make any concrete contribution towards her child's upbringing did not really astonish Marie Louise. It was only a repetition of the way she herself had been raised to be utterly dependent in all things on her *ayah*, all contact with her parents having been strictly official. What did amaze her, on the other hand, and at the same time awaken a subconscious jealousy, was Napoleon's behaviour towards their son.

There was nothing of imperial protocol in his paternal pride or adoration of the baby. Whenever he was able to snatch a few moments of relaxation, he called for his little king and, what secretly horrified Marie Louise, *actually played with him*. The household was iron-corsetted by etiquette. This facet was non-existent where father and son were concerned. Baron de Menéval, one of that company of the faithful few, gives the best accounts of this domesticity. He relates that beneath the shocked gaze of the empress and Madame de Montesquiou, he often saw the ruler of Europe rolling on the floor with the baby, tickling him, making clucking noises, then joining in the child's shrieks of laughter.

'She' (Marie Louise) 'was so unsure of herself that, when she took the little prince from his nurse's arms, the Emperor rushed up, seized him himself, smothering him with kisses . . . One day when the child leant forward to grab a morsel of food – I can't remember exactly what it was – his father had held out to him, he' (Napoleon) 'pulled it out of his reach teasingly. Thinking this rather funny, the emperor did this again, but the third time the child turned his head and refused to take it even when his father wanted to give it to him. The emperor was astonished at this, but Madame de Montesquiou observed that the child did not like people trying to be funny with him, and that he was "proud and sensitive".

' "Proud and sensitive," repeated the emperor. "That is splendid. Ah, how I love him." '

Marie Louise made no attempt to assert what authority she might have been able to claim regarding the running of the nursery. She did not want to. In her carefree isolation she devoted herself to dallying with the arts, her life drifting along in placid monotony.

At eight o'clock the *Femmes Rouges* entered her room, pulled the curtains, half opened the shutters, and brought her the papers chosen, of course, by the emperor and including *Le Mercure, Le Journal de Paris, Le Journal des Modes et des Dames* and the *Gazette de France* (no foreign papers were allowed). Breakfast in bed: chocolate or coffee, and Viennese-type pastries the *chef* Lebeau had learnt to bake. At nine o'clock, under the supervision of the *Femmes Rouges,* she was bathed and dressed by the *Femmes Noires.* When the emperor was busy, as he was usually, the other meals, the daily drive or walks, were taken alone with the duchess of Montebello.

Though he himself was not a booklover, it was Napoleon who chose his wife's reading material. He is supposed to have said that he was anxious for her to get an idea of *la delicatesse des sentiments et des usages de la Société* which, he thought, could be gleaned by studying the forty-three volumes of Restif's *Contemporaines.* Suspicious of novels and novelists, he nevertheless allowed the purchase of works by Chateaubriand, Madame de Genlis and Anne Radcliffe. With so much time on her hands Marie Louise was, herself, an avid reader. Records show that during her four years as empress she spent 28,630 francs at Rousseau's bookshop, and had a permanent account with at least six others.

For her painting, two masters were approved: Prud'hon and Isabey. Since these were highly remunerative appointments, one is not surprised to find that Isabey obtained the post thanks to the combined machinations of the duchess of Montebello and Dr Corvisart, who took it for granted that their efforts on his behalf would earn them a 'rake-off'.

Marie Louise herself had talent. The present writer has seen, in Parma's Glauco Lombardi museum, several attractive canvases attributed to her brush which had a near-professional touch.

Music, however, was her great love. She was a most excellent pianist. In the exercise of this natural gift, she was allowed an astonishing independence by Napoleon who so far forgot his chauvinism as to order for her a Broadmann from Vienna when she expressed her dissatisfaction with her Pleyel.

Her Paris music professor was Paer, the director of the court theatre and composer laureate. A very mediocre composer, he was a distinguished teacher. Thanks to him, Marie Louise attained a technical perfection in her playing that brought her near to the virtuoso class. In addition, she was a talented harpist and singer, possessor of a small, true, limpid soprano of the lyric-cum-coloratura type, perfectly suited to the interpretation of such Mozartian 'soubrette' roles as Zerlina or Suzanna. Furthermore, her appreciation was genuine rather than super-ficial. She loved Beethoven and was not afraid to admit this at a time when, in court circles, he was looked upon and condemned as a revolutionary both musically and politically. Yet, in many ways, her musical expression was as limited by etiquette as all other aspects of her life.

In Vienna, the royal family occasionally held little private concerts when, in much the same way as during a typical late-Victorian or Edwardian *soirée*, each guest would be expected to perform his or her piece. Napoleon, on the other hand, looked upon the arts from a political rather than a social point of view, and in any case was determined that the empress must always be on so exalted a pinnacle vis-à-vis the rest of humanity – the Bonapartes included – that he would never have permitted such a departure from court etiquette.

Deprived as she was of normal human relationships, it was inevitable, though unfortunate, that Marie Louise came to depend more and more on the duchess of Montebello, and that in her craving for some object on which she could lavish her deep resources of affection, her passion for her *dame d'honneur* absorbed something of the adoration of her early love for Victoria de Poutet. In marked contrast, not in the least heart-ruled, Louise Lannes exploited her imperial mistress's slavish devotion to the full without reciprocating one iota of affection or loyalty.

95

'She' (the duchess of Montebello) 'was the only person the empress was allowed as a personal friend, the only one living near her, the only one who accompanied her on her outings and who, in Napoleon's absence, kept her company. It was natural, logical, even necessary, that she' (Marie Louise) 'should conceive either a passionate affection or a profound hatred for her, but she was incapable of hating anyone.

'This exclusive friendship entailed a complete subjection, a complete subordination of the ideas, affections, sentiments even, of the Empress to those of the Duchess of Montebello . . .'

The duchess, who suffered from ingrained misanthropy, was more than ever set on poisoning the empress's mind against all those who surrounded her, and it was not long before she felt herself so secure that she was able to make adverse, though veiled, comments about the emperor himself. One day, after being reprimanded by Napoleon for giving Marie Louise a purge without first consulting Corvisart, she did not actually answer back but, as soon as Napoleon had left the room, remarked acidly, 'I'm so glad Mr Etiquette has left us in peace. I get very bored by long sermons.'

By this time Marie Louise was so much under the duchess's influence that she made no attempt to defend her husband. In fact, Constant says, it was soon difficult to determine who was the mistress, for Marie Louise would often slip out of bed to prepare breakfast for her *dame d'honneur* and serve it, herself, in her bedroom; while during Napoleon's prolonged absences on campaign, the duchess's portrait would replace that of her husband on her dressing table.

Yet, from start to finish, the duchess had not the slightest liking for Marie Louise, nor was she to show her any more gratitude than she had done to the emperor. She accepted favours, attentions, fabulous gifts, as though they were hers by divine right. It may be argued that she was a woman who had given her love to her husband and children to the exclusion of all else, that when her husband had succumbed to his battle wounds only maternal love had survived and that for the rest of humanity hers was a heart of stone. It would be charitable to urge this argument as an excuse for her behaviour; but her intense materialism, her willingness – eagerness, rather – to exploit every circumstance for personal gain, the final callous betrayal of those to whom she owed everything, would seem to discredit the theory of eternal

The Emperor Francis II (I) of Austria

Prince Metternich

Napoleon I Emperor of the French
and King of Italy

Marie Louise Empress of
the French and Queen of
Italy

mourning, suggesting rather a cold-blooded, grasping, un-principled egoist.

In September, Napoleon felt obliged to undertake another tour of Holland. Deprived of its vassal king, Louis Bonaparte, the country was now merely a French province, without the least semblance of national independence. The change, Napoleon knew well, was not to the people's liking. Though not counting on bringing about a miraculous change of heart, he still retained a certain faith in his own personal magnetism and hoped that an imperial visit, accompanied once more by the daughter of the emperor of Austria now empress of the French and mother of France's future emperor, might impress the Dutch as a symbol of temporal power, an alliance of past and present against which any form of resistance, moral or physical, was doomed before it had even had time to take shape.

Marie Louise's health, however, had to be taken into consideration. She was still suffering from lack of proper medical attention and a sane convalescence after the 'little king's' birth. She was losing her hair which showed no sign of recovering its former blonde sheen. Even in the summer she was subject to feverish colds. She was tortured by frequent bilious attacks – though these may well have been brought on by her passion for Viennese pastries which she was incapable of resisting – nor had she regained any of that plumpness which had so delighted Napoleon, a lover of buxom women.

Finally it was decided that for the first part of the tour, basically military rather than political, Napoleon should go on ahead while the empress, following in easy stages, should join him in Antwerp. The idea of this separation, short as it would be, appalled Marie Louise even though their prolonged honeymoon had, to all intents and purposes, been ended by their son's birth. Napoleon, however – purely for her sake – was adamant. A typical Napoleonic tour of inspection – it was again the coastal defences, and the latent possibility of a descent on the English coast which interested him – involving hours on the road, little sleep, uncomfortable lodgings, tiring visits, eternal receptions of back-breaking monotony, could prove as dangerous as a second pregnancy.

With a bad grace, accompanied by storms of weeping, Marie Louise gave way. She was a very unhappy young woman confronted by the spectre of this first, albeit brief, separation from her husband, for the very simple reason that she loved him.

'My husband is leaving for the Island of Walcheren,' she wrote to Victoria. 'It is the unhealthiest place you can possibly imagine, and as it is the first time I can't accompany him, I'm feeling very unhappy . . .'

Within a few hours of Napoleon's departure, having clung to him as if he were leaving for an expedition in darkest Africa, she was writing him a frantic, lovelorn letter: 'All that I long for is a message calling me to your side. I long to be held in your arms and to tell you how much I love you . . .'

Napoleon had promised he would write every day, and, though he was certainly not an inspired letter writer, he kept his word even though most of the letters could be better described as scribbled notes. The first came from Boulogne, composed hastily on the evening of September 21st:

My good Louise,
    I've just received your letter which has made me very happy because it is as sweet as you are. I've been at sea all day. I chased an English cruiser for four leagues.* The weather is superb. My health is excellent. I hope yours is too, as it's very hot. I beg of you to look after yourself. You know that dust and heat are bad for you. You are right in letting your thoughts fly to one to whom you mean everything.
                                                    Nap.

And the following day:

My good Louise,
    I have received your letter of the 20 Sbre. I spent all day with my troops. I leave here, and will be in Ostend, tomorrow. I will be with you at the time we agreed upon. I was pleased that it rained today; it won't be so dusty and the journey won't be so tiring for you. I'm anxious to hear that you have arrived at Laeken in good health. I hope you'll like the Belgians and be happy amongst them. You know how much I love you, and you are quite wrong if you think that my

* This is probably an exaggeration. It is generally thought that all that happened was that Napoleon supervised the fire of a shore battery at a cruising British man-of-war.

many preoccupations could in any way affect my feeling for you. Good-bye Dear one. Tomorrow I'll be near you. I will write from Ostend. (unsigned)

Marie Louise was in a hurry to answer this letter which was waiting for her on her arrival in Laeken. After assuring Napoleon that the journey hadn't tired her in the least, she went on:

'. . . The time passes very slowly without you, and if this separation were to last many more days, I should die of grief, and I hope you won't go chasing the English again. I hate them more than ever for delaying you for another day, and perhaps even longer; but if you break your promise to me I shall not forgive you at all. Please let me have news of you regularly and I for my part will not let a day pass without writing and telling you everything I'm doing. Goodbye, my dear one. I hope you're not worn out by your journey and that it will not be long before I know the joy of being held in your arms.
　　　'Your faithful and loving wife – Louise.'

Arriving at Laeken on the 23rd, Marie Louise was received enthusiastically by the citizens of Brussels. Unfortunately, though the journey had been deliberately unhurried, she was tired and quite unable to respond to the ovations greeting her. All she could think about was rest and the reunion with her husband which finally took place at Antwerp on the 30th.

As planned, the rest of the tour was conducted at a leisurely rhythm, Napoleon making a few lightning visits, one of which – to the fleet lying off the mouth of the Helder – necessitated another three-day separation. During this absence Napoleon, who was particularly anxious that Marie Louise should make herself popular with the Dutch, gave her the order to spend money liberally, and went as far as allowing her to make whatever purchases she desired without supervision. She obeyed gleefully. Even after seventeen months in the affluence of Paris, the apparently unlimited imperial purse more or less at her disposal, she could not forget the comparative penury of her extreme youth in Vienna's chill and impoverished splendour. Spending, for the sake of spending, was an enthralling pastime: 'The manufacturers have been having a very hard time, and been obliged to dismiss two thirds of their employees; they are not doing any business at all. The Mayor told me this so pathetically, that I felt obliged to buy liberally. I was also told that the poor factory girls had prayed really hard to God for three days that I would help to relieve their misery, for unless I did, they would not be able to buy bread this winter. Amongst many things they'd made were two foot muffs. But these were so terribly dear that I told them I'd buy them when I was expecting my second son – but you know I'm not in a great hurry for this to happen. But I have bought the most beautiful material to make night-dresses, and lots of other things, but what they've cost is a secret. I'm also bringing back tea pots from Boucaran' (Bokhara) 'and old Chinese lacquer which I found in the loveliest shop imaginable in Amsterdam . . .'

For once, Marie Louise was popular. Napoleon would have liked to prolong the tour, but the Dutch autumn was proving too rigorous for most of his entourage. They were being stricken with colds and chills, were appalled by the prevailing damp and miserably depressed by the water-logged countryside. Napoleon also had his private reasons for wanting to get back. He longed to see the little Napoleon who, he learnt from one of Madame de Montesquiou's letters, had cut his first four teeth and could now say 'Papa'.

Returning via Cologne, Liège, Givet and Mezières, the cortège reached Compiègne the evening of November 10th.

Both father and mother were enchanted to find their son in such boisterous good health thanks to Madame de Montesquiou's near fanatical care. But happy moments with the little boy were now Napoleon's sole relief from worries.

France's economic situation had worsened, and the notoriously turbulent Parisians were restive. There was no more enthusiasm when the emperor passed by in the streets. The new faces turned in his direction were more often sullen than smiling. News from abroad was even more disturbing. Those whom he counted among the best of his marshals – Masséna, Soult, Marmont – were being trounced in battle after battle by Wellington; the 'running sore' showed no sign of healing. At the same time, English influence was making itself felt in all the seaboard countries of northern Europe. Worse still, this influence was now so strong in Russia that, in diplomatic circles, it was considered almost as a covert alliance between the two countries. Often, and with great bitterness, Napoleon remembered the czar's words at Tilsit: 'If you really dislike the English, then we should soon be in agreement. I've nothing but complaints to make about them myself . . .' There were even moments – though for the time being they were few and far between – when he began to have doubts of Austria's sincerity.

And so once more he decided that the best antidote for depression was ordered gaiety. Whatever happened, court life must not reflect the Master's torments. There must be dancing, music. Everybody must be cheerful, even dissipated, behave as though the only care in the world was the necessity of outdoing in splendour the reception offered by one's neighbour. Thanks to imperial decree, 1811 passed into 1812 on the crest of a wave of fêtes, galas, receptions, whose glittering façade was only exceeded by the monumental boredom of those obliged to take part in this ordained merrymaking.

A typical evening of this period is described by Baron de Bausset: 'One had to arrive just before half past eight. One entered the salon, which was a sort of waiting room, just outside that of the Empress. The women were seated, the men on their feet. The lights, the heating, the crowd, made it so hot that one often felt ill.

'Towards nine o'clock, the women were shown into the Empress's presence. A few minutes later the door of the salon was thrown open. An usher announced, "The Emperor". The Emperor entered preceded by the Grand Chamberlain, the Grand Equerry and the Grand Marshal. The Empress followed the Emperor, and she in turn was followed by her *dame d'honneur*, the Ladies of the Household and, finally, the women guests. Once the ladies had passed, the men fell in step behind them as far as a long hall at the far end of which was a stage. At this point everyone was allowed to be seated, and this was always the signal for a certain amount of jostling among the men, as there were never enough chairs for all the guests.

'The Emperor was seated in an armchair in the middle of the front row. The Empress, on his left, also had the right to an armchair. On either side of them – on ordinary chairs – were the princesses in order of seniority. The performance was usually a mediocre comedy or a sort of musical comedy with a small cast.

'The performance over, we trooped back in the same order. In the first salon, tables would have been set up for "loto" or some sort of gambling game, and in the Empress's salon, there would be three gaming tables; one for the Empress, the other two for the princesses. Those who were to play had already been detailed by the Chamberlain. The ladies only played for the sake of appearances, as no stakes were allowed. During this time, the men had to stand, all crowded together, and would be inspected, as if on parade, by the Emperor, walking up and down in a rather mincing way, twiddling his snuff box. He would address one by name, another he honoured with a few words, many he ignored completely. Occasionally he would start a conversation, but this would soon be interrupted by cavernous yawns. At exactly half past ten he returned to his own apartments. This was the signal for departure. Men and women jostled each other in the general rush for their carriages. One would have said a group of schoolchildren who'd just been given a holiday . . .'

Napoleon was still careful not to mention his secret fears to Marie Louise. He felt that it was of the utmost importance that her letters to her father should not betray the slightest anxiety, and retain their unmistakable spontaneity. In this he was successful, for at the height of this last winter of peace, she wrote to her sister Leopoldine: 'We are having such a wonderful time in Paris. In Vienna you haven't the faintest idea of what fun everybody has here . . .'

It was, on the surface, a round of gaiety unprecedented, which lasted till mid-February. Yet it was during this time, while Paris was dancing, that the empress's fate was sealed. In between public appearances at which he was unable to hide the fact that, not only was he bored to distraction but that his thoughts were elsewhere, Napoleon had come to the melancholy conclusion that war with Russia was almost inevitable. Already orders for vast troop movements eastwards across Europe to the line of the Vistula had been issued.

It was a terrible decision, and one which he made with the deepest foreboding only after deducing that the czar meant to take the initiative and launch his masses towards Paris, absorbing like a snowball the manpower of those vassal states (and most certainly Prussia) across which they moved.

These fears were justified.

Though he had refused to allow his sister to replace Josephine, the czar was infuriated by the Austrian marriage. By some strange, circuitous thought process, he considered it at the same time an insult and a betrayal. His spite was directed entirely against Napoleon. For Francis, he felt only pity, combined with sympathy. By the end of 1811, Alexander was openly in touch with the British government and encouraging trade with Britain in all Russian-dominated ports, thus flagrantly defying the blockade. He was also negotiating an anti-Napoleon alliance with Bernadotte who, now Sweden's heir apparent and having no more respect for his former master and benefactor than his former creed, was stirring up trouble with Prussia. He had started negotiations with Austria, promising Francis – via Metternich – the whole of Moldavia, half of Wallachia and a free hand in Serbia in return for an active role in the march on Paris. Most dangerous of all, from Napoleon's point of view, he was in touch with Talleyrand, arch-intriguer and utterly amoral leader of the Bourbon underground.

The general yearning for peace dominating French thoughts was a further problem. The call-up of reservists, followed by conscription, was bound to add to Napoleon's embryonic – for the moment – unpopularity. This he feared above all things, only too well aware – despite the king of Rome's birth – of the basic fragility of his dynasty, on which he set such store yet which, by reason of being self-created, was still without true roots, threatened both by those who hankered for a return to 'legitimacy' and those who remembered the republic with nostalgia. With bitter frustration he contrasted his position with that of the Austrian royal family. Three times in less than twenty years, during Francis's reign, he had beaten Austria to her knees, inflicting the most humiliating terms of peace on her; yet the weak Francis, because of five centuries of royal blood in his veins, remained on his throne, his popularity unshaken. But for him, Napoleon – and this he recognised only too well – one minor defeat on some distant battlefield, and he risked losing all.

Though in early 1812, as has been said, Napoleon did not entertain any serious doubts of Francis's loyalty – so intensely family-minded, he could not conceive of a father making war on his own daughter or betraying his son-in-law, and had no inkling of Metternich's power nor of Francis's abandon – he felt that nothing should be left to chance. For this reason, it occurred to him that family ties might be tightened by a family reunion.

He knew that Marie Louise longed to see her father and stepmother, so what, he asked himself, could be more calculated to charm the Austrian emperor than the spectacle of his daughter's happiness? Furthermore: a cordial, intimate, family meeting between two imperial families would provide hesitant neutrals – Prussia, in particular – with a public show of power solidarity which, in turn, should discourage a friendly response to Russian flirtations.

It was thus that the idea of the Dresden meeting germinated.

By mid-March, talk of war, most of it gloomy, was so much in the air that Napoleon felt obliged to take Marie Louise into his confidence. Carefully he played down the seriousness of the situation, the dangers of the coming campaign which he studiously avoided referring to as war. The czar, he explained, was being rather silly. He was not a very stable character, and at that moment was the victim of British guile. Like a naughty boy, he had to be taught a sharp lesson but, after the correction had been administered, there was not the slightest doubt that he would be prepared to listen to reason. The coming campaign would be nothing more than a military promenade, a show of force. He even indulged in the cliché – to be so popular in August 1914 – that 'it would be all over by Christmas'. But in the meantime, before starting off on this military promenade, he meant to make arrangements for a happy little family gathering in Dresden.

The thought of impending war did not worry Marie Louise in the slightest. She believed implicitly the explanations put to her, and was convinced that even if the Russians did show fight they would soon be annihilated in record time by her invincible husband. On the other hand, as Napoleon had hoped, she was wildly excited at the thought of seeing her parents after more than two years' separation. She rushed to write to her father: '. . . The Emperor sends you his compliments and wants me to tell you that if there is a war, he will take me with him as far as Dresden where I would stay for two months and hope to see you. You can't imagine, dear Papa, the joy that overwhelms me at the thought of this possibility. I'm sure you won't deprive me of the pleasure it would give me if you brought my dear Mama and my brothers and sisters too. But please, dear Papa, don't mention this to anyone yet, because nothing is definite at the moment . . .'

The festive season was over. Napoleon realised ruefully that three years of peace had made him flabby. He had put on weight in an alarming way. He spent the month of April toughening up, re-adapting himself to long hours in the saddle. Every day there was an organised hunt in the *Bois de Boulogne*. When possible, Marie Louise was by his side. She had grown to love riding. Galloping with her husband she was able to forget, albeit momentarily, her increasing tendency to hypochondria, freeing herself at the same time of the tyrannical bonds of etiquette since she had become such a hard rider that none of her ladies was able to keep up with her. Napoleon appreciated this. 'Often he' (the Emperor) 'would awaken the Empress at dawn and, apart from an equerry, an A.D.C. and two guards, they would be alone on these mad gallops . . .'

In the meantime, the *Grande Armée* was concentrating on the Vistula. The disgruntled marshals had left – with extreme reluctance – their luxurious castles, their Paris houses, and said goodbye to wives and mistresses, cursing the emperor to whom they owed everything as they did so.

In the interim, the Dresden rendezvous had been arranged and, on May 9th, Napoleon and Marie Louise set out on the road to the Saxon capital.

Never before had Napoleon left France so quietly to embark on a campaign. The comedy that this was to be a mere military promenade was played out to the last. In Paris there were no parades. There were no bombastic proclamations aimed at working up the citizens to a state of martial fervour, no distribution of imperial eagles on the *Champs de Mars*, no universal prayers for victory in churches and cathedrals; no glittering squadrons escorted the royal carriage.

Le Moniteur of that morning printed a casual paragraph, a masterpiece of understatement: 'The Emperor left Paris today for a tour of the *Grande Armée* units stationed on the Vistula. Her Majesty the Empress is accompanying His Majesty as far as Dresden where she hopes to have the pleasure of meeting her august family. She will be back in July at the latest. The King of Rome will spend the summer at Meudon where he has been in residence for the past month. His teething is now completed, and the King enjoys the best of health. He will be weaned at the end of this month.'

Chapter VI

The journey across France was conducted on the same quiet note, and it was a journey which Marie Louise thoroughly enjoyed. She drove in the same carriage as her husband. Halts were made more or less incognito. There were no tiresome receptions, no parades, no lengthy speeches to be suffered with bored indifference.

Once across France's frontiers, however, there was a complete change. In view of the tense situation, Napoleon was incapable of relaxing in the company of his vassals. They, he was convinced – perhaps erroneously – must be made to remember who was the master, who it was who issued orders which brooked no questioning, and to whom all honour was due.

Typically, at Mainz Napoleon had decreed that he and the empress should be lodged in the palace of the Teutonic Order. It did not matter that the palace had been converted into a school for artillery officers. Students and staff had to move out in bulk for the imperial visitors' one-night stay.

On May 16th, after having received lip-service homage from the grand duke and duchess of Hesse-Darmstadt and the prince of Anhalt, the cortège entered Dresden late in the evening. Officially, Napoleon and his empress were guests of the king and queen of Saxony; but again Napoleon, as master, had made it clear that he would be taking over the palace, and the royal family could count themselves lucky that they were allowed to retain a small wing for their own use. In fact, all through his stay Napoleon behaved as if he were the host, palace and city his.

Everything had to be French. Glass, silver, even furniture had been brought from Paris. A full staff of servants from Compiègne, including four cooks, took charge. Only French uniforms were allowed to be seen in the courtyard. The Tuileries had moved to Dresden.

On May 17th other vassal rulers of German states arrived, among them the king of Prussia and the crown prince, all summoned to be present at, and be suitably impressed by, the spectacle of the affectionate meeting of the two super-monarchs and their families, united, one and indivisible, by marriage's sacred bonds.

Marie Louise had hoped to be allowed to drive out to meet her father and stepmother before their official entry on the 18th. Reluctantly, Napoleon had to veto this. Even the emperor and empress of Austria must realise that he, Napoleon, was the master; that it was he who had summoned them to this family reunion, that he was not only their host but sole director of Europe's – including Austria's – destiny. Besides – Marie Louise was unaware of this – he would be holding private talks with his father-in-law, during which he wished to be reassured that certain rumours of Francis's lukewarm support for his Russian adventure were unfounded. Hypersensitive, he feared that the spectacle of Marie Louise, racing informally to meet her father, might be twisted into indicating a sign of weakness on his part. A little tearfully, but automatically submissive, Marie Louise bowed to his verdict.

If, however, either Napoleon or Marie Louise could have had a glimpse into the minds of their guests, as they neared Dresden escorted by their surprisingly modest suite of only eleven men and four women, they would have been both shocked and surprised.

Francis himself was anxious to see his daughter and, despite past humiliations, still retained, vis-à-vis the French emperor, a weak man's admiration for the strong. In addition, he was genuinely grateful to Napoleon for converting a marriage of political expediency into an affair of the heart bringing undeniable happiness to a much-loved child. Essentially honest, he regretted that the tokens of esteem and affection he would be obliged to exchange with his son-in-law would of a necessity be hypocritical since, as a patriot, he had sworn to put country before family and sublimated himself to the virtual domination of his chancellor Metternich (who, nevertheless, always referred to him as 'The emperor, my master'), whose policy, he knew, was directed to the destruction of French hegemony.

By Francis's side, the empress Maria Ludovica was a small, frail but burning bundle of hate.

When Napoleon's invitation was received, she had been loud in her protestations that it was an impertinence, an insult, and that never under any circumstances whatsoever would she agree to meet the 'usurper'. The emperor could go, if he wished, running like a little dog to the master's whistle; she herself had no intention of leaving Vienna. Metternich eventually persuaded her to change her mind by pointing out that since Francis was so easy-going, so easily influenced, her presence at Dresden was essential as an antidote to the Corsican's blandishments.

Yet another surprise for Napoleon was the presence, uninvited, of Metternich himself.

The Austrian chancellor's plans were working smoothly. The two colossi – France and Russia – were, he hoped devoutly, about to bleed each other white. In anticipation, he had done everything to ensure that while Austria would appear committed she would not be involved in the blood-letting. In the March of that year he had signed a treaty with Napoleon that in return for 'compensation in Illyria in the event of losses in Galicia, for a guarantee of Turkish integrity and for certain more indefinite advantages', Austria would place at the disposal of the French emperor a corps of 30,000 men. It was laid down, however, that this corps should form the right wing of the *Grande Armée*, be an independent command under an Austrian general and receive orders only from Napoleon himself. The man chosen to command this corps was Prince Schwarzenberg, an able diplomat but with no practical experience of command on the battlefield.

No sooner was this treaty signed than Metternich had a secret message delivered to the czar, assuring him that the Austrian contingent would afford 'the least possible assistance, advance the least possible distance, and commit the least possible injury . . .'

Whichever of the two giants proved to be the winner, Austria had taken out a good insurance policy. It was essential that it should not be compromised by Francis's vacillation. With this in mind, Metternich was determined to be present whenever the two monarchs met at the conference table.

The meeting, which took place as arranged on May 18th, was notable for the pleasure both father and daughter displayed at seeing each other once more after a two-year separation, and the lamentable failure of Napoleon's efforts to charm his vinegary young mother-in-law.

Despite his height (five feet two inches only) and his vanishing waistline, Napoleon had had so much success with women that he was convinced that he had only to turn on his charm to disarm the most militant female hostility. For this reason he had flattered himself that, although the Austrian empress was reputed to hate him more than the Devil himself, he would soon succeed in winning her over.

Had Maria Ludovica been a normal woman, this might have been the case. But she was not. She was a sick woman, as well as an incurable neurotic, warped by her hatred of Napoleon, the man whom she considered not merely the representative but the embodiment of the misfortunes which had befallen her family.

Napoleon was soon aware that his famous charm had no effect at all on this fanatical young mother-in-law whom he was soon likening to 'an asparagus stalk dipped in vinegar'. She saw no reason to shelter behind even a conventional diplomatic in-difference. She shivered with disgust when he embraced her, stiffening when he attempted a plebeian hug which he hoped would convey a non-diplomatic message. When, at meals, he devoted himself to entertaining her, she feigned a quasi-total deafness which left him baffled and irritated. At the little concerts which invariably followed an official dinner, and during which Napoleon was in the habit of ignoring the musicians and carrying on uninterrupted conversations, Maria Ludovica pretended that she was a fanatical music-lover and demanded total silence.

What was even more serious – and played happily into Metternich's hands – was the fact that Maria Ludovica, who had never reciprocated her step-daughter's affection, now grew to hate Marie Louise.

Perhaps inevitably, she was acutely aware of her position as the poor relation. Though conditions had improved in Austria after two and a half years of peace under Metternich's guidance, the Viennese court was still, comparatively speaking, extremely hard up. The Austrian retinue was reduced to the bare necessity not from reasons of modesty but, rather, by reason of the harsh dictates of a near-empty purse – this in all-too-marked contrast with the exaggerated opulence of the Napoleonic suite.

In her naive delight at being able to play the role of Lady Bountiful, Marie Louise had brought, literally, coachloads of presents for her *liebe mama*. There was no question of refusing these gifts but, having accepted them, the *liebe mama* complained to Francis, 'I'm afraid our poor Louise has become impregnated with the Corsican's vulgarity.'

This caustic attitude, however, did not prevent her making

daily visits to her step-daughter at the moment of the latter's morning 'toilette'. On these occasions Marie Louise, still naively unaware of the fact that her step-mother hated the sight of her, begged her to look through her immense wardrobe and help herself to anything she wanted. As Napoleon remarked bitterly on St Helena: 'She used to ferret round every morning while Marie Louise was dressing, and never left empty-handed.' Nor did Maria Ludovica's depredations limit themselves to clothes. By the time she left Dresden her jewel boxes, pathetically empty on arrival, were crammed with rings, necklaces, bracelets lavished on her by Marie Louise and accepted with secret greed but an outward comedy of disdain.

Commenting on Maria Ludovica's hatred, Raymonde Bessard remarks: 'If Marie Louise talked naively of her husband's kindness, or if she made "some not very tactful comparisons between her old and new countries", she was treated as a renegade by this jealous woman who would not admit such a change of mind. This last conquest of Napoleon's only served to swell Maria Ludovica's rancour. Implacable from then on, helped by Metternich, she was to devote herself to the destruction of the Franco-Austrian alliance. This woman, one might say, was the source of Napoleon's misfortunes.'*

Maria Ludovica proved herself an excellent instrument of Metternich. She never lost the opportunity of trying to turn Marie Louise against her husband; but this had no effect. Either Marie Louise was obstinate, being still in love, or else the poison was too subtle for her to absorb. With Francis, however, Maria Ludovica scored a great success which won her Metternich's deep appreciation.

Napoleon was not happy about the conditions attached to his employment of the Austrian corps. He had hoped, therefore, that when they met he would be able to persuade Francis to take personal command of this corps and that the spectacle of the two great emperors marching to war, hand-in-hand as it were, would have a decisive propaganda effect. To begin with, the Austrian emperor was attracted by the idea although, other than half-heartedly at Austerlitz, he had never assumed the almost automatic monarchical role of commander-in-chief of his armies. It may be that he nurtured a secret hope that if he were to distinguish himself in the campaign, he would find his tragically lacking

* Raymonde Bessard, *La Vie Privée de Marie Louise*, Hachette, 1951.

self-respect and then, morally armed, might feel himself in a position to break some, at least, of the shackles binding him to his chancellor. Through Metternich, Maria Ludovica got to hear of his wavering – 'to prevent her husband' (Francis) 'being caught up in this adventure, thus strengthening his ties with France, she employed all possible means, reproaches, prayers and tears . . . so the Emperor did not go, did not allow himself to be influenced by his son-in-law; he remained fettered to his wife and to Metternich . . .'*

When on May 29th, a Friday, Napoleon left Dresden to join his *Grande Armée*, he was a sadly disillusioned man. He realised that he had failed to win over Maria Ludovica, even though he failed to gauge the passionate intensity of her hatred, putting it down instead to 'petty jealousy' at the sight of the wealth and luxury enjoyed by her step-daughter. More deeply still was he disappointed by his failure to persuade Francis to ride by his side. Unwillingly he was obliged to admit to himself that Austria was now more of a neutral than an ally. He still refused to envisage, could not conceive of, Austria as a future enemy, and that within little more than a year. On the other hand, he was most careful not to let Marie Louise share his fears and suspicions, and was delighted that it had been arranged that she should remain a few more weeks with her parents, accompanying them to Prague, before returning to Paris. He entertained, in fact, a slender hope that her continued presence might revive Francis's flagging enthusiasm for the French cause.

Marie Louise was in floods of tears. She made a dramatic scene of heart-broken grief as she took leave of him, again extorting from him the solemn promise to write every day and swearing that she would not know a moment's happiness till he returned. The scene took place in front of the Austrian imperial couple. Francis's eyes filled with tears. Maria Ludovica remained tight-lipped, contemptuous. Napoleon, well satisfied by his wife's public display of devotion, drove east with his comparatively small escort.

Once again it can be stated emphatically that, not withstanding the drama, Marie Louise's grief was genuine. As usual she had to pour out her emotion on paper; this time it was to her lady of the wardrobe, Madame de Luçay: 'You know me well enough to judge how sad and unhappy I am. I do try to control my feelings, but I shall stay like this until I see him again.'

* Raymonde Bessard, op. cit.

And of the coming journey to Prague: 'It's the only possible consolation which enables me to bear my husband's absence . . .'

And when, late that evening, a despatch rider brought a letter from Napoleon, written only a few hours after his departure, she clutched it to her hysterically.

My sweet Louise,

As I am stopping for a hurried luncheon, I'm taking advantage of the halt to write to you and implore you to be gay and not upset yourself. I'll keep all the promises I made you; so our separation won't last long. You know how much I love you, and I must be assured that you are calm and well. Good-bye, sweet friend, a thousand kisses.

Nap.

And two days later another, equally hurried but optimistic:

My friend,

I received your three letters all together. I was very sad at being two whole days without news of you. It makes me unhappy that you are so sad, and I'm grateful to Princess Therese for taking you for a drive. I am in very good health and will be leaving tonight for Thorne where I shall be staying for several days. Give my regards to your aunt and to the king of Saxony and his family. You are quite right to think of me. You know I love you and I hate not seeing you two or three times every day. But I think in three months it will be all over.

Goodbye, my sweet love (*Adio, mio dolce amore*),

All yours,

Nap.

Marie Louise entered Prague with her parents on June 6th.

This was a real, and happy, family reunion. All her brothers and sisters had gathered to welcome her. The city was *en fête*. Even Maria Ludovica could not spoil the spontaneous gaiety prevailing. Marie Louise was radiant, and for once managed to throw off her awkward shyness on the round of official occasions, dinners, receptions. Everyone remarked on how well and happy she looked and, unlike Maria Ludovica, brothers and sisters were enchanted by, and touchingly grateful for, the sumptuous gifts offered to them, which included not only clothes and jewellery but rare plants sent specially from Paris, bulbs, toys, chocolates and crystallised fruit. In addition, Marie Louise received a (for him) long letter from Napoleon – then in Marienberg – who, still believing in the efficacity of presents, gave her detailed instructions as to who was to be included in the list:

My good Louise,
My presentiment wasn't wrong. I had four of your letters half way, the other three arrived this morning. I'm surprised you haven't received mine. I sent two to my Minister in Dresden to pass on to you. It must have been a great joy for you to see your brothers and sisters again. Please tell Prince Charles what a great admiration I have for him. I suppose you gave Prince Clary a present, as you were staying with him you should have done. If you haven't, you must do so when you leave Prague. Montesquiou* will, I suppose, have done the necessary as far as the household is concerned; one must be very generous and give lavishly. I have ordered presents to be sent to the ladies of the Empress: that to Madame Lagiski† (*sic*) should amount to £50,000 at least. You must not give gold snuff boxes, that is in bad taste, but rings of £1,200, £2,000, £3,000 and £6,000. Talk it over with the Grand Chamberlain. Give plenty of money to those who wait on you. I imagine Montesquiou has given you your June allowance so you can spend plenty. Jardin should have arrived to train your riding horses. Be nice to your father and the whole family. Tell your father how fond I am of him, and offer my respects to the Empress. Let me know whether it is customary for visiting sovereigns to offer presents to the Burgraves when they visit Prague. And try to work out what you can give when you leave so that your visit is remembered. Get anything you want sent from Paris. Goodbye, my friend, you know how much I love you. I want to hear that you are well and happy and have got rid of that naughty cold. Never allow anyone to make an adverse comment on French policy in front of you. All yours,
Nap.

* Husband of the king of Rome's governess, Madame de Montesquiou.
†Madame Lazansky, Marie Louise's old governess.

While at Prague, the emperor Francis increased his daughter's already overgrown retinue by the addition of twelve honorary chamberlains. Among them was a certain general, Count Adam Albert von Neipperg. The general was in many ways a remarkable man.

He came of an old Swabian family. His great-grandfather, Eberhard Frederic von Neipperg (1655–1725) was a field-marshal; another ancestor, Wilhelm Reinhard (1684–1774), after being imprisoned for signing a treaty handing over Belgrade to the Turks, was eventually amnestied and became Austrian commander-in-chief. Adam Albert's father, Leopold, chose a diplomatic career and became an ambassador before his death in 1792. While accredited to Paris in 1774, a handsome and dashing young French officer was a frequent visitor to his salon.

Count Leopold was a man of genius. He invented the first writing machine in 1762 while in Naples and, as Max Billard has suggested, was 'influenced by the love of machinery rather than the machinery of love': whereas the countess was a romantic soul and soon violently attracted by the young Frenchman. Again, to quote Billard: 'Their early relations were innocent as a German idyll, but soon became more intimate, resulting eventually in the birth of the future General Neipperg.'

Probably Leopold was ignorant of the fact that the child christened Adam Albert might not have been his. In any case, he was brought up as a Neipperg, educated at Stuttgart and Strasbourg, and adopted an army career at the age of fifteen. Even at this early age, despite possible Gallic blood in his veins, Adam Albert conceived a fanatical hatred for France and the French. This hatred was fanned when, after seeing action at Jemmappes and Neerwinden, he was severely wounded at Doelen (September 14th 1790), battered by sabre cuts from the saddle and left for dead on the field.

It was not until the next day he was picked up and taken to hospital where he came very near to ending his career, as he spoke French so fluently that he was suspected of being an *émigré* and, as such, would have been shot out of hand. It was some time before he recovered from his wounds, his treatment including the removal of his right eye, almost hacked from its socket by a French sabre.

Eventually, he benefited by an exchange of prisoners, was posted to the Austrian army in Italy and took part in the battles of Carsona, Novi, Trebbia and Marengo. Promoted general at the age of 37, he reverted to his father's role of diplomat, being appointed ambassador to Sweden in 1810.

He was extremely popular in Stockholm. He was an ardent supporter of a close alliance between Russia, England and Sweden, making it known – unofficially – that despite Marie Louise's marriage it was only a question of time before Austria, also, would be an active member of such a league. Showing himself to be as skilled a diplomat as he was a soldier, he was able to persuade the crown prince, the ambitious Bernadotte, that his interests would be best served by taking up arms, at the right moment, against his old friend and benefactor, Napoleon.

Highly intelligent, well versed in the arts, he was an excellent amateur poet and musician. There was yet another field in which Adam von Neipperg shone. Madame de Stael herself, temporarily exiled in Stockholm, remarked that, 'With his one unbandaged eye he could devastate the fair sex in half the time another man could accomplish the fact with two.' She spoke of him as the 'German Bayard': 'The title of the *Chevalier sans peur et sans reproche* became him well, for he was as daring in love as he was dauntless in war . . .'*

There had been a number of affairs, verging on scandal, which only Neipperg's great reputation as a soldier allowed him to live down. A Countess Trento had her marriage annulled so as to legalise her liaison with her one-eyed lover but, before this could happen, Neipperg had already tired of her and was deeply involved with Countess Teresa Ramondini who also happened to be married. This detail, however, did not deter von Neipperg. The Ramondinis were living in Mantua. As in a scene from a romantic novel, the countess escaped from her home to the shelter of Neipperg's waiting carriage in which they travelled to Milan where he installed her in a rented villa. This affair lasted until 1814. The couple were married in 1813, but not before the countess Teresa had presented Adam von Neipperg with five children. Again there was considerable scandal, but Viennese society was permissive enough to place services to the fatherland above moral considerations.

At Prague there was no personal contact between Marie Louise and von Neipperg. As far as Marie Louise was concerned he was simply one of a number of Austrians whom, for politeness' sake,

* E. M. Oddie: op. cit.

she had been obliged to include in her suite. For his part, Neipperg was not in the least interested in his temporary appointment. He was one of those who had been profoundly shocked by the marriage and, as a woman, he found the French empress most unattractive; he preferred small, dark women.

Marie Louise had also become very gallicised. She was no longer happy in Austrian company. At the same time, the French members of her household were getting extremely bored and longed to be back in their beloved Paris, overcome by that nostalgia which even today makes all things non-French abhorrent to the French. For Marie Louise, the joy of family reunion was wearing thin, and when the time came to leave Prague she shared their impatience to be 'home'.

The eighteen-day leisurely journey to Saint Cloud started on July 1st. For the first six days Marie Louise travelled with her father, who left her at Egra. On July 7th she reached Wurzburg where she was lavishly entertained by her uncle, the grand duke, whom she had so reproached for his passion for Caroline Murat. She enjoyed herself, but also gave signs of increasing hypochondria aggravated by sexual frustration: 'My health is good though yesterday' (July 9th) 'I had a nasty attack of stomach cramps', and on the 10th, 'My arm hurts, as a result it is swathed in poultices which make the room stink . . .'

Marie Louise's physical ills were largely imaginary, but she was psychologically disturbed. She had been delighted to see everybody again after a two years' absence, and was supremely ignorant of the hatred she had inspired in her stepmother, believing, on the contrary, that, charmed by so many gifts, *liebe mama* loved her all the more dearly. On the other hand, she now shared increasingly with each passing day her French entourage's longing to be back in France. She had come round to their way of thinking that Paris was the *only* city in the world and that others, so-called, were nothing but overgrown villages; that only things French were of any intrinsic value, and that France held the monopoly of world culture. She had, in fact, become more French than the French and was in a hurry to impart her reactions to her husband.

Already fearing that his promised military promenade was not going according to plan, her letter brought a brief ray of light to the dark background of Napoleon's gloomy forebodings. He replied: 'I am so pleased that you are happy with the French people and hold them in your esteem. And really you do put me on too high a plane, but then I know you are prejudiced and I love you for it because all my happiness depends on you. You know how devoted I am to you. Kiss my son. How I long to see him. He must be a big boy by now, and very good I hope. *Adio mio bene*. All yours. Nap.'

But though she felt French, Marie Louise showed very soon after her return that she was still incapable of relaxing in the company of French people, with the notable exception of the duchess of Montebello.

Once installed at Saint Cloud, she plunged back into that same detachment which had already earned for her such adverse criticism and so many enemies. She made it quite clear that she had no wish for the companionship of anyone but her *dame d'honneur*, and that she intended to cut down on the normal run of entertainment and public appearances, duty and apanage of her position as sovereign in her husband's absence. The day after her arrival (July 19th), the principal officials and dignitaries of the state summoned by Cambacérès to present their homage and congratulations on the empress's safe return were told, after they had been waiting some considerable time, that the empress was fatigued and that the ceremony was put off till the following day. As one of the irritated dignitaries remarked: 'Even if the other' (Josephine) 'had been dying, she'd have been there with a smile and a gracious word for everyone.'

But for the fact that Napoleon, knowing her hatred of public functions, had laid down a strict programme – theatre on Thursdays, Mass followed by a diplomatic reception on Sundays – she would have led as retired a life as Queen Victoria after the prince consort's death.

Referring to these bi-weekly appearances, Frédéric Masson says: 'Apart from a few semi-official visits to the Queen of Spain' (Julie Clary, Joseph's wife) 'these were the only occasions on which she showed herself in public.'

That she was unhappy can be gleaned from her constant bemoaning of her grass-widowhood: 'God grant,' (she wrote to her father) 'that I will see the Emperor again soon, because this separation is crushing me and I do not have the courage to fight my depression.'

And to Madame Mère of whom, despite the old woman's near-peasant blood, she was slightly in awe: 'I'm in good health as the Saint Cloud air agrees with me and I'm living a very quiet life, though when one is so sad, one does not want any form of amusement, and one is only happy when one is all alone and able to give way to one's private grief. That is why it is such a strain for me when I'm obliged to meet people. We must pray most fervently that this will soon end and that it will not be long before the Emperor returns victorious to us, for I know that till then I shall not have a moment's happiness.'

If, as some claim, these letters were dictated by a mixture of tact and policy, there can be no doubt as to the genuineness of her emotional outburst to Victoria de Crenneville: 'You are quite right in thinking that I must have spent August 25th' (Marie Louise's name day) 'less happily than on previous years. You know me well enough to be assured that when I'm unhappy I really *am* unhappy, and yet do not show it. And so you can judge for yourself how miserable I am without the Emperor and that I will be till he returns. I never stop worrying and tormenting myself. If a day passes without a letter from him, I'm plunged into the depths of despair, and when one does arrive I'm only consoled for a brief hour or two . . .'

Nevertheless, in between her lamentations at being husbandless, she found time to complain of her health. Often she refused to eat and soon lost the agreeable plumpness she had regained as a result of the journeys to Dresden and Prague. Incontestably, most of these complaints – migraine, feverish colds, stomach disorders, rheumatism – were imaginary or greatly exaggerated. The irritable Dr Corvisart frequently said so, much to her fury, so that one day we get a triumphal entry in her diary: '*At last* he' (Dr Corvisart) 'has admitted that I am ill!'

On the contrary, matters which should have caused her sleepless nights – the war fast turning to disaster in Russia, and deteriorating conditions in France – worried her not in the least. Hers was a childlike confidence in the emperor's invincibility and dynastic stability.

Never was this insouciance better illustrated than at the moment of what is generally known as *The Malet Affair*.

Of all the inhabitants of France, Marie Louise was perhaps the only one who did not realise, as autumn passed, that the war in Russia was in fact already and disastrously lost. Though Napoleon had won his 'good battle' at Borodino on the banks of the Moskova river, which victory he had been convinced would bring the czar racing to beg for peace, the 'victory' had cost him 9,000 killed, including twelve generals, and 21,000 wounded, among these latter Marshals Davout and Rapp. It would have been better for Napoleon if he had not been victor for, despite inconclusive results, the fact that he remained master of the Borodino battlefield induced him to commit the fatal error of continuing his march on Moscow.

Remembering the fate of the Swedish king Charles XIII, the French emperor should have adhered to his original plan; an advance as far as Smolensk only, installation in that town for the winter, re-concentration and renewal of the advance – if necessary – in the spring of 1813. Again, having blundered, against the advice of all his marshals, by departing from this sound strategy, he made a second and even more deadly mistake in not giving the order to fall back from Moscow on Smolensk when it became evident that the czar had no intention of asking for terms, before the onset of the Russian winter with all its attendant horrors. Yet he insisted in delaying in the capital until the first snow had fallen, thus condemning tens of thousands of men to certain death.

No news of this was allowed to infiltrate to Marie Louise's ears. Napoleon's letters were devoted mostly to bulletin-like reports of his own health, enquiries as to that of Marie Louise, and pathetic demands for more detailed news of his son, the 'little king'.

On September 3rd:

My friend. I've received your letter of the 19th. I leave here tonight to carry on the advance to Moscow. It's now the same sort of weather as when we were at Fontainebleau. The granaries are full, the fields covered with vegetables so the soldiers are all right which is a good thing. All goes well. My health is good. I hear yours is perfect. Embrace the little King on both cheeks. *Adio, mio ben.* Nap.

Even after Borodino, the tone was equally casual: '. . . Yesterday I beat the Russians; their whole army 120,000 strong . . .' A short catalogued report of mutual losses, then, 'My health is good, the weather fresh . . .'

The only time when a genuinely personal note can be detected is shortly after the entry into Moscow:

My friend. I've already written to you from Moscow, but I had no conception of this city. It has 500 palaces furnished French style and with incredible luxury, several imperial palaces, barracks, magnificent hospitals. All this has disappeared, consumed by fire the last four days. As all the bourgeois homes were wooden they burnt like matches. It was the governor and the Russians who, mad with rage at being defeated, set fire to this beautiful city, 200,000 inhabitants are reduced to despair, the streets, and misery. However, there's enough left for the army, and the army has discovered all sorts of riches, as in this chaos everything is being pillaged. This is a terrible loss for Russia and her commerce will suffer severely. These miserable creatures went as far as to carry off or destroy the pumps. My cold is finished, my health good. Goodbye, my friend. All yours, Nap.

It was not surprising, therefore, that the morning of October 23rd, as Marie Louise was taking her morning walk leaning, as usual, on the duchess of Montebello's arm, she showed a most remarkable *sang-froid* when Prince Aldobrandini suddenly appeared, almost staggering, livid and stammering: 'A revolution has broken out in Paris. We must leave immediately.'

She was rather annoyed at her walk being interrupted and had to be convinced by both Madame de Montebello and Madame de Montesquiou that it would be better to make a move to St Cyr, where there was a presumably loyal garrison, before she would even give the order for a carriage to be harnessed up. However, before this order could be carried out an A.D.C., the comte de Verdun, arrived at the gallop, calling out: 'Don't worry! It's all over!'

Though Marie Louise was still smiling as she read the report handed her by the count, and was in the best of humours when Cambacères arrived with further details, this ill-conceived, amateurishly-carried-out plot had come perilously near to success.

Colonel Malet, its instigator, was of noble birth but a liberal. He had embraced the Revolution's principles with fervour, so much so that he disapproved most strongly of the 18 Brumaire *coup d'état* and was soon flirting with those planning to overthrow the consulate, though cunning enough not to allow proof of his activities to fall into the hands of the police. In spite of this he was imprisoned in La Force but, considered comparatively harmless, transferred to a form of mental hospital in 1809 where he was kept under rather half-hearted surveillance. There he remained for three years working out further plots – purely theoretical – for overthrowing the emperor. Unfortunately – for him – news of serious setbacks on the Russian front, accompanied by rumours of the emperor's death, inspired him to take action.

During the night of October 22nd, accompanied by a fellow detainee, a royalist priest named Lafond, he walked unchecked out of the hospital (Dubuisson) with a mass of papers, proclamations and orders he had managed to get printed clandestinely. The basic idea was to spread the news that Napoleon had been killed in battle, then take advantage – though how was far from clearly defined in their minds – of the resulting confusion.

The two men picked up two more accomplices, then went to the house of a Spanish priest who – although it is not explained how – had managed to get possession of a collection of high-ranking army and police officer uniforms. Suitably dressed, the four men then went straight to the nearest barracks, commanded by a Colonel Soulié. There Malet, pretending to be General Lamothe, an officer of impeccable reputation, announced the emperor's death, the re-establishment of the Senate and his – Soulié's – promotion to the position of *Commandant de la Place de Paris*. The colonel, delighted by this unexpected advance, called all the officers at that moment in the barracks, read them the proclamation handed him by the false General Lamothe and then, at the head of an infantry company, marched to the La Force prison to free General Lahurie, who had been implicated in the Moreau plot, and an anti-Bonaparte Corsican, Bocchiciampi, prefect of the Seine. The plotters' next move was to arrest Baron Pasquier, Savary, the real chief of police, and Desmaret, head of the secret police, while they were still in their beds. All three were then taken to the La Force prison and locked up in the cells Lahurie and Bocchiciampi had just quitted.

Malet then went to the Babylon barracks and informed General Robbe of the emperor's supposed death. As gullible as Colonel Soulié, the general, without questioning, obeyed Malet's orders to march his troops out of the barracks and take over all the posts guarding the roads leading to Paris.

It was just dawn when Malet, dazzled by such easy success, set out to arrest Count Hullin, official *Commandant de la Place de Paris*. Hullin, less naive than Soulié and Robbe, demanded proof of the emperor's death. Infuriated by this first show of opposition, Malet fired a pistol point blank into Hullin's face, pushed past his victim's bloody corpse and rushed into the adjoining office occupied by General Doucet, Hullin's chief-of-staff. Doucet recognised Malet immediately and, before the latter had time to reload his pistol, denounced him to the escort who, changing allegiance as easily as they had done their leaders but an hour or so earlier, arrested him to cries of '*Vive l'Empereur!*', then hurried off to seize Lahurie. A couple of hours later, Malet and Lahurie were in the La Force cells from which Pasquier, Savary and Desmaret had just been released by totally confused gaolers falling over themselves to implore forgiveness.

For the rest of the morning chaos reigned. The troops had no idea whose orders they should obey and it was not until Clarke, the war minister, issued a proclamation denouncing the plotters and denying the emperor's death, that order was restored.

It had been a close-run thing.

For a brief moment, Malet had been virtual master of Paris. But for General Doucet's perspicacity and courage, Napoleon's reign might well have ended as he was battling westwards to the Beresina.

Retribution was swift. Of the twenty-five plotters arrested, fifteen were condemned to death and shot the same day. As well as Malet and Lahurie, the guileless Robbe and Soulié were among those to face the firing squad.

Cambacérès had fully realised the danger and was extremely irritated by Marie Louise's complacency when she remarked: 'After all, what could they have done to me? Am I not the daughter of the emperor of Austria?'

He must have been tempted to make some reference to great-aunt Marie Antoinette, but contented himself by replying: 'Upon my faith, Madame, Your Majesty is fortunate in being able to look upon matters so philosophically. Perhaps you did not know that it was the intention of the conspirators to put the king of Rome into a home for lost children.'

She was not impressed. She wrote to her father: 'I am not at all alarmed by trouble stirred up by a few lunatics, for I know how loyal and devoted the people are to their Emperor . . .'

With that, the affair was forgotten, and Hortense, who came

hurriedly to visit her the following day, noted: 'I have never seen her looking better.'

Napoleon's reactions, however, were very different. Marie Louise's casual letter mentioning the *affaire Malet* reached him on November 6th when he was two days' march from Smolensk. Realising to the full the gravity of its impact, it was for him almost as cruel a blow as the spectacle of his *Grande Armée* disintegrating before his eyes. What did it matter that he was emperor, that his wife was the Austrian emperor's eldest child, that the blood of one of Europe's oldest reigning families ran in his son's veins? His dynasty, which meant more to him than anything else in the world, had still not taken root. Against his will, he had suspected as much. Here was the proof. It was enough for a bare rumour of his death to circulate for all to collapse like a straw hut in a hurricane. The stark truth wrung from him the agonised protest: 'At the first hint of my death, on the order of an unknown person, officers lead their regiments to break down the prisons, arrest the highest in the land . . . But what about the King of Rome, your oaths of allegiance, your principles? You make me tremble for the future! Was there no one to cry "The Emperor is dead! Long live the Emperor!"?'

Haunted by the spectre of a potentially disloyal capital, he could stand it no longer. The war was lost. The empire must be saved. His presence with the army no longer served any useful purpose. He must get back to Paris with the least possible delay.

Calling a meeting of senior officers, he put the case to them squarely, having the good sense to point out at the same time what might happen, if not to their persons, certainly to the vast fortunes they had amassed thanks to him, should the Bourbons return to the Tuileries or a second republic be proclaimed. It was the master argument and, sure of their interested loyalty, Napoleon made his preparations for departure.

First he drew up the famous document known as the XXIX bulletin to be published in *Le Moniteur,* which put the full measure of the calamity to the French people – a veritable 'blood, sweat and tears' document, in which was published a sober estimate of losses, the recognition of failure, the whole summed up in the words *l'affreuse calamité.*

Then on December 5th, forty-eight hours after the bulletin's despatch, accompanied only by Caulaincourt, he left Smorgoni in an open sledge, a survivor of his army, his power, one might add his glory, passing through the lands of his allies, his vassals, like a ghost vulnerable to the least puff of misfortune's tempest, yet possessor still of a name capable of inspiring terror and commanding respect.

After the Malet scare Marie Louise made a few visits to Paris, notably to the theatre and an exhibition of modern art showing, chiefly, the works of Franque, Gérard, Prud'hon and Isabey; but though the Saint Cloud palace was inadequately heated – 'It's so cold that one is continually waking up during the night, and in spite of all the clothes one heaps on the bed it is impossible to get warm' – she stayed on, feeling that a few physical discomforts were more than compensated by isolation. However, her entourage began to complain bitterly of colds due to damp river mists, and in view of the approaching coronation anniversary ceremonies the return to the Tuileries was fixed for the end of November, much to the delight of those who had christened themselves 'the Saint Cloud deportees'.

Paris was uneasy. No great enthusiasm was shown during the ceremonies, reduced in any case to a minimum; salutes of guns, *Te Deums*, but no parades, no fireworks, no public festivities. On December 8th, Marie Louise paid an official visit to the opera where the ovation greeting her was noticeably tepid. At last, on the 17th, *Le Moniteur* published the XXIX bulletin. 'It burst in silence, but was like one of those explosions which can scarcely be heard but yet splits a mountain. The whole edifice was shaken; from that moment on, everybody realised its fragility and awaited the fall.'

Once again, Marie Louise was singularly unaffected. She went to the salon that same afternoon, and a private performance of the comedy *L'Homme du Jour* in the evening.

At half-past eleven the following evening, Marie Louise had just gone to bed. The *femme rouge* on duty, Mademoiselle Katzener, was about to close the doors and prepare for bed herself, when she heard footsteps in the adjoining room. She had been terrified by the implications of the Malet affair, and promptly jumped to the conclusion that an attempt was about to be made on the empress's life. Her terror was heightened when the door was suddenly flung open disclosing two men so muffled in furs as to be unrecognisable.

Though certain that her last minute had come, Mademoiselle Katzener gave a piercing scream and rushed to try to prevent their entrance at the risk, so she imagined, of her own life. As she did so, the shorter of the two flung open his coat with a dramatic gesture. It was the emperor.

During this time, alarmed by her *femme rouge*'s screams, Mari Louise had jumped out of bed and was standing shivering in her nightdress, not knowing what to do or in what direction to attempt escape. Still confused, she suddenly felt herself seized and carried back to the bed she had just vacated, a familiar voice whispering passionately in her ear.

Chapter VII

All that mattered to Marie Louise was that her husband had come back to her. 'I am sure you will share with me' (she hurried to write to her father) 'my joy at seeing my husband again after a separation of over seven months. I can't think of a happier way to begin the New Year.'

Even though she saw less of him than before, she did not care. The presence she loved, that gave her strength and confidence, was by her side; nagging loneliness belonged to the past. She put on weight, colour returned to her cheeks, and this in spite of the fact that Napoleon, feeling that she could no longer be kept from reality in a rose-tinted, make-believe world, had explained with almost brutal candour the situation's gravity.

During the long race across Europe from Smorgoni to Paris, and the long silences broken only by bouts of thinking aloud to Caulaincourt, and after his first meeting with his ministers when he had repeated his reproach, 'And did not one of you gentlemen give a thought to the king of Rome?', Napoleon was more deeply convinced than ever that his 'legitimacy' must be forced on the people; a legitimacy that at the same time must spell 'continuity'. Obsessed, he reached the conclusion that the empress must be officially proclaimed regent, in case of his absence or decease, and that both empress and king of Rome must be crowned by the pope himself. These, he felt, were the measures which would definitely consolidate his dynasty, discourage Bourbon and republican aspirations, and confirm the shaky Austrian alliance.

This latter consideration had assumed a major importance.

In his frank talk with his wife, Napoleon deliberately omitted any mention of his suspicions that 'papa Francis' was being subjected to almost intolerable pressure not merely to stay neutral in case of a future conflict but even to change camps. He had been disgusted and thoroughly disillusioned by the behaviour of the Austrian contingent in Russia. With a skilled negativeness that fringed on genius, Schwarzenberg manoeuvred the Austrian troops so as to be absent from the scene of action; and if indeed they had fired any shots, they had been directed rather towards the heavens than the supposed enemy. Already, this puppet corps safely withdrawn to its homeland, Austria had signed a tentative armistice with Russia, and Napoleon had learned on the best authority that Metternich intended, when inevitably hostilities were renewed, to offer Austria's services as mediator.

Prussia in the meanwhile had also signed an armistice with Russia, soon, Napoleon knew, to be changed to an offensive alliance. At the same time Sweden, whose foreign policy was now in the hands of Bernadotte, was making active preparations to join in this new coalition and a march on Paris in the coming spring. From Vienna there came a further rumour that if France was not prepared to accept the 'mediator's' terms, then Austria might well make the allies' cause her own in the name of peace. The 'war of revenge' party now dominated in Vienna where the empress Maria Ludovica and one of Francis's younger brothers, the archduke Maximilian, had joined the rabidly anti-Bonaparte faction which called itself 'The Friends of Liberty League'.

In spite of all this, however, Napoleon refused, though admitting the danger, to allow himself to believe that a father could deliberately set out to ruin his daughter, a grandfather his grandson. Furthermore, such a probability could be ruled out definitely once the double coronation by the Pope had taken place. In the meantime, he begged Marie Louise to write still more frequently to the Austrian emperor, chatty letters which nevertheless should contain frequent references to her husband's love and deep esteem for his father-in-law, and the French people's fanatical devotion to their emperor and the baby king of Rome.

Of the proposed regency, Marie Louise wrote: 'For the moment, the date is not yet fixed. But you can be certain, my dear Papa, that this move of the Emperor's, his confidence, flatters me; God grant, though, that I am never called upon to exercise the powers of Regent, for I should be doing so only under the saddest of circumstances . . .'

By that time, Francis was aware of the role he was likely to be called upon to play. He was prepared to play it, unwillingly perhaps, but since he had sold himself morally to Metternich, he either could not, or would not, turn back. From this moment on, therefore, the basically honest, pious Francis shows himself to be a thorough hypocrite in a rather despicable game of deception for the imagined good of his country!

This double game is evident in his reply to his daughter's letter: 'I have just had the news that you are to be crowned and appointed Regent. You must indeed consider this decision of your husband's as the greatest and most flattering expression of his confidence. But if it is the will of Destiny, follow the example of your ancestors, follow the advice of your old father who does have a certain experience in the matter of government. Seek, first of all, happiness in the love of the people whose fate has been confided to you, assure peace at home and abroad. By this love you will safeguard your son's rights and assure him the heritage created, and to be left to him, by his father. My one and only wish at this moment is for such a peace and to be able to protect, as far as is possible, your husband from any dangers to which he may be exposed . . .'

A little later Francis was to write that he intended to send Prince Esterhazy to represent him at the coronation as being 'the most important man of his court thanks to his wealth and possessions' together with Prince Schwarzenberg 'to give Europe definite proof of the Austrian court's sentiments by causing the commandant of the auxiliary corps to make his appearance at the French court at the side of his (former) commander-in-chief . . .'

Willingly deceived, Napoleon stated: 'War with the Emperor Francis would be a *monstrosity*. I believe in the honour and piety of my father-in-law . . .'

And, not to be outdone in this double game, Metternich told the French Ambassador in Vienna: 'Even if you were to break our alliance with France today, tomorrow we would ask for it to be re-established in exactly the same terms and under the same conditions, for our alliance is founded upon our natural and permanent mutual interests . . .'

While sharing her husband's naive conviction that she was helping matters, Marie Louise continued to send, monthly, fabulously expensive gifts from Paris to her step-mother who professed to despise, yet readily accepted, them, and letters to her father, always with the same *leit-motif*: 'The Emperor tells me to send you all sorts of affectionate messages on his part . . . the Emperor is always speaking so warmly about you; not a day goes by without him saying how fond he is of you, especially since meeting you at Dresden . . . the Emperor tells me to assure you of his really genuine friendship for you . . .'

Marie Louise receiving a deputation

Marie Louise painting a portrait of her husband

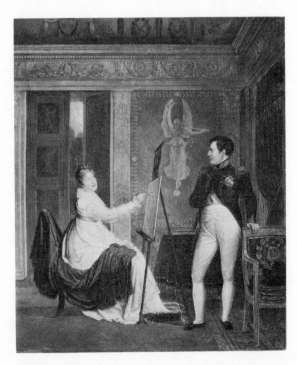

Marie Louise and the King of Rome

Marie Louise and her son from
a miniature by Isabey

Early in the New Year (1813), however, Napoleon's coronation plans received a severe setback.

In January, on the pretext of a hunting expedition accompanied by Marie Louise and a reduced household, he paid a surprise visit to Fontainebleau. The real reason was to see the pope, Pius VII, a virtual prisoner at Fontainebleau, with the object of arriving at a reconciliation, of drawing up and signing a new concordat, and extracting from the pope a promise to crown, in the very near future, both the empress and the king of Rome. Already, to pave the way for their reconciliation, Napoleon had written to Pius VII: 'Couldn't we arrive at some much longed for agreement by which we could put an end to the differences separating the Church and the State; for my part, I am very eager to accomplish this, and it now depends entirely on Your Holiness . . .'

The pope's reply, delivered by Cardinal Joseph Doria, seemed hopeful – enough at any rate to decide Napoleon to make the unannounced visit the evening of January 19th.

So as to ensure surprise, no preparations had been made to receive the imperial party. It was bitterly cold – seven to eight degrees below zero centigrade – and the palace notoriously draughty. By the second day everyone was complaining of chills, bad food, uncomfortable quarters; everyone, that is, except, for a change, Marie Louise herself who, profoundly devout, had always been worried by the relationship existing between the French court and the papacy, and was more than anxious to be received by the pope, in person, and given his blessing. In fact, remarked one of the entourage, morosely, 'The empress has never appeared to be so happy.'

On January 25th she wrote to her father: 'We have been at Fontainebleau for the last six days, where the Emperor has arranged the affairs of Christianity with the Pope. The Pope seems very contented. He is gay and in good spirits, and the treaty was signed a quarter of an hour ago. I have just left him. He is a handsome man with a most interesting face; I am sure you will be as happy as I am to learn this news . . .'

On the 27th, feeling that all the terrible problems regarding the future, which had tormented him for so long, were at last solved, Napoleon left Fontainebleau for Paris.

He called a meeting of the privy council, on February 1st, to draw up the final form for the regency act and set a tentative date for the double coronation. March 7th was suggested and semi-official notices to this effect were sent out to the vassal rulers in the hope that warning of the coming ceremony might have a salutary effect on the waverers exposed to the czar's blandishments.

A few days later, however, there was a setback. The cardinals, who just under three years previously had refused to attend the imperial wedding and were qualified by Napoleon as the 'black' cardinals, had called on the pope, urging him to change his mind. He still hesitated to do so but, as an indication that he might, a sum of 300,000 francs sent by the emperor towards 'expenses' was returned without comment.

As a counter move, an anxious Napoleon had the terms of the new concordat printed in *Le Moniteur* though, it was noted, he did not dare to mention the coronation in his speech at the opening seance of the Legislative Corps. No comments were forthcoming from Fontainebleau.

A second date, March 15th, was mentioned to the ministers of state. Nothing happened! But on the 23rd Napoleon, replying to an address from the Legislative Corps, stated: 'As soon as the preoccupations of war leave us a moment of respite, we will recall you to this capital, together with the notables of our Empire, to be present at the coronation of the empress, our well beloved spouse, and of the prince imperial, the king of Rome, our very dear son. Our heart is moved by the thought of this most solemn occasion, at the same time religious and political. We will press forward with this so as to satisfy France's desires . . .'

The very next day, March 24th, the pope retracted publicly. He stated that pressure had been brought to bear on him and that his infallibility had not stood up to the test or protected him from making a mistake that weighed heavily on his conscience. In an official letter to the emperor, he informed Napoleon that he withdrew his signature placed on the concordat of January 25th.

Though furious and bitterly disappointed, Napoleon realised that he was helpless. A further attempt at coercion would certainly prove abortive and might do immense harm. The coronation so dear to his heart had to be abandoned, but the proclamation of the regency, he determined, must be made before his departure for the front.

Originally, this was meant to be a national occasion, a grandiose ceremony for the benefit of the public; but since it now could no longer lay claim to any religious significance, Napoleon felt that such a ceremony would be a waste of both time and money. Instead, reduced to its simplest expression, it took place before a small selection of the notables, and the household.

From her apartments the empress was escorted to the council hall of the Elysée palace and led by the emperor to an armchair on the left of his own. Cambacères then read a speech stating that the emperor, wishing to make public showing of his supreme respect and confidence in his beloved spouse, the empress and queen, invested her with the right to be present at Cabinet meetings and conferred on her the title of regent.

Marie Louise then rose to her feet and read a shortened, simplified version of the prepared oath of allegiance:

'I swear fidelity to the Emperor. I swear to conform to the Acts of the Constitution and to observe the rules laid down by my husband the Emperor in the exercise of my duties as Regent; to consult, in the employ of my authority, only my love and devotion for France and my son, and to hand over to him at his coming of age the powers confided in me. I swear to maintain the territorial integrity of the Empire, to respect and enforce respect for the laws of the Concordat and freedom of worship, civil liberty and the irrevocability of the sale of national property; never to raise a tax other than for the needs of the State, conforming to the Monarchy's basic laws, to maintain the institution of the Legion of Honour, to govern with the sole object in view the interests, the happiness and the glory of the French People!'

The ceremony was over. To lend it a popular angle, orders had been given that no doors in the palace were to be closed, but no mention is made of any uninvited guest.

On April 4th, Marie Louise received a deputation of thirty senators to whom she delivered her maiden speech. She read it, one of the senators noted, with difficulty, with a pronounced German accent and a tendency to stress the wrong syllables:

'Gentlemen, my august and well loved husband, the Emperor, knows how my heart overflows with my love for France. The daily proof that the nation gives us of its devotion only increases these sentiments and my pride in the grandeur of your nation. My soul is weighed down with grief when I see the hopes of peace, which alone can make me happy, receding. The Emperor is deeply afflicted by the numerous sacrifices he is obliged to call upon his people to make; but since the enemy, instead of trying to bring peace to the world, seeks to impose shameful conditions

upon us and everywhere preaches civil war, treachery and dis-
obedience, the Emperor is obliged to call upon his ever victorious
armies to confound his enemies and save European civilisation
and its monarchs from the anarchy which is threatened.'

These seem, indeed, strange words put into her mouth by an
ex-revolutionary and republican, a repeat of the very same appeal
which had roused her own people twenty-odd years ago to march
on regicide France. There was, however, a strong thread of
realism between the staccato phrases of this brief discourse. The
warning was addressed chiefly to the vacillating German states.
In the last twenty years the majority of the German rulers had
been replaced by puppets of Napoleon's; puppets, whether of the
old or new order, of ancient families or adventurers hurled to
the top by the eruption of Napoleonic power. If the empire fell,
their petty thrones would topple with it. The message was clear,
but Napoleon no longer had either the moral prestige nor the
material power to enforce it. Less than a year ago the emperor
of the French was still the colossus whose word no one dared to
question. Now, with the approach of spring and a new campaign,
the vast majority of these rulers were convinced that the end of
French domination in Europe was very near, and were either
frantically contacting the czar, hoping by a change of allegiance
to hang on to their possessions, or else waiting for the first
opportunity to defect, as was to happen sometimes in the middle
of a battle.

Yet in spite of these worries, Napoleon and Marie Louise were
able to snatch moments of acute happiness, in which the little
king united them the more intimately. The crisis also had a
salutary effect on Napoleon's mind and physique. There had been
moments during the Russian campaign when it had seemed as if
his brain were clogged. He was incapable of taking the vital
decision at the right moment; his refusal to commit the Old
Guard at Borodino lost him the only chance of turning the
Russian retreat into a rout, perhaps of winning the war. His body
had been equally sluggish; his movements, usually so brisk,
painfully slow. But, as the trial of strength approached with the
budding leaves of 1813, 'amazing paradox', the accumulation of
misfortune had an invigorating effect on him. Like certain violent
remedies, it reacted on his nervous and muscular systems
bringing about the miracle of complete rejuvenation.

'Anyone who had not seen him for some years, would have

thought himself confronted with the Napoleon of Austerlitz and Iena. He had lost weight, refound his vigour, his agility, his perpetual urge to be on the move, and from his fined down features shone the piercing look that was his at Arcola. His vivacity, quickness, precise speech, his working capability were unimpeded, one would have imagined oneself in the presence of a happy monarch, confident in the future. It was incredible, but with disaster upon disaster heaped upon his head, Nature had seemingly plunged him in a magic bath from which the over-weight, listless, tired man had emerged with all the fire of a soldier a bare thirty years old . . .'*

On the other hand, Marie Louise, despite her official standing as regent, had not improved as an empress or, rather, as empress of the French. The gap between her and her household had widened. Apart from the duchess of Montebello who was still adored, and the countess de Luçay whom she looked on as a necessity to her well-being, she cordially disliked her cohort of ladies, a dislike heartily reciprocated.

During the first three months of the year, Napoleon insisted that the spectacle of Paris daily life should give the world an impression of complete confidence in the future. Without being maintained at the heady rhythm of early 1812, fêtes and receptions must continue, even though he himself were too busy to put in the briefest of appearances. Unfortunately Marie Louise, whose only wish was to remain cloistered with her husband, was always in a vile temper at these functions, encouraged in her moods by the duchess and further beset by the shyness she had still failed to dominate. It was the same story when the emperor, anxious to improve her popularity with the masses, took her with him to visit an orphanage, or old soldiers at *Les Invalides* – the latter including four centenarians, veterans of Fontenoy – or drove out to the suburbs, stopping his carriage haphazardly to chat with any passer-by. She did what she was told, woodenly. She never had a word to say on her own, agreeable or disagreeable. Her face remained without expression, and for good reason. She was hopelessly bored. Yet she was more in love with Napoleon than ever before, and complained bitterly to Victoria de Crenneville that she was not pregnant again.

*   *   *

* Marcel Dupont: *Napoléon en Campagne.*

133

Praying that, despite the thwarting of his coronation plans, the regency act had made his position more stable than during the Russian campaign, thus eliminating the dangers of another Malet affair, Napoleon left Paris on April 15th to assume command of his reduced army. Marie Louise once again was inconsolable, though her grief was untinged by fear.

This time, however, she could not shut herself off from the nation's affairs. She was regent: nominal ruler of France.

Nominal was indeed the word. Napoleon was at heart an arch-anti-suffragette. He did not trust any woman's judgment or capabilities beyond the frontiers of bed, nursery and kitchen. The regency proclamation had been aimed chiefly at impressing Austria, not to relieve him of responsibilities incumbent during his absence. A genius, he was isolated by his lack of confidence in his fellows.

Even though surrounded by three such (comparatively) trustworthy and competent advisers as Cambacères, de Champagny and de Menéval – the latter prevented from following the emperor as a result of extreme debility resulting from his nightmare experiences in Russia – Marie Louise had no real power. Her every move was controlled by a volume of conditions and dictats laid down by the emperor himself. She was not allowed to sign an army promotion above the rank of captain; she had the right to preside at the senate but not to propose a subject for discussion or initiate a law. On the death of a senator, she had not the power to name his successor. Even her right to preside was limited. She was not allowed to be present if *quelque affaire délicate* was on the minutes, this because strict orders to the effect that 'Ministers are forbidden to discuss any matter with the Empress that might worry her' had been given. As regards police matters, Savary, duke of Rovigo, also had his express orders: 'She' (the empress) 'is too young to be troubled by police details.'

However, to bring the empress's name more frequently to public notice, Napoleon had decided to suppress the normal *Bulletins de la Grande Armée*, replacing them by *Nouvelles de l'Armée* signed by the empress. But these *nouvelles* were composed by Napoleon and only allowed to be published after detailed instructions from him: 'I send you the *Nouvelles de l'Armée* for the 25th and 27th. You will summon the Arch-Chancellor and give the order for that of the 25th to be published first of all in *Le Moniteur*. You will retain that of the 27th and you will order it to be published the day after the publication of that of the 25th. You will also have the enclosed note inserted in *Le Moniteur*.'

According to Masson: 'He' (the emperor) 'dictated every act of the Regent's, from a *Te Deum* to be celebrated, an ordinary letter to be written or the granting of a favour. From a distance he followed her slightest movement and would permit of no departure from his rulings. Thus, one morning the empress received the arch-chancellor while she was still in bed. Immediately the following letter was despatched. "It is my wish that in no circumstances whatsoever, or under any pretext, will you receive anyone, whoever he may be, while you are in bed, such an act could only be permitted for someone over thirty years of age . . ." '

One can gather, therefore, that Napoleon was indulging in fantasy when, in his efforts to ensure Austria's neutrality, he wrote to the emperor Francis: 'These days the Empress is my Prime Minister.'

Marie Louise, for her part, was quite content with her false title of regent, happy to do exactly what Cambacérès, acting as Napoleon's mouthpiece, ordered; happy above all not to be called upon to make an independent decision, longing only for the war to end and her husband's return, and praying that this separation would truly be the last.

'Nothing that she did was of her own initiative. She stayed just what the Emperor wished her to be, and as Nature had formed her, passively obedient. If therefore she made a mistake, it was because she was following the directions of Cambacérès, or those – far more dangerous – of the Duchess of Montebello, for it was the Emperor who had imposed on her these counsellors, mentors, guardians. If fault there was, it was he and he alone, who was to blame . . .'*

In the meantime, Napoleon's personal letters maintained their usual staccato mixture of facts, but show more comprehension for her real and pseudo ailments, stressing at the same time the need to remain cheerful and not to worry.

On April 18th he wrote:

My good friend, I have received your letter of the 16th. I am grieved to hear about your health not being all it might be, and that you are making it worse by being upset. Good-bye, my

* Imbére de Saint Amand: *Marie Louise et le Campagne de* 1814. Hutchinson, 1891.

135

dear Louise, love me as I love you, as far as this is possible on the part of *someone of your sex*. All yours. Your husband.

And a few days later:

My sweet Louise. I've just received your letter. I wish I were with you. Seeing you near me and passing my life beside you is very dear to me. I'm upset by what you say about the little King; I hope he is now eating normally again. Please let me know that he is quite well. There was a little business in the streets of Veimar (*sic*), we beat a regiment of Prussian hussars and took fifty men including one of Bluker's (*sic*) aides-de-camp. It's scarcely worth mentioning.

Adio, mio ben. Nap.

On April 30th came disturbing news. The Austrian contingent that had been with Napoleon in Russia, which was not taking part in the campaign but which Napoleon liked to think was, on paper, still part of his army, was officially withdrawn on Metternich's advice. Napoleon was alive to the obvious menace for the future. He wrote hurriedly to Marie Louise:

. . . Papa Francis isn't behaving very well. He has withdrawn his contingent. They are trying to drag him into the war against me. Call M. Fleuret* and say to him, 'They are trying to drag my father into a war against us. I have sent for you to request you to write to him that the Emperor is fully capable of dealing with the situation, he has a million men under arms and I warn you that if my father listens to the Empress's (Maria Ludovica) cackling, he's laying up a store of trouble for himself. He doesn't know the nation, its energy, its devotion to its Emperor. Tell my father from me, his beloved daughter, who has the interests of the land of her birth so much at heart, that if he does allow himself to be pushed into this, the French will be in Vienna before 7*bre* (*sic*), and he will have lost the friendship of a man who is genuinely attached to him.' Write to him yourself also in the same vein, for his own sake rather than mine, because I have seen this coming for some time and I'm ready. *Adio, mio dolce amore*. Your Nap.

* Austrian Chargé d'Affaires in Paris.

Dutifully, Maria Louise did as she was told, but the letter was a great and totally unexpected shock for her. She realised for the first time that rumours of Austrian hostility, to which she had barely bothered to listen, had, after all, some foundation. In spite of it, she still could not conceive that such a rank betrayal on her father's part were possible. Her heart had not changed; she was still naive, credulous, taking words, spoken and written, at their face value. Instinctively, if uncomprehendingly, however, she sensed the shadowy menace for, from that moment on, an ill-disguised anguish is noticeable in her letters to her father. More than a hollow echo of her husband's words, they are an expression of mounting distress: '. . . You can be quite sure that the Emperor desires peace. I cannot tell you how many times he has said that once this war is over, he will never go to war again but devote himself entirely to domestic affairs and to his family, but he cannot sign a peace which would dishonour him in the eyes of France. If he were forced to give up territory now incorporated with France, he would have the whole nation against him. He is so brilliant, so determined, that nothing can stand up to him, and he will return with a lasting peace. At the moment rumours are circulating, which I pray may be unfounded, and untrue. It is said, my very dear papa, that you have withdrawn your corps of troops and that you wish to make war on us. Such an eventuality would be quite unbearable for me and you can be sure, my very dear papa, that you would gain nothing by such an action. I can tell you, between ourselves, that the Emperor will soon have a million men under arms and as I know this nation and its devotion to its Emperor so well, I can assure you he could double this number if needs be. The Emperor has often said to me, "The Prince of whom I am fondest is your father, and if he allows himself to be dominated by the Empress, he will regret the loss of my friendship." You cannot imagine how strong the rumour is here, it's mentioned in a report I've just been reading and that is why I had to write to you. Believe me when I say it would be more than I could bear . . .'

Incredibly, to begin with, it looked as if Napoleon's threat, his power to crush all opposition, was no frightened boast. These letters were followed by news of the astounding victories of Lutzen and Bautzen, the French emperor's triumphal entry into Dresden, and that, panicstricken, Prussians and Russians had asked for an armistice.

137

Anxious to prove his genuine desire for peace, Napoleon made a mistake which constituted a major step towards his downfall. Instead of following up his advantage and destroying the two demoralised armies, he agreed to the proposed suspension of hostilities, and to withdraw his forces twelve leagues from the line of the Oder river. Probably he regretted and realised the enormity of his error within a few hours of the temporary 'cease-fire', for he was heard to mutter, 'If the allies are not genuine in their desire for peace, this armistice may well prove fatal.'

On the other hand, he had no real choice in the matter.

It was true that these three major victories in the space of six weeks could be termed miraculous, for the newly reconstituted *Grande Armée* was an imposing force in numbers only.

In January 1813, two levies of 350,000 and 180,000 men had been raised, bringing the total number with the colours to the same as that which had crossed the Niemen the previous year. But it would have been almost permissible to describe this new army as a horde, rather than an organised fighting force. Most of the half-million conscripted men were youths of nineteen or twenty years of age, baptised *Les Marie Louises* – immortalised by Raffet – by the few remaining veterans.

By the time they found themselves marching eastwards to the Rhine, few of them had had time to master the most rudimentary elements of foot drill or weapon training. It was hoped that en route they might, during halts, be able to snatch a few hours to learn what movements they were expected to make in response to certain basic commands, and at least how to discharge their muskets in the right direction. Unfortunately, they were boys who had passed their early childhood during the lean days of the 'Terror'. At the end of a day's march they were too exhausted to do anything but swallow a quick meal and drop down to sleep. When they experienced their baptism of fire, the majority were still incapable of loading their muskets.

Even more serious was the state of the cavalry. Fifty thousand horses had been lost in Russia and, despite all efforts, only a bare thirteen thousand remounts had been collected. The majority of these animals were what one could have termed 'sorry nags' rather than potential chargers. Worse still, most of the recruits drafted into the cavalry were from the towns, and had no idea of riding. Like the infantry, they were directed to the front untrained: there was no time to put them through even the briefest courses of equitation or sabre drill.

At this period of military history, the cavalry was the arm which could turn defeat into disaster, an ordered retreat into a wild flight, a *sauve qui peut*. Lack of a competent corps of cavalry weighed heavily against Napoleon. Both at Lutzen and at Bautzen, enemy forces could have been totally destroyed. As it was, unharassed by the French cavalry, Russians and Prussians, in spite of their enormous casualties, were able to keep their forces intact and withdraw to fight another day.

It is easy, with all details and records at one's fingertips, to be wise more than a hundred and sixty years after the event. One can see, today, that Napoleon's most logical move would have been to recognise the situation in Spain as hopeless, to have cut his losses, allowed Ferdinand to return to his throne in Madrid, and recalled his quarter of a million veterans to Germany. Wellington's army in the Peninsula would have ceased to have had a legitimate *raison d'être* and, reinforced by the trained and battle-tried Spanish divisions, Russians and Prussians could have been destroyed, Austria, for reasons of self-preservation, kept neutral.

Such a possibility did occur to the French emperor. But he was victim of his own power, conquests and prestige. He was terrified that compromise might be interpreted as weakness, perhaps fear. He looked ahead, but not far enough.

'I was ready to make concessions,' he confessed later at St Helena, 'but I felt the moment was too critical. A false step, an unconsidered word, could have destroyed what was left of my prestige . . .'

There was another factor forcing him to agree to this more than unwise armistice. As has been pointed out, the morale of his marshals and senior generals before setting out for Moscow had left much to be desired; now it was deplorable. Even Ney 'the bravest of the brave' was lethargic, unwilling to take risks, permanently complaining. Nor did it improve matters that between April 20th and May 28th four of Napoleon's oldest companions in arms, Marshals Bessières, Duroc, Bruyères and General Kirgener, were killed in action. Shortly before his fatal wounds, Duroc, one of Napoleon's most devoted adherents, was heard to exclaim: 'This has been going on too long. Not one of us will survive.'

Napoleon was deeply affected by the deaths of these old friends, especially by that of Duroc for whom he wept, as he had done for Lannes, and feeling that too much blood had been spilt, he welcomed the armistice demand, though recognising its potential danger.

It was to cost him his empire, his wife and his son.

News of victories alleviated Marie Louise's fears. *Te Deums* were sung to celebrate Lutzen and Bautzen, and it was with a sense of profound relief that she heard her husband and Metternich were to meet to discuss terms for 'final' peace at Dresden. She was even happier when, some days later, a letter from Napoleon arrived, telling her to leave Paris immediately and join him at Mainz:

> My friend. I want to see you. You will leave on the 22nd and sleep at Chalons, at Metz the 23rd, arriving at Mainz the 24th where I will join you. You will travel with 4 carriages of the 1st service, 4 of the second, 4 of the 3rd; you will bring with you the Duchess, 2 chamberlains, 2 pages, a doctor, 2 *femmes rouge* (*sic*), 2 *femmes noires*, and your dinner service. Start getting ready. Count Gafarelli* (*sic*) will command the escort. Please pass these instructions to the Arch-Chancellor. Goodbye my friend. You will have time to hear further from me before you leave. All yours. Nap.

Marie Louise had no way of knowing that this sudden whim of her husband's was prompted by a premonition that their days of happiness were counted, and because, possibly for the last time, he wished to relive those moments of *bourgeois* husband-and-wife existence he had snatched during the first eighteen months of their marriage. She had no idea that the final break between France and Austria had been rendered inevitable as a result of Napoleon's stormy interview with Metternich at Dresden's Marcolini Palace on June 26th. How could she? Only the briefest reference to it had been made in Napoleon's letter of the 27th:

> My good friend. I had a long and very tiring talk with Metternich. However, I'm in good health. What you say

* General Count Caffarelli.

140

about the little King being jealous makes me laugh. How I long to see him. Give him 3 kisses from me. Have you seen the elephant in the *Jardin des Plantes*? I hope we'll be able to negotiate a peace in a few days. I long for it, but it must be an honourable one. *Adio mio bene.* All yours. Nap.

It was extraordinary that after a meeting which had effectively destroyed all his remaining illusions and, realist that he was, driven home to him that the end of the empire – *his* empire – was inevitable, he could remain so outwardly calm, and write in so casual a vein.

Before meeting Metternich, Napoleon had no inkling of the 'take it or leave it' terms with which he was likely to be confronted. Soon after Lutzen he had had an interview with an Austrian envoy, Count Bubna. The count had made it clear that Austria would expect 'considerable territorial sacrifices' as the price of neutrality, to which the angry Napoleon had reiterated his 'no dishonourable peace' maxim. By the time Bubna departed, Napoleon was aware of the fact that Austria was re-arming rapidly, nor had he any illusions as to this new army's ultimate objectives.

In Vienna, Metternich was well satisfied by the trend of events. Each day was proving the justification of his policy. While Russians and Prussians were profoundly discouraged by the April–May campaign, Metternich was delighted. Allied defeats served to restore Austria to her former domination. On the continent, she was now arbiter instead of poor relation. Though no military genius, the Austrian chancellor knew that the French army was incapable of winning a decisive victory. Napoleon might still hold a few tactical trump cards; strategically, he was finished. But by early June Austria's re-armament was not quite completed. For this reason, Russians and Prussians were advised to sign an armistice to play for time till, by the end of August at latest, an Austrian army of close on quarter of a million men would be ready to take the field.

Certain that the sheer weight of numbers must eventually crush the French, Metternich looked beyond the mere military aspect of the struggle. Napoleon must be made to fill the role of warmonger in history's verdict, the man who had refused the peace terms offered him.

This would not only salve the conscience of the emperor Francis, tormented by the thought of the hurt he was about to inflict on his daughter and of promises made to his son-in-law callously to be broken, but of those at the Austrian court, among them the archduke Charles, who were as scandalised at the thought of their country dishonouring a treaty as they had been by the French marriage. In addition, Metternich counted on discrediting Napoleon in the eyes of his fellow-countrymen. Well aware of the nation's longing for peace and the faltering morale of the military leaders, at the same time counting on Napoleon's rejection of the so-called peace terms he would be offering, he gave a promise before leaving Vienna that in case of rejection Austria would formally declare war on France.

The Chancellor's hand was still further strengthened when, on arrival at the Marcolini Palace, a woebegone, rather contemptible Berthier met him, insisting, 'Do not forget that Europe requires peace and especially France will have nothing but peace . . .' Berthier did not have the honesty to add that no one desired peace more fervently than the French emperor.

From the beginning of their interview, Metternich behaved as if the war were already won. It was not a true discussion between the two men. The Austrian, realising his power, was delivering an ultimatum, making no attempt to disguise his personal hatred of the man he felt to be at his mercy.

The 'terms' he proposed made Napoleon gasp. France must give up not only Illyria but abandon all interests in Poland, Spain, the Confederation of the Rhine, Switzerland and the Netherlands. Exasperated, he rounded on Metternich, accusing him of treachery, even of blackmail.

'What?' he said at last, 'You wish to tell me that my father-in-law agrees to this outrage? It is *he* who has sent you here? What sort of a position does he wish to place me in vis-à-vis my own people? He's making a strange mistake if he thinks a mutilated throne a fit setting for his daughter and his grandson.' Then, suddenly as though overcome with weariness, he added sullenly, 'I see it now. I made a terrible mistake marrying an Austrian archduchess.'

Sneering, Metternich replied, remembering that he had been one of the principal instigators of the marriage: 'Since Your Majesty wishes to hear my opinion, I would say quite frankly that Napoleon, the *Conqueror*, did make a mistake.'

'So,' said Napoleon, 'the Emperor wishes to dethrone his daughter!'

The answer came quickly.

'Whatever fate may be in store for his daughter, the emperor, my master, is above all a sovereign, and the good of his people takes precedence in all his actions.'

The futile argument dragged on for eight hours, Napoleon trying desperately to make an implacable Metternich listen to reason. Finally, as they were about to separate, Napoleon tried to smile. He said:

'Let me tell you something. You won't make war on me.'

Metternich's reply was brutal.

'You are lost, sire.'

Napoleon knew it was true. It was the principal reason for his call to Marie Louise to join him.

It was Francis, in the end, and not Napoleon who informed Marie Louise that war between France and Austria appeared inevitable. She was appalled, but so sure of Napoleon's power to conquer that her first reactions were pity and fear for Austria: 'I received your letter three days ago. It grieved me so much realising that the last hope of peace had vanished. You must be as horrified as I am. I pity you with all my heart my dear papa. I am persuaded that this war will bring disaster in its wake. Count on me, my dear papa, remembering that if later I can help you, I will do so willingly . . .'

Having written this letter in a spirit of genuine compassion for her parents, Marie Louise started off for Mainz on July 23rd, happily and studiously beginning a new diary, even more detailed than that which she had kept on her trips to the Netherlands. 'It was on July 23rd that I set out on my journey to Mainz. Never had I undertaken one so happily, being enchanted at the thought of seeing the Emperor again after three long months of separation, but I'm afraid Madame de Montesquiou thought me very stony-hearted when I said goodbye to my son without a tear (which doesn't often happen). I left at six in the morning determined to travel day and night if necessary so as to reach Mainz by the 25th. The road is very pretty as it winds round Paris; on leaving the barrier one sees Rancy on the right, the park is magnificent but the château very small. The Emperor wanted to give it to me but I had the good sense to refuse it as I did not feel like bothering with an estate, and I was more than pleased when later I found out that it only produces 30,000 francs, whereas 60,000 francs have to be spent annually on its upkeep . . . We lunched with the post-master (at La Ferté-sous-Jouarre) who has a rather nice house. The road is even prettier as one approaches Château Thierry; the valley narrows with woods and charming villages on either side. Château Thierry is a badly constructed little town; the road divides, one fork leading to Chalons, the other to Etages, the property of the Duchess's (Montebello) father. She talked a lot about an estate called St Martin du Bois near Etages which she hopes to buy when she retires and her services are no longer needed.

'When she talks like this I find it very difficult not to get angry. Nevertheless it is true that in the delightful present day society the morrow is always uncertain. The sovereign who is amiable today, treating you as a friend, may well exile and then forget all about you tomorrow; for this reason I'm always praying to God that I may never have a sovereign's heart. As far as I'm concerned I feel that if one of my friends were to be disgraced today, he would only be all the more dear to me . . .'

After this bit of moralising, there are further details of the countryside and a great deal of grumbling about accommodation and food at Châlons-sur-Marne, and the inevitable complaint about health; a violent attack of indigestion, this time through eating too much sour cream. Next day they reached Verdun. 'After passing Dombasle we reached the descent to Verdun, which is very steep, from which one can see Verdun and all the surrounding country, which looks very ugly. Whilst we were passing over the heights, I noticed a number of English who are recognisable from their appearance and impertinent manner . . . There are more than 900 English prisoners, all officers. Little girls presented me with a basket of *bonbons* while we were changing horses. Verdun is renowned for its sweetmeats . . . The road is very ugly till within a league of Metz.

'I admired this splendid road the Emperor had made over the hill; one really cannot take a step without coming across some improvement or important work which has been carried out on the Emperor's instructions.'

The night was spent in Metz, a city which she stated had 'a melancholy air about it'. There was a tiff with the grand equerry,

Prince Aldobrandini, about the time of the next day's start. 'Prince Aldobrandini made me angry by saying that we could not leave before six in the morning. Knowing we had 56 leagues to travel I was in despair at the thought that the Emperor would arrive before me. I suggested four o'clock, but he was obstinate and though I, too, can be stubborn as a Breton, I had to give in...'

Her fears were not unfounded. The journey lasted all day and most of the night. 'We dined at nine in the evening at Kirchen Boland in a magnificent mansion belonging to a Frankfurt merchant who is said to have an income of £100,000 a year. The park is as lovely and the house as luxuriously furnished as any in Paris. It was pouring with rain and we still had 15 leagues ahead of us. I tried to relax as best I could in the carriage, but we progressed so slowly that by four in the morning we were still a league from Mainz. I could then see the Rheingan and Hunsruchen mountains, and at five we entered Mainz by a gate through the ramparts. Everybody had got so tired of waiting for us that they had gone to bed and I was delighted when General Foulin brought me a letter from the Emperor saying he would not be arriving before the 27th. I went straight to bed but could not sleep ... I spent the whole of the next day watching the Bridge of Boats and the Frankfurt road, knowing that was the way the Emperor would be coming, and thinking he might arrive a day early. However, my watch was in vain and I went to bed half dead from lack of sleep. In fact everyone was so tired when the Emperor did arrive he traversed the salons where my pages and women were sleeping without anyone hearing him. I will not attempt to describe my joy at seeing him again. It was something that cannot be written, only felt. He looked well and was in good spirits ...'

For both husband and wife this brief interlude at Mainz marked the end of their mutual happiness, as indeed Napoleon's forebodings had warned him it might well do. As far as possible he tried to be alone with his still very youthful empress, cutting down official ceremonies to a minimum. They waited on each other at breakfast. He sat beside her when she reclined in her bath; and when, glowing like a lobster, he stepped from his steaming tub, it was Marie Louise who insisted on replacing Constant and massaging him with his beloved eau-de-Cologne.

Marie Louise, however, still kept up her diary, caustic and revealing. 'On the 28th the heat was still unbearable. In the morning I was visited by the old Prince of Nassau, with his wife and two daughters. The mother is very witty but the daughters hideous. The elder, who is as fat as Prince Schwarzenberg, had been married only three days to a Baden prince, when she was divorced by him because she'd become infatuated with one of her father's grooms . . . The Emperor and I embarked on the Rhine, then had a beautiful walk in the sunset . . . I also saw the Prince of Nassau and the Prince of Isenberg. The Emperor, I'm glad to say, put an end to these visits and we spent the morning together as usual. I read extracts from *Gil Blas* to him; he asked for the bit about Doctor Sangrado which made him laugh a lot; I laugh too, but only in secret, having a profound respect for doctors . . . On the 30th the Grand Duke of Baden came to see us. How tedious these visits are. I'm afraid (I) must show my feelings by my expression for, on meeting my friends, I've so much to say I'm choked, whereas with other people I find the greatest difficulty in the world in forming a single sentence.'

They had a bare four days together for the Emperor, awaiting Austria's declaration of war almost hourly, left Mainz on August 1st. 'On the 1st, after Mass, the Emperor decided to depart immediately. The carriages weren't ready before four. I was obliged to be present at the dinner to which he had invited his entire Household, but have now learned to control myself and put on a show of gaiety.

'I tried to be calm till the Emperor entered his carriage, as he felt so much grief at this parting, I did not wish to add to his distress. My courage upon this occasion satisfied me . . . the evening passed very sadly, and I pray I shall not have many like it. I gave orders for my departure the next day. It was so lonely in Mainz . . .'

The very next day, though, Marie Louise's passion for the duchess of Montebello was reawakened by the need to fill the gap left by the absent husband, in a desire for an object for her affections. The French ladies apparently made fun of the unfortunate princesses of Nassau and Marie Louise wrote indignantly: 'Their' (the ladies') 'behaviour made me very angry, only the Duchess' (Montebello) 'refrained, but she is a perfect woman the like of whom has never before been seen . . .'

The empress and her cortège moved down the Rhine as far as Cologne, and then returned to Paris via Aix-la-Chapelle (Aachen) and Rheims. For most of the journey she was bored, tired and depressed, continually catching cold – or so she imagined – accusing her accompanying doctor, the chevalier Bourdier, of being an idiot. Barely had she settled down at Saint Cloud, when she had to be off on another tour, this time to Cherbourg.

Chapter VIII

On August 12th Marie Louise wrote to her father: 'I am still terribly worried about the result of the negotiations going on; God grant that there won't be a war; I can't bear the thought of it, and if there is one I pray you won't be mixed up in it because I'm appalled by the thought of the disastrous consequences it will have for you . . .'

Napoleon was so determined that she should not be unduly distressed that he continued to treat her as a pampered, sheltered child. She did not know when she wrote this letter that war had already been declared on the 10th, and that a powerful Austrian army, commanded by Prince Schwarzenberg – the archduke Charles had refused command in a campaign he qualified bluntly as 'dishonourable' – had taken the field with Russians, Prussians and Swedes.

Cambacères – while Marie Louise was still hoping the worst could be avoided – received, on the 12th, a communication from Napoleon in which he trusted that 'Austria will soon be made to regret most bitterly her mad claims and infamous treachery', and ending, 'I wish the Empress to carry out the visit to Cherbourg, and that she be not informed of what has happened until her return . . .'

Before the official tour could be organised, however, Marie Louise learnt the truth from her father who, still torn between his sense of duty and paternal affection, tried to minimise the gravity of the situation: 'Above all don't worry' (he wrote, whether genuinely or hypocritically, it is hard to say) 'this particular war is quite different to the former ones we have waged. I am not, and never will be, your husband's enemy, and I count on the fact he will not be mine . . .'

Further 'consolation' came from Napoleon on hearing that his plans had been thwarted: 'Don't be too upset by your father's behaviour. He has been tricked by Metternich. I want you to be brave . . .'

When one thinks of the grim atmosphere of modern warfare,

the bitter passions aroused between warring peoples, the vindictive fury of the victors, it is with a sense of unreality that one reads of the amical correspondence passing almost daily between two of the principal adversaries. Some communications border on the affectionate. Napoleon was anxious to assure Francis that no obstacles would be put in the way of his correspondence with his daughter and, in reply, Francis included a letter for Marie Louise with the remark: 'which' (the letter) 'I know I could not entrust to safer hands than those of Your Imperial Majesty . . .'

The object of the Cherbourg visit was to bestow an imperial blessing on the occasion of the opening of the Cherbourg docks. 'First of all' (Napoleon decreed) 'so that she' (the Empress) 'can enjoy the impressive spectacle of the sea pouring into the dock area, and also to add the right touch of official solemnity . . .'

The inauguration of this new harbour, capable of sheltering a considerable fleet, meant much to Napoleon, still dreaming of a descent on the British coast. There was also another reason for his wish that the empress should make her presence as regent felt in the provinces. As France's frontiers became directly threatened, Napoleon feared unrest at home. He was haunted by the thought of another, but better-organised, Malet affair. He knew that republicans and royalists alike were stirring, especially the latter. Once again, therefore, with false and unfounded optimism, he wished to play the card of the prestige he still deluded himself into thinking had resulted from his marriage with the daughter of the last of the Holy Roman emperors.

Most of the country through which Marie Louise would be travelling was notoriously pro-Bourbon. There had been several incidents the previous year. At Caen, eight people – four men and four women – had been executed for subversive activities. After Bautzen, rumours had been spread that the emperor was severely wounded in the hope of inciting an uprising. Deserters, anti-Bonapartists of all tendencies, roamed the forests in bands, many of them armed. Civil war was in the air. Yet Napoleon was apparently confident that Marie Louise had only to show herself, stammer a few hesitant words, and all would be well.

Savary, chief of police, was more realistic in his appreciation. In his opinion the proposed tour entailed distinct risks. He was dogged by the fear that an attempt might be made to kidnap the empress and, in any case, he had no confidence in the empress's theoretical charm. General Caffarelli was again in command of the large escort deemed necessary for Marie Louise's safety, and to him Savary addressed a few serio-comic admonitions: 'Try to see that the Empress is punctual when a set hour for some function has been notified; a well known courtier once said, "Punctuality is the privilege of Kings"; and he was right. So for God's sake my dear friend, don't let's have any of this eternal hanging about, which only infuriates and sets evil tongues wagging . . . This journey will create either enthusiasm or indifference, and in the case of the latter would do a great deal of harm . . . Frankly were I in your place, I would pluck up the courage to tell her that the country wishes to love, and be loved by, her; but for God's sake, my friend, see that there's none of this *iciness*! You follow me?'

It is not known whether Caffarelli did act on his friend's advice. It is unlikely. And even if he had 'plucked up the courage', it is doubtful whether he could have escaped the duchess of Montebello's vigilance. One can only say that if he did manage to whisper a few phrases of judicious advice in the imperial ear, they were ignored. Upset by her father's betrayal, tired by the journey, convinced that she was in a parlous state of health, she was even less forthcoming than on previous occasions. As if searching to reach the supreme heights of gaucherie, she was not even present at the great moment when the barriers were broken and the sea poured in to fill the docks.

Her own words leave no doubt as to her mood: 'I left Saint Cloud for Cherbourg at eight in the morning of August 23rd, feeling very depressed and therefore completely uninterested in the undertaking for I detest travelling more than ever. Moreover I am certain my expression must depress everyone, for I feel so sad and have no desire to hide my feelings; separation from my son, who during the Emperor's absence is my one consolation, also upsets me very much. Altogether I was in such a vile mood that I didn't say a word during the first part of the journey and was quite oblivious to the beauties of the landscape.'

The evening was spent at Evreux and here, too, fuel was added to the furnace of the empress's bad temper: 'We arrived at Evreux at five o'clock. The postilions drove much too fast into the town and nearly crushed a brigadier-general between our carriage and the houses which really frightened me. On any journey there are far too many of these alarming incidents, and doctors who always scold when one returns ill, should forbid generals to get caught in wheels and postilions to fall off their horses. After dinner I received the town authorities who bored me with ridiculous speeches . . .'

Next day, en route for Caen, she forgot to grumble: 'On passing through Lisieux, I was welcomed in a truly touching manner. Generally, throughout Normandy everybody is so devoted to their Emperor, and the enthusiasm of these good people impressed me very much . . .'

This entry is a tribute to the deceptive state of euphoria still surrounding the empress. In fact, Lisieux was a centre of anti-Bonapartism, and Savary heaved a sign of relief when he learned that the cortège had arrived safely in Caen. Caen, however, witnessed the return of Marie Louise's black mood. She mentions that the city was 'rather picturesque', but: 'After dinner there was the usual task of receiving the local authorities. Rank is truly a mixed blessing for one is obliged to hold such receptions however tired one may be, and to laugh even when one feels more like weeping; and one is never pitied . . .'

There were much the same complaints at Bayeux: 'After Mass the Bishop kept me waiting a good quarter of an hour while he was disrobing; usually I laugh at this sort of thing, but this time I was furious. I was ill and knew I was catching cold. I am sure as they saw me go by, the inhabitants of Bayeux must have remarked "What an ugly, bad-tempered Empress!" '

On reaching Cherbourg: 'I was pleased to find myself once more in the house I had occupied two years ago, bringing back memories of that previous journey when I was so happy and light-hearted, but what a difference now!'

There are complaints however about her apartments: 'My room is the Emperor's former bedroom, looking on to a miserable little courtyard where nothing can be seen and which seems to pick up all the bad smells from the kitchen . . .'

As regards missing the ceremony, Marie Louise tries to excuse herself, utilising the diary to express her apologia: 'At last at six o'clock, the Minister (Navy) came and took us down a slope at the side of the dam where it was so cold that two shawls and a fur-lined coat weren't able to keep me warm.

'The water was already seeping in through two apertures making a sort of cascade, but the dam itself showed no sign of breaking. Monsieur Cachin was in a foul temper, because his *coup de théatre* had not come off.

'At half past seven, the water level had not risen and I was in such a bad temper at having to wait for so long for nothing, that I went back to my apartments. At nine o'clock, the Minister arrived in a dreadful state to tell us that the dam had given way and that we hadn't been there to see it. "It's still a magnificent sight; will you come back for a moment to look at it?" So we hurried back at quarter past nine. The dock was full and the water as calm as if it had been there for centuries!

'I shall never forgive myself for having missed the spectacle, the more so as it was my reason for my journey to Cherbourg.

'The night was fine and warm which was surprising as the day had been so cold. We entered the carriages again to watch the 10,000 rockets which were to be fired from the Roule Fort, but as misfortunes never come singly, Prince Aldobrandini lost the way and we meandered through the town with the result that we were half an hour too late. But perhaps that was no great misfortune.

'Malicious tongues say that the 10,000 rockets were in fact only five or six, and even these did not go off . . .'

The rest of the short stay in Cherbourg was given over to more receptions and official entertainment, the latter failing to amuse the disgruntled empress: 'In the evening there was a theatrical performance in an ugly, badly lighted hall which held only 400 people. The play was *Le Petit Matelot* into which verses referring to me had been introduced which drew everyone's attention to the fact that I was present. This infuriated me and made me feel so embarrassed that I didn't know where to put myself.

'I can't stand this brazen flattery, especially when it fails to ring true, and particularly when they say how beautiful I am. I only appreciate one form of flattery, that is when the Emperor says "I am pleased with you" which makes me want to do even better, but this evening I was so angry that I coughed for over an hour, and would have liked to have given everyone a sound beating . . . I am always amused at some fêtes because some people dance so badly. I noticed one lady who raised her foot so high off the floor we could see her leg right up to the knee, and a gentleman who danced like a lobster opening its claws . . .'

The last day in Cherbourg, the 31st (August), there was good news from Germany: 'I was most agreeably surprised to hear of the great battle of Dresden which cheered our last evening in Cherbourg enormously. Everyone was enchanted, but my joy was not entirely unmixed, for although we had won a battle, that would not bring the Emperor back to me; this thought poisoned all my happiness . . .'

Sorrow, however, did not prevent her from indulging in an outburst at Rouen on the return journey because she had not had a letter for some (unspecified) time. She seemed to forget that her husband was engaged in what was, literally, a life and death struggle. 'Today I was in a very bad temper not having news of the Emperor. He is erratic. I'm sure he is not thinking of me. Ah, it is only we women who are constant in love. Men are so frivolous that one should not take them too seriously; unfortunately I do and will punish him by not writing for at least a week, that will teach him . . .'

She was indeed in such a bad temper that, describing Cambacères' brother: 'The Arch-Chancellor's brother is here. He is a bishop and a freak; somebody suggested to me that he should be put in a glass cage, preserved as a curiosity labelled "The sea monster" . . .'

And there is the last entry of the existing diaries: 'We dined in a dirty inn at Meudon and arrived at Saint Cloud at one in the morning, where, straightway I promised myself that this journey should be the last.'

If Marie Louise had hoped to pick up the thread of an indolent existence after her imagined hardships, she was to be disappointed. Napoleon's confidence in his lieutenants was fast vanishing; that in his family already evaporated. As he saw it, his only hope of that continuity so dear to him reposed in the regent's hands till his son's coming of age.

The victory of Dresden – 'I really thrashed Swarzen (*sic*) and the Emperor Alexander. Papa Francis's soldiers have never been worse . . .' – had in no way affected the inevitable fatal issue.

The allies had indeed lost a major battle, more than 10,000 dead and wounded, close on 20,000 prisoners. For them it was a drop in the ocean. A slender chance of total victory was again lost by lethargy, the semi-cowardice, the almost deliberate inefficiency of the tired, disgruntled marshals. Vandamme, dilatory, failed to trap the fleeing enemy in the Bohemian mountain passes. Had he acted with his usual vigour, most of the Austrian army would have been annihilated and Austria obliged to sue for peace. And barely had the despatches announcing the Dresden victory left for Paris than there came the news that

Oudinot had been routed by Bernadotte at Gross-Beeren, and Macdonald crushed by Blücher at Katzbach, losing 3,000 killed, 20,000 prisoners, 100 cannon and 2 standards.

'Unless I am present in person, everyone makes the most idiotic mistakes,' Napoleon cried despairingly.

He was not the only person to realise this. Bernadotte knew it. It was on his advice that, after Dresden, the allies refused battle when the forces opposing them were commanded by the Emperor, and fell on those led by his marshals who were now easy prey. To make matters worse, Vandamme, overcome by remorse at the thought of his failings, launched a hopeless attack on the heights of Kulm, allowed himself to be surrounded, and was forced to surrender *en masse*. Soon news, even more alarming than that of his marshals' bungling, began to reach Napoleon. German contingents still included in the French army were going over to the enemy.

Once more, Napoleon's thoughts turned to France, the regent, the 'little king'. For the first time he asked himself the stark question; would it not be better, for his dynasty's future, if he were to die on the battlefield? It was an eventuality to be considered seriously. So many of his oldest, closest friends had been killed at his side. From the very beginning of his career, he had never hesitated to expose himself to enemy fire. In future he would be even more reckless; he would invite death. In the meantime, however, the regent must be seen by the people, not merely as an imperial ornament but in her role as sovereign in her husband's absence.

Marie Louise was, for her, unusually calm, making no reference in her private diaries or letters to the fact that on October 7th she was to address the senate.

She acquitted herself with honour. The speech which Napoleon had written was short and to the point. One observer remarked that her German accent and clear, but heavy, pronunciation lent power and solemnity to the discourse.

'Senators, last year the principal powers of Europe, disgusted by England's machinations, allied their armies to ours to obtain world peace and the re-establishment of all peoples' rights. But, due to war's hazards, hidden passions have come to the fore. England and Russia have enmeshed Prussia and Austria in their net. Our enemies wish to destroy our allies and so punish them for their fidelity. They wish to bring war to the heart of our lovely homeland, to avenge themselves for those triumphs which carried our eagles victorious into their estates. Better than anyone I should know what would be the fate of our people should they allow themselves to be vanquished. Before mounting the throne to which I was called by my august husband, I had the highest opinion of the courage and energy of this great race. This opinion has only increased after what I have witnessed with my own eyes. Associated for the last four years with my husband's most intimate thoughts, I know what he would think of a withered throne, a crown shorn of all glory. Men of France, your country, honour, your Emperor, call to you.'

Clarke, minister of war, then rose to give substance to this brief allocution. He appealed for 160,000 men of the 1815 class and 120,000 from that of 1814 and immediately preceding years, warning at the same time that even greater calls on the country's manpower might be expected in the very near future, while giving frank details regarding the coalition forces and the horrors of possible invasion.

It was a sombre début for the regent as a speaker but, nevertheless, Talleyrand, the soul of sarcasm, admitted she had done well: 'She was neither too brazen nor too timid. She showed a certain dignity combined with tact and self assurance.'

Her bearing, in fact, may well have confirmed Talleyrand's tentative opinion that the safest game to play in the approaching crisis was that of the regent and the future Napoleon II.

The Prince of Benevento was as shrewd as he was unscrupulous. His brain was the equal of Metternich's but his behaviour, the path he set himself, from beginning to end was dictated purely by self interest. Unlike Metternich, patriotism, mistaken or otherwise, played no part in his deliberations.

Although he had been in contact with Napoleon's enemies ever since Erfurt – where he had suggested to Alexander: 'The French people are civilised, the Russians are not; the Russian Emperor is civilised, the French Emperor is not. Therefore the French people need the Russian Emperor,' urging him not to allow himself to fall under 'General Bonaparte's' spell – he was far from feeling assured that a restored house of Bourbon would best serve his purpose. How much better, perhaps, a regent guaranteed by the European powers, surrounded by a small circle of advisers. Heartily despising the mental powers of all such advisers, and in particular those of Cambacères, Savary and Berthier, he had no doubt that his would soon be the unique influence behind this youthful regent who was still within two months of her twenty-second birthday. Of one thing he was absolutely certain: Napoleon himself was finished.

Napoleon shared this opinion but, at the same time, still retained a faint though rapidly dissipating belief in miracles. The one chance left, as he saw it, was an eleventh-hour reconciliation with his father-in-law.

On October 16th during the opening phases of the three-day battle of Leipzig, 'the Battle of the Nations', the French, though once more heavily outnumbered, again defeated the Austrians, this time at Wachau. One of the prisoners was a general, Count Meerfeld, who by a strange twist of fate had been one of the negotiators of the Campo Formio armistice, and had later accompanied the emperor Francis when, defeated, the latter had come hat in hand to solicit peace terms after Austerlitz. Meerfeld, reversing the previously held roles, was willing to bear Napoleon's suggested terms to the Austrian emperor.

Cornered, Napoleon agreed to most of the conditions put to him three months previously by Metternich. He would give up Poland, Illyria, the Rhine Confederation, Spain, Holland, the Hanseatic cities; he would withdraw all French troops from Germany and fall back to the west of the Rhine. Meerfeld promised to bring back an answer the next day. He never returned. In spite of all the amicable sentiments that Francis had reiterated in his letters to Marie Louise, he could not or would not act independently of his allies and contrary to Metternich's will, all of them firmly set on Napoleon's destruction.

The battle was resumed with increasing violence. By the evening of the 18th, it was all over. His army reduced to a bare 40,000 men, Napoleon was forced to fall back, through Germany, beyond the Rhine. Luckily for him, the bulk of the allied armies had been so badly mauled they were in no fit state to follow up.

However, before reaching the river, a flanking force of 30,000 Bavarians and 20,000 Austrians who had not taken part in the Leipzig slaughter, managed to straddle Napoleon's line of retreat at Hanau. In a fierce engagement, this allied force was routed by 10,000 of the Old Guard. On November 2nd the first crossings took place and, by the evening of the 3rd not a French soldier was left on the eastern bank.

Handing over command of the troops standing guard on the west bank, divided between Marmont, Mortier and Macdonald, Napoleon set out for Paris, arriving at Saint Cloud at 5 o'clock the evening of the 9th.

For most of the month of October, no news had been received at Saint Cloud. There were plenty of rumours, most of them justifiably pessimistic; but nothing official.

'One evening all the despatches' (of Leipzig) 'arrived together. In the Duke of Cadore's apartments' (Secretary of the Regency) 'the table was set for forty: twenty ladies, twenty ministers and grand officers. Everybody looked anxious; people were whispering in each other's ears. To the generals' wives it was announced, "There's no need to worry. Your husband is all right." Monsieur de Rémusat gave himself an air of great importance, having had a couple of lines from Monsieur de Nansouty* and making out that he was completely in the know. Not a single senior Guard's officer was badly wounded and, what was of prime importance, "All the members of the Emperor's household are in good health." Details were asked for; none were available. Everybody went to bed with profound misgivings, and so matters remained for the next thirty-six hours. It was two days later, on opening the newspapers, that four bulletins could be read: the daily statements of the army of October 4th, 15th, 16th and 24th, the hopes, the plans, the victory, the "disaster" – the actual word was there. "The enemy, badly shaken after the battles of the 16th and 18th, regained his courage, ascendancy, and the victory after the *disaster* of the 19th. After so many brilliant successes, the French Army has now lost its supremacy!"'

There is a theory that when Marie Louise read these bulletins, irrefutable proof that her husband was no longer the invincible warrior she had always, since her childhood, dreamed him to be, she lost all interest in him; that in her heart, no longer able to revere him as a demi-god and master of Europe, the greatest trembling at the mere raising of an eyebrow, the seeds of the betrayal which was to hurt him beyond all others were already germinating. 'The admiration reinforcing her conjugal love

* A cavalry general.

157

collapsed. She wept for herself, at the same time as she wept for his defeat.'*

It is a neat theory. It tidies the explanation of Marie Louise's extraordinary sentimental *volte-face* of the next few months, her near-hysterical statements to the world in general at the time of the Hundred Days, yet it does not stand up to too close examination.

In spite of the catastrophe of Leipzig, the irresistible conqueror was still valid in Marie Louise's mind. To her the Beresina, Leipzig, were merely names of no profound significance. Nor was she really interested in politics, still less in battlefields. She took Napoleon's invincibility for granted, but without pride. It was not Napoleon, emperor and soldier, who meant so much to her, but Napoleon the man, the husband. Far from being repelled by the revelation of his fallibility, she would almost have welcomed defeat if it had meant peace and a return, this time on a permanent basis, to the semi-bourgeois prolonged honeymoon of the first year of their marriage. During the next sad, anxious two and a half months it is also obvious from the petulant, reproachful tone of her letters that she had no idea that the end was so near. Her depression was caused by the certain prospect of further separation rather than from a sense of doom. 'You cannot imagine' (she repeated during the uninterrupted correspondence with her father) 'how upset I am that you are mixed up in this war against your son-in-law. God grant we will soon have peace. The Emperor longs for it, everybody here longs for it; but one can't make peace without negotiations, and up till now I gather you have not been exactly helpful. I am sure the English are behind this.'

Francis's sententious reply shows how completely he was now dominated by Metternich who indeed saw eye-to-eye with England, as far as the Bonapartes were concerned: 'I received your letter of December 12th (1813) yesterday and am very glad to hear you are well. Thank you for your New Year wishes and please accept mine in return. As for peace, you may rest assured that I desire it just as much as you do; as does the whole of France and, I hope, your husband. Only in peace can happiness and well-being be found, my views are modest and all I hope for is the basis of a peace which may be durable; but just hoping isn't enough in this world we live in. I have many solemn obligations to my allies and, unfortunately, the problems revolving round

* Raymonde Bessard op. cit.

the question of the, I hope soon to be attained, Peace are extremely complicated. Your country has caused profound upheavals; from whichever angle you view the matter there are just causes for complaint and provocation to hostilities . . . In England there is no ill will but differences of opinion are considerable and it needs time before they can be straightened out; after that the matter is in God's hands . . .'

Napoleon made no objection to this correspondence, but he no longer held out any hope that 'Papa Francis' would succumb to the pull of family ties; the father had been replaced by the subservient politician. The emperor was saddened and puzzled. Under no circumstances would he have behaved in a similar way. He was fully aware of the uselessness of his own family, yet it never occurred to him to turn on them nor to deprive any single one of an iota of the wealth and privileges they enjoyed thanks to his genius.

Joseph chased by Wellington from Madrid, Louis deprived of the Dutch throne for suspected sympathies with the enemy, yet still allowed to call himself king, Jerome a fugitive from Westphalia but accompanied by the faithful Catherine – all hung about in Paris scheming, squabbling, bitterly jealous of each other and their benefactor, desperately trying to think up ways and means of saving something of their undeserved fortunes when the inevitable fall came about. Even more despicable was the behaviour of Caroline, actively goading her brave but weak husband to listen to von Neipperg's blandishments – successful with Bernadotte, the one-eyed von Neipperg had been sent on a similar mission to Murat – and, in return for the right to continue on the Neapolitan throne, join openly with the Allies.

At this tragic moment, Napoleon's only real joy was the company of his son who, just under three years old, was a handsome, sturdy and highly intelligent little boy, already imbued with the sense of his own dignity.

Madame de Montesquiou tells a story of the 'little king' which has something of the aura of an *image d'Epinal*. So long as he was accompanied by his governess, Napoleon had no objection to the child breaking in on his cabinet meetings. On one occasion, however, he escaped, ran down the corridor, but was refused admission by an embarrassed guard who said:

'Sire, I cannot open the door for Your Majesty.'

'I am the little king.'

'But you are alone.'

At that moment Madame de Montesquiou appeared and, in a triumphant treble, the little boy shouted:

'Open for the king!'

Whereupon the guard, anxious to placate, flung open the doors, announcing:

'His majesty the king of Rome.'

Every moment that could possibly be spared, Napoleon spent with his 'little king', reawakening once more Marie Louise's latent jealousy. He liked to dress him up in miniature uniforms, and was inordinately proud of the interest taken in his public appearances by the Parisians. Even when he was studying his maps, planning the next campaign, the little boy would often be on his knee moving the coloured flags representing divisions, corps, armies. And later, before a slightly embarrassed Marie Louise, the young Napoleon would dance up and down, clapping his hands and chanting: 'We're going to thrash Papa Francis! We're going to thrash Papa Francis!'

New Year's Day 1814 was given over to the usual official ceremonies; distribution of presents after mass, review of the Paris garrison, state banquet followed by a ball, just as though the situation were normal. But it was to prove to be the last normal day in the empire's short ten years of existence.

On that day, against all Napoleon's expectations – he was convinced that the threatened offensive would not be launched before spring – Blücher crossed the Rhine at the head of 120,000 men without a single casualty. The marshals ordered to protect the west bank had retreated hastily without firing a shot. A mass of close on 400,000 enemy soldiers were – as a result – moving slowly on Paris.*

Once more, Napoleon's principal preoccupation was for the future of his dynasty. As an individual he was obsessed by the idea that he no longer existed, of a glorious death, sword in hand, on the battlefield.

After frantic preparations, the principal officers of the national

* Already, on December 21st, Schwarzenberg, in command of a Russo-Austrian army of 250,000, had violated Swiss territory and was poised for an attack. Napoleon, however, had not expected the advance to get under way for some weeks.

The Empress Josephine

The Imperial Family

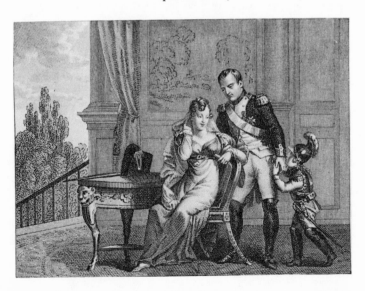

The King of Rome and 'Mama quiou', Madame de Montesquiou

The Duchess of Montebello

guard were called, after mass on Sunday, January 23rd, to the Hall of the Marshals, in the Tuileries.

It was a desperate, theatrical gesture.

Napoleon had planned a dramatic entrance into the hall, himself by one door and, simultaneously, Marie Louise, followed by Madame de Montesquiou carrying the 'little king' in her arms, by that facing the assembled officers.

This careful staging was slightly marred by the fact that, as usual, Marie Louise was late. Napoleon, however, spent a few minutes of waiting by chatting amiably then, when the far door at last opened, went across and took the 'little king' from his nurse's arms. A brief pause before he and Marie Louise, each holding one of the child's hands, advanced to within a few paces of the officers who, automatically, had fallen silent.

'Gentlemen,' he began, 'part of France's territory has been invaded. I am about to place myself at the head of the army and, helped by God and the valour of my men, I hope to throw the enemy back beyond our frontiers. Should the enemy approach the capital, I entrust the Empress and the King of Rome, my wife and my son, to the courage of the National Guard; I will be taking my departure untroubled, knowing that their safety lies in your hands. To you I leave the care of that which, after France, I hold most dear in this world. You will protect them, will you not? You will protect them?'

The question, in a voice dark with emotion, was twice repeated.

'A clamour broke out, arms were raised in an oath of fidelity. Officers wept, others breaking from the ranks ran to kiss the Emperor's hand. For a moment he had to support the Empress who, her face bathed with tears, seemed about to collapse. Then he picked up the little King and walked slowly in front of these deeply moved men who, at that moment, vowed their entire devotion to him. He felt sure of them. Once again, his eyes shone. He was no longer the livid, harassed man of the past few weeks. He was rejuvenated. His smile had returned. Once more he imagined his star was shining. His imagination carried him beyond the plains of Champagne, face to face with the enemy. No further doubt existed; he would conquer.'*

The moment of exhilaration was, however, but a passing flash of light against the sombre horizon.

* Octave Aubry: *Le Roi de Rome*, Plon, 1937.

On the 24th the text of the regency act was checked and again signed, last details attended to, secret documents burned.

Not feeling that she could bear to be alone when her husband actually took his departure, Marie Louise invited Hortense to share their last meal. It was far from being a cheerful evening, as Hortense has noted in her memoirs.

Napoleon made a gallant attempt to introduce an atmosphere of false, optimistic gaiety, but Marie Louise was plaintive and tearful, while Hortense was filled with premonitions of approaching ruin. There are, indeed, many who suggest that though she cordially hated her husband, Louis, she had always been in love with her stepfather.

'Come now, Hortense,' he said, teasing them, Marie Louise for her unrestrained tears, his step-daughter and sister-in-law for her doleful expression, 'Is everybody in Paris frightened? Can you see the Cossacks in the streets already? Let me tell you, they're not here yet, and I haven't forgotten how to do my job.'

Morbidly practical, Hortense replied: 'You have only fifty thousand men, sire.'

'And me,' said Napoleon sharply. 'That makes a hundred and fifty thousand,' and, turning to Marie Louise and putting his arms round her, 'Don't cry. Try to calm yourself. You'll see, we'll be going to Vienna to chastise Papa Francis.'

But, according to Hortense: 'The Empress never stopped crying and the Emperor, trying to console her, went on embracing her and murmuring, "Don't be so upset, have confidence in me, do you think I've forgotten how to do my job?" '

At midnight the carriage to take Napoleon east towards Châlons and his headquarters was waiting at the door, but he could not tear himself away. At two o'clock, however, he got up abruptly and left the room. He went to his son's bedroom. Madame de Montesquiou was awake instantly. Napoleon gestured to her to keep silent and approached the ornate cot on tiptoe. The little boy was asleep, his face framed by yellow curls faintly outlined against the pillow by the slow-burning night light. Napoleon bent over him, kissed him on the forehead, then hurried out without saying a word. With Marie Louise and Hortense, both of them now weeping, he hurried down the corridors to the waiting carriage. Very near a complete breakdown, Marie Louise clung to him, sobbing loudly. It is likely that his remark the previous day to the legislative assembly had been repeated to her – 'Within three months I will either have returned victorious to Paris, or be dead!' – for it was only after a genuine physical effort that he was able to disengage himself from her arms.

For a moment husband and wife regarded each other tensely, the silence being broken at last by Marie Louise murmuring between sobs, 'When will you be back?'

Napoleon hesitated for some seconds before replying sombrely, 'That, my dear one, is God's secret.'

Then, turning, and without another word, he went out into the courtyard. A brief interval, the noise of a door being slammed, and the two women heard the sound of hooves on cobbles gradually dying away in the distance.

Chapter IX

Since he pinned so much faith on the principle of the regency, it was a pity Napoleon had so little faith in his wife's abilities, or those of her advisers. His surveillance during the brief campaign preceding the collapse was severer than it had been the previous year. Cambacères remained arch-chancellor without whose official permission, which in turn came from the emperor, the empress herself could do nothing; while La Bouillerie controlled the *Trésor de la Couronne* which meant, in effect, that Marie Louise was unable, on her own initiative, to authorise the expenditure of a single franc. To complicate matters, dominated by his congenital nepotism, Napoleon named his brother Joseph, whose cowardliness, inefficiency and doubtful loyalty he had so often castigated in the past, lieutenant general of the empire.

More or less a refugee in Paris after running away from Wellington, Joseph could scarcely claim to be king of Spain; but with a childish obstinacy he clung to the royal title and Napoleon, indulgent as always, had decreed that he should be known as king Joseph or, simply, 'the king'. He was allowed to wear the uniform of the grenadiers of the guard – we have no record of what the *grognards* said when they heard of this – and maintain a household. This title of lieutenant general, conferred verbally, was never confirmed in writing. It is probable that Napoleon did not intend that it should be taken seriously. Nevertheless, as soon as he left Paris, Joseph began to interfere in every department of the regency's diverse functions. The tragedy of the moment was enhanced by the fact that his every move only served to hasten the allied victory.

With his army of a bare fifty thousand men confronting the allied steamroller, this *Campagne de France* was also a campaign of despair. Yet in the first three weeks it seemed as if the miracle upon which Napoleon counted might, against all predictions, be realised. Before leaving for the front he had said that it was time everybody put on once more their 'boots of '93'* and had boasted to Hortense that his presence alone on the battlefield was worth a hundred thousand men. For the moment it seemed as though he had not been exaggerating. This swan-song as a great commander was, in many ways, his most brilliant exhibition of military virtuosity. Strategically, tactically, his judgment proved faultless, his eye for the instant situation unerring.

Though the marshals were practically in a state of rebellion,† the junior officers, the men in the ranks, still adored him. In rapid succession came the victories of Brienne (January 28th), Champaubert (February 10th), Chateau Thierry (February 11th), Vauchamps (February 14th) and Montereau (February 20th). In each of these encounters, Napoleon found himself outnumbered by at least two to one; most of his troops were the rawest of recruits. Despite the odds, his presence alone, his uncannily exact decisions when, and where, to strike, combined with a skill of manoeuvre unsurpassed, won him the day.

In early February, victory bulletins raised the Parisians' original pessimism to an equally dangerous pitch of optimism, especially as the bulletins failed to mention the bloody reverse of La Rothière two days after Brienne, or the fact that lack of cavalry, combined with the sheer exhaustion of the infantry, the heavy price paid – by late February the imperial army had lost nearly half of its effectives – and again because of the marshals' total inability to carry out orders to harass the retreating enemy, not one of these victories had proved decisive. The history of 1813 was repeating itself. The marshals knew this and, once again, were clamouring for 'peace at any price'.

On the other hand, the coalition armies were badly shaken. Schwarzenberg, Blücher and the czar had believed that after Leipzig the French would never again be able to put an army in

* Napoleon refers to the miraculous victories of literally ragged republican armies over Austrians and Prussians in 1793.

† Just before Leipzig, what is known as 'the first revolt of the marshals' had taken place. Napoleon had conceived the brilliant plan of marching on Berlin. This move which had every possibility of success would have obliged the Russians to sue for peace and discouraged the diffident Austrians from continuing as active belligerents. The marshals, however, led by Ney, Berthier and Macdonald, were appalled by the thought of adventuring still deeper into hostile territory rather than beating a hasty retreat to the Rhine's western bank. They said they would not obey 'such a mad order'. Against his better judgment, Napoleon gave way. The result was Leipzig.

the field. In this they were encouraged by the lack of resistance offered to their crossing of the Rhine, a formidable natural obstacle for an early-19th-century army. These February defeats, the loss of a large number of senior officers, some fifty thousand men, a mass of material, halted them temporarily, at the same time bringing to light certain divergences of opinion as to future operational plans, even as to the war's objectives.

At this stage there was a slender chance of that 'peace with honour' which for so long Napoleon had been stressing was his one desire and once again the emperor's hopes were based on Austria. Letters still passed uninterruptedly between Marie Louise and her father. On February 17th, three days after Vauchamps, Napoleon had a plea for suspension of hostilities despatched to the emperor Francis: on the 23rd Prince Wenzel of Lichtenstein arrived at French headquarters with the Austrian emperor's reply and a demand for an armistice.

Napoleon received this envoy with mixed feelings. After La Rothière, and before the brilliant action at Champaubert, he had felt the end was near. Bad news assailed him from all sides. Joseph plied him with letters emphasising the bourgeoisie's deplorable morale, the Paris 'mob's' seething discontent. No replies had been received to Marie Louise's appeals to her father. The huge allied army was outflanking him from the south. Murat, in a despicable effort to save his throne had, as a result of von Neipperg's diplomatic needling, actually joined forces with the Austrians instead, as Napoleon had expected, of creating a diversion in Italy. Talleyrand, for some strange reason a member of the regency council instead of occupying a prison cell, was known to be in touch with the czar.

On February 8th, harassed, profoundly depressed, Napoleon had written Joseph a long letter containing a passage he was to regret the rest of his life:

> . . . If the battle be lost and news of my death reach you, see that the Empress and the King of Rome leave at once for Rambouillet; give orders to the Senate, the Council of State and the army, to re-group on the Loire . . . But do not let the Empress and the King of Rome fall into the enemies' hands. If I live you must obey me. But if I die, my son and the Empress Regent, for the sake of France's honour, must not allow themselves to be captured. Remember what Philip V's

wife said. Indeed what would be said of the Empress? That she abandoned her son's throne! The allies would put an end to everything by carrying him off as a prisoner to Vienna. I am surprised you don't realise that . . . For my part I would rather my son had his throat cut than that I should see him brought up in Vienna as an Austrian prince, and I have a high enough opinion of the Empress to be sure she shares this view so far as is possible for a woman and a mother . . .

Yet only two days after these sombre reflections he was writing to Marie Louise:

My good Louise – Victory! I have destroyed 12 Russian regiments, taken 6,000 prisoners, 40 cannon, 200 limbers, captured the army commander and all the generals, many colonels, and I lost only 200 men. Have the cannons of Les Invalides fire a salvo and publish this news everywhere. I'm chasing Sachen' (commander of one of Blucher's corps) 'who is near Ferté-sous-Jouarre. I'll be at Montmirail and closing in on him by midnight. Nap.

Encouraged by his successes, Napoleon made another determined attempt to touch his father-in-law's repressed paternal instincts, a letter which he felt could now be written from strength rather than construed as a broken man's plea for mercy.

After beginning, 'My brother and very dear father-in-law' he set out a tableau of his triumphs over the Russians and Prussians, warned that a battle from which he was certain to emerge victor – between French and Austrians – was imminent and stressed the grief that such blood-letting between erstwhile allies would cause him: 'Matters being as they are,' (he continued) 'I suggest signing a peace with Y.M. immediately, on the basis you prepared at Frankfurt,* and which I and the French nation have adopted as our ultimate concession . . . If harder concessions should be imposed on the French, peace would be of short duration. There is not a Frenchman living who would not prefer death to conditions which would make us slaves of England, and mean that France could no longer be counted as a great power . . . Do you want your flag outraged and insulted by England as it

* A Treaty which offered France her natural boundaries, that is to say, the Rhine and including the port of Antwerp.

has been in the past? What interest can Your Majesty have in putting Belgium under the yoke of a protestant prince* whose son will, one day, ascend the English throne?'

And finally:

'May I be permitted to remind Your Majesty that, in spite of the harm you have done me by invading my territory and your forgetfulness of the ties uniting us, my feelings remain unchanged, and I am much afraid that if you refuse peace, such an act on your part will bring you untold misfortune and many evils . . . One single word from Your Majesty can put an end to this war, assuring the happiness of not only your own people but of Europe . . . Hence I write to Your Majesty, my recent ally, who because of the strength of his army and the extent of his Empire is regarded as the driving force of the coalition . . .'

Undoubtedly Napoleon should have signed the peace granting France her 'natural frontiers' immediately, but he was both suspicious and resentful. He could not forget the fraudulent 1813 armistice. He knew that the allies were disorganised by defeat and heavy losses and feared that the offer might, as before, be nothing but a time-gaining ruse. One more victory, this time really decisive, was necessary. Encouraged also by the fact that the prince of Lichtenstein mentioned specifically that the emperor Francis had no wish to assist in a Bourbon restoration – 'My august sovereign, the Emperor, would never lend his aid to such a step' – he was heard to say that evening:

'The allies will repent of their insolence. They will see that I am nearer to their capitals than they are to mine.'

And when, next day, there came a messenger under a flag of truce suggesting that terms be discussed at Lusigny,† he repeated

---

* Prince Leopold of Saxe-Coburg, who married Princess Charlotte, daughter of George IV, and who later ascended the Belgian Throne. He was Queen Victoria's dear Uncle Leopold.

† It is indicative of the general chaos of this campaign that, while fighting was in progress and these negotiations in hand, another congress whose object was to agree upon suitable peace terms was being held at Chatillon, attended by representatives of the powers concerned. Caulaincourt represented France; Count Stadion, bitter enemy of France, Austria; Count Ramisovski, Russia; von Humboldt, Prussia. Three plenipotentiaries from England were present: Lord Cathcart, Lord Aberdeen and Sir Charles Stuart. Caulaincourt was faced with a hopeless task. He had been ordered to obtain 'peace at any price' but, after Montereau, came a note from Napoleon: 'Your attitude must remain the same: you must do everything to secure peace, but it is my will that you sign nothing without my direct order.'

loudly enough to be heard by everybody: 'I am nearer to Vienna than you are to Paris.'

A triumphant letter was sent back to Joseph: '. . . I am at Troyes. The enemy envoy pursues me with flags of truce asking for a suspension of hostilities . . . A few days ago they thought that I had no army. Now they say I have massed all my veterans and face them with picked troops only. That is what fear does. It is important that Paris newspapers give full publicity to this fear . . .'

To Marie Louise the emperor's letters, though little better than situation reports, were cheering and, indeed, miraculous. They were also filled with instructions: 'Have a thirty-gun salvo fired for the Montereau battle . . .'

'When I write giving orders you in your turn must write to the Minister of War, signing the letter yourself, and say "because of such and such a success won by the Emperor on such and such a day, etc." . . .'

'You must always keep the Minister of War directly informed regarding military details . . .'

Often the letters ended, 'Write to your father . . .' and, invariably, 'My health is excellent. Embrace the little King for me.'

The atmosphere of victory was enhanced on February 27th when standards captured from the enemy were officially presented to the regent.

'Madame,' said Clarke, the war minister, in his official speech, 'when Charles Martel defeated the Saracens in the plains of Tours and Poitiers, the capital was bedecked with the trophies won from but a single enemy. Today, when dangers no less grave menace France, your august husband, after even greater triumphs, presents you with these standards captured from the three great powers of Europe . . . These pledges of French valour are for us the emblems of even greater triumphs to come, should the enemy in his obstinacy determine to prolong the war . . .'

Marie Louise, again making a good impression, replied: 'Duke of Feltre and Minister of War, it is with the most profound emotion that I contemplate these trophies you present me on the orders of my august husband, the Emperor. In my eyes they represent that certain security enjoyed by my country. At the sight of them may all Frenchmen spring to arms. May they rally to their monarch and their father. I know that their courage led by his genius will soon free our homeland.'

The same evening she was writing to her father: '. . . It would be bad policy on your part to try to force a dishonourable peace on us, one which, in any case, would not last. Everybody here is prepared to die rather than accept such conditions. Try also, my dear Papa, to put yourself in my position. It would be such a terrible blow for me I could not survive it. I beg of you, my very dear papa, to think of me and my son. You know how devoted I am to you, and how grateful to think that I have your paternal love.'

It was not only to her father that Marie Louise was asked to write. On February 25th she received one of the strangest letters Napoleon with his meagre respect for women ever penned. 'My friend. Send for the Duchess of Castiglione. Tell her to write to her husband' (Marshal Augereau) 'and tell him that he's half asleep when by now he ought to have freed Mont Blanc, reached the Ain and routed the enemy. Tell her to write to him in this sense and suggest he fights better. My health is good, the weather fine but chilly. All yours. A kiss for the little King.'

Both Marie Louise and the duchess did as ordered. It was no good. Augereau, formerly brutal and energetic, was affected by the prevalent fear of losing the material benefits conferred on him by his emperor. His ineptitude in mid-March lost the chance of a crushing victory, so much so that Napoleon cried out: 'Everybody betrays me. No one fears or obeys me any longer!'

At this moment, according to General Segur: '. . . fortune hung on a single thread; a little more and the coalition would have collapsed under its own weight, and France would have been saved. With the exception of the Prussians, the enemy's staffs imagined they were caught in a trap. The emperor Alexander suggested that a victorious advance from Moscow to the Seine was enough, that they should not expose their flank to a second Marengo . . .'

In the end, it was the oldest of the allied commanders, the septuagenarian Marshal Blücher, who refused to be intimidated or affected by his allies' pusillanimity. Ignoring the Chatillon conference and the fact that parallel negotiations for an armistice were under way with the czar and the Austrian emperor, he regrouped his badly mauled divisions to march independently on Paris, following both banks of the Marne. Informed of this manoeuvre on the night of the 26th, Napoleon left Troyes, the town he had entered two days previously, hoping to intercept the Prussians somewhere on the axis Arcis-sur-Aube–Sezanne. At the same time, inspired by Blücher's example, the retreating Austrians halted and faced about. The brief hope of an armistice, of peace, much to the marshals' horror and loudly-voiced distress, belonged to the past. In chorus, they blamed the emperor for his dilatoriness in signing.

As abruptly as the wheel of fortune had swung in his favour, it was now to swing in full circle against him.

There were to be a few, a very few, more minor tactical successes but, once set on their objective, the allies could not fail to gain the upper hand by sheer weight of numbers alone.

On March 1st, on the initiative of Lord Castlereagh, each of the allies agreed to keep a contingent of 150,000 men in the field till the war was won, and a standing army of 60,000 permanently with the colours for a further period of twenty years after the conclusion of peace, in case a resuscitated France be tempted to embark on a war of revenge. Known as the Treaty of Chaumont, this agreement was kept a secret from Caulaincourt who, however, was presented the following day (March 2nd) with an ultimatum to the effect that, if allied terms limiting France to her *pre-Revolutionary boundaries* were not accepted by the 10th, the peace congress would be broken up.

In a long detailed exposé of the situation, the duke of Vicenza made it clear to Napoleon that, in his opinion, the terms, harsh as they appeared, should be accepted if anything were to be saved from the wreck. It included the telling phrase: 'Your Majesty can no longer deceive yourself. Our ranks are far too thin to triumph over so many foes. Our dangers are too real, and the hours left us are counted. Possibly Your Majesty will consider these reflections as due to weakness. I am nevertheless convinced that the time has come when nothing should prevent me from making them.'

Napoleon treated this communication with contempt, but was unwilling to break off negotiations altogether. With great difficulty, Caulaincourt persuaded the allies to extend the final date of their ultimatum, and on the 15th handed them the French emperor's counter propositions. Napoleon agreed to give up conquered territory east of the Rhine and in Italy, but insisted on retaining Antwerp, Mainz and Cologne. At the same time he demanded indemnities for Prince Eugène and his sister Elisa.

The allied representatives were outraged. The propositions, they claimed, were an insult, and it was a letter from Metternich to Caulaincourt which concluded this futile conference: 'If the conditions of this counter project are the Emperor Napoleon's final terms, then peace is impossible and the fate of Europe will be decided by arms . . . In fact we are possibly nearer peace as the result of the breaking off of these ridiculous parleys . . .'

Obstinately, Napoleon still hoped. Any hint of bad news was forbidden in the French newspapers. General Moreau,* who had surrendered Soissons, was arrested, tried by court-martial and shot on the *Place de la Grève*. Anybody spreading defeatist rumours was to be considered as a traitor. Above all, the empress was not to be alarmed. And yet in the middle of these torments, at a time when many contemporaries confirmed that never had his claims to greatness been more justified, he showed himself intensely vulnerable to the most human of weaknesses: jealousy.

A number of Marie Louise's letters had given him the impression that she was seeing a great deal of King Joseph. In one she disclosed that she had shown him a translation of one of her letters to her father.

Napoleon could never rid himself of the conviction that no woman had the strength to resist the approaches of a would-be seducer, that given the opportunity to stray from virtue's path she would inevitably do so through sheer moral feebleness. The mental picture of his wife in his brother's arms momentarily ousted from his mind the agonising problem of saving France from the allied hordes. His angry reproach was despatched by galloper to Paris.

My good Louise. I have just received your letter. I have sent yours to your father through the outposts. I am angry that you showed your father's letter and your reply to the king. You have too much confidence in that prince. Such communications should be for my eyes alone. Everybody now betrays me. Am I destined to be betrayed by the king as well? It wouldn't astonish me and I could survive it. The only thing that would be too much for me would be to learn that you were indulging in secret relations with the king and no longer felt about me as before. Beware of the

* Not to be confused with General Moreau of the Moreau plot, who was killed in battle fighting with the allies in 1813.

king; he has a bad reputation with women and nasty habits which he picked up in Spain. If you want to make me happy, never show any of my letters, or your father's, or your replies, to the king and keep him at arm's length. Once more I beg of you, don't let the king into your confidence or into your presence if you have any regard for my happiness. All this makes me rather sad. I needed the affection of my people but am accustomed to being betrayed; but from you such a thing is unexpected and would leave me inconsolable ...

The bewildered Marie Louise, aghast at the storm she had raised so innocently, hurried to reply:

My dear Friend. I received your letter of the 12th' (March) 'half an hour after midnight and would have answered immediately had I not been suffering from a severe fever accompanied by a splitting headache, but I feel a little better at the moment and hasten to write to say how upset I am that you could think I trusted the king more than I do you and that I could have any secrets from you. I pray you do not really believe this, as such a thought would make me most desperately unhappy. Please realise, on the contrary, that I love you most tenderly and that all I wish for is the opportunity to be able to prove it. I'm cross with myself for having spoken to the king about my father's letter though all I did was to translate a few phrases to calm him down as he seemed to have lost his head ...

It is, perhaps, unlikely that Napoleon had any real doubts as to his wife's fidelity, but he did have misgivings as to Joseph's political loyalty. Rumours persisted that, like Talleyrand, Joseph was hoping to save himself by backing the regency, gambling that Napoleon would be persuaded to abdicate in his son's favour, in which case he, Joseph, might retain a position as *eminence grise* of the new régime. As before, Napoleon, overloyal to his family, refused to take any action. A sharp reprimand, skirting the subject of Marie Louise, and that was all. The king was left to carry on with his schemes unimpeded. 'I am sorry to learn' (the letter ran) 'that you have been talking to my wife about the Bourbons and the reactions of the Austrian Emperor. Your character and mine are very different. You like to coax people and follow their ideas, while I require submission and to have people follow mine. Today as at Austerlitz, I am master . . .'

The same day he despatched a rebuke to Savary, Minister of Police: '. . . They' (the people of Paris) 'must realise that I am the same man that I was at Austerlitz and Wagram, that I will not tolerate intrigue in the country, that there is no other authority than mine, and that the Regent alone enjoys my confidence. King Joseph is weak. He busies himself with intrigues which could be the State's undoing, and certainly his and that of those who listen to him, if he does not mend his ways speedily . . .'

Strangely enough after this threatened crisis he wrote to Joseph on March 16th again charging him with the responsibility of the fate of both Marie Louise and the king of Rome. What inspired him to do this is one of history's unsolved problems, for the letter was almost a replica of that which he had written only eight days previously,* and ended with the gloomy reflection: 'The fate of Astyanax, a prisoner in Greek hands, has always seemed to me to be the most tragic of all times.'

One thing may be said in Joseph's favour. He was more than careful to see that Marie Louise was not troubled by pessimistic reports. Because of this and her husband's non-committal letters, she was able to write on the 21st in reply to a further plea that a well-worded letter to her father might still help towards the conclusion of the tragically illusive peace:

. . . I am so pleased by the way matters are progressing. I hope all will continue to go well. All my prayers are for this. I want you to enjoy the happiness you deserve. All Paris is ringing with good news.† Everybody is talking about battles won, and above all of peace. I wrote to my father as you asked me to do. I would like to think my letters have a good effect, but fear this is not the case. My father never listens to me when it is a question of affairs of State. I haven't seen the king. He hardly ever comes to see me in the morning and I'm so glad because I know that's what you want. Your son embraces you: he is wonderfully well. My health is excellent, the spring really suits me, and it has been so fine I have been able to ride. It does me so much good, but what would do me even more good would be to

* see pp 166–7.
† A highly erroneous statement.

see you again. I love you and kiss you most tenderly. Your
faithful friend. Louise.

She had not the slightest idea when she composed this letter
that during the next twenty days the course, not only of her life
but of Europe's history, was to be changed irrevocably.

Even at this late stage of the campaign, the allies were still prey
to doubts as to their ability to destroy the apparently rejuvenated
tiger. In fact, as Bainville* points out: 'For yet a few more days,
Napoleon was able to cling to the illusion of victory. The enemy
believed him to be everywhere. From March 16th to 19th, he
forced them to fall back in confusion, terrified that their lines of
communication were about to be severed and that the people of
Argonne, Burgundy and Lorraine would be falling on their rear.
But on March 20th, Augereau† turned his back to them, evacuated
Lyons at the approach of an Austrian corps and retreated to
Valence. Thus the southern army the Emperor had been relying
on to create a diversion proved to be useless . . .'

More than ever, Napoleon knew that by a simple mathematical
calculation the allies, with their vastly superior numbers, could
not fail to destroy him. He could still, perhaps, win a few more
indecisive skirmishes which made such good reading in *Le
Moniteur*, but there were no replacements for his casualties
whereas with the allies two men could take the place of each one
who fell. Only some master stratagem could now save France
and his dynasty.

In this moment of dire stress, Napoleon's thoughts turned to
Russia. He had been obsessed by the thought that at all costs
Paris must be held. But the Russians had not bothered about the
fate of Moscow! He did not imagine for one moment that the
Parisians would be prepared to gut their beloved city but, on the
other hand, even if Paris did fall – temporarily – into allied hands,
if he were to raise the local populations astride the enemy supply
lines, at the same time rallying the scattered garrisons isolated by
the allies rapid advance, then, he reckoned, the allies' very
numbers would prove a major handicap. They could be starved,
denied supplies, ammunition, reduced in reasonable time to a
defenceless mob. Let them continue their ponderous advance on

* Jacques Bainville: *Napoléon*, Fayard 1931.
† see p. 170

the capital; he would turn east, cut their lifeline, oblige them to embark on a retreat as disastrous as that of his own in 1812. The Rhine, if they got so far, would prove to be their Beresina!

It was at this stage that, on the 23rd, Napoleon wrote the historic letter to Marie Louise in which, most unfortunately, he gave away his basic plan. Such a departure from the normal tenets of security was all the more incomprehensible in view of the fact that he knew that hundreds of Cossacks roamed the countryside, their principal task being the interception of couriers and despatches:

My friend, I've been continually in the saddle these last four days. The 20th I occupied Arcis-sur-Aube. The enemy attacked me at six in the evening, but the same day I beat him and killed 4,000. I took two of his guns and he took two of mine, so that on that score we were equal. The 21st the enemy army took up positions to protect convoys between Brienne and Bar-sur-Aube. I have decided to drive on to the Marne and fall on his communications, so as to push him back from Paris, and rally my garrisons. This evening I will be at St Dizier. Goodbye, my friend. A kiss for my son. Nap.

The despatch rider bearing the letter was captured by a troop of Cossacks and the letter sent to Blücher. The old marshal had copies taken and then gallantly arranged for the original to be forwarded to Marie Louise, accompanied, according to popular legend, by a bunch of flowers.

Some historians are inclined to believe that this incident, resulting in the disclosure of the vital secret, was the direct cause of the plan's failure. This is very unlikely. Undoubtedly the captured letter confirmed Napoleon's proposed future moves, but they were already suspected and already causing considerable alarm at allied headquarters.

A conference of allied commanders and chiefs of staff was immediately called and met the following day at Pougy, a small village between Arcis and Brienne. It opened with the reading of Napoleon's letter. Initial disagreement on the appropriate counter steps to be taken was profound. In spite of Russia and Leipzig, Napoleon's presence on the battlefield was still able to produce a hypnotically stultifying effect on his opponents. The king of Prussia suggested that the whole allied line should be pulled back so as to secure the Rhine bridges, while Schwarzenberg stated urgently that it was 'against all the established rules of warfare to contemplate driving on Paris while the French field army under the emperor was still intact'. The czar, Alexander, appears to have been the only one, at this moment, who remained unruffled. Victory was within their grasp, he insisted; retreat would be a cowardly act of folly. Finally, a compromise was reached. The bulk of the allied army would march obliquely on Châlons to reinforce Blücher, and would try to trap the French in the neighbourhood of St Dizier.

As preparations for this manoeuvre were under way, the czar received more captured letters, this time from Paris, and addressed to Napoleon. One of these, from the minister of police, Savary, implored the emperor to head for the capital as quickly as possible, where general morale was at its lowest ebb, and where very 'influential people' were obviously waiting for the allies' arrival. To begin with, Schwarzenberg did not consider the news important enough to warrant a change of plan. The czar, on the other hand, was of the opinion that it revealed the key to the situation. Rather than risk another costly and possibly disastrous battle in the St Dizier area, they should push straight on, and at top speed, to Paris. Amateur psychologist, the czar, with certain justification, considered that he knew the Parisians well enough to be sure that resistance would be feeble and, once overcome, would not be revived by suicidal patriotic fervour; too great a proportion of the population was too deeply imbued with sybaritism for there to be any serious risk of such an eventuality.

After a vigorous exposé of his ideas at a second conference held between Sommepuis and Vitry, the czar was able to win over his hesitant, still somewhat fearful, allies. Ignoring Napoleon, the allies, by forced marches, then resumed their thrust on Paris.

It proved to be a master stroke.

Marmont's and Mortier's divisions, numbering a bare twenty-eight thousand men, the only regular troops covering the approaches to the capital, were routed at Fere-Champenoise on the 25th. The two marshals, however, managed to rally the remnants of their divisions and fall back on the suburbs but, to all intents and purposes, Paris was practically without defence.

Two days later Napoleon heard of the disaster. He was appalled.

He had been absolutely convinced that his threat to their communications would make the allies turn back and head for safety. He was now faced with a grim choice.

As a soldier he knew that the sound course was to forget about Paris for the time being and continue with his plan. On the other hand, he had no faith in those he had left behind, or the people of Paris. There would be little point in annihilating enemy supply convoys if, in the meantime, Paris were to acclaim the return of the Bourbons, and Louis XVIII were to take over the Tuileries' imperial apartments. When General Sebastiani urged him not to be diverted by the threat to the capital and call for a general national uprising against the foreigner, he replied: 'That is a wild dream based on memories of Spain and our own Revolution. It is useless to call upon a nation which has destroyed the priests and the nobles, and in which I myself have destroyed the Revolution.'

As Saint Amand* points out: 'To defend Paris against two hundred thousand allies, to protect the city with barricades, to sound the tocsin, to determine to conquer or die, required both patriotism and religious conviction. It called for monks, like those of Saragossa, to set the Holy Sacrament in the path of the invaders, fanatics, like the men who burned Moscow, who chose to see their city in flames rather than in the hands of foreigners. Paris was moved by a very different feeling – a yearning for peace.'

It was not until the very end that Marie Louise fully realised the situation's gravity, and then surprised everyone, accustomed to her hypochondria, her petty grumbling, her apparent lack of stability and fortitude, by her calmness and dignity in the moments of greatest trial.

News of the allies' rapid advance reached Paris within a few hours of the Fère-Champenoise battle and, as always in such cases when news is carried by defeated troops, was considerably exaggerated. Nevertheless, it caused panic. The very word 'cossack' was enough to numb most individuals with terror. This terror was heightened by another of the eternal spectacles resulting from invasion; the blind flight of the inhabitants of towns and villages before the invaders' path.

By the evening of the 27th, allied cannons, harassing the remnants of Marmont's and Mortier's divisions attempting to

* Imbère de Saint Amand: op. cit.

178

re-form, could be heard distinctly in the city's southern and eastern suburbs. Nobody could pretend any longer that the situation was not critical. The question, therefore, became automatic: should the regent, the king of Rome, the regency council and high dignitaries of the imperial government remain in the beleaguered city, possibly to share its fate, or escape beyond the Loire while there was still time before Paris was completely surrounded?

To settle this urgent problem, a meeting of the regency council was called for the evening of the 28th. Several of those who took part have left records of this meeting which initially decided the fate of the empire, notably Savary and Clarke. It was significant, perhaps, that the regent herself, nominally president of the council, hardly said a word throughout the proceedings and has herself left no written record.

Clarke was the first to speak. He advocated flight. The next speaker, the minister of state, Boulay de Meurthe, took completely the opposite point of view. In a fiery speech he pointed out that the departure of the empress would precipitate not only the end of the regency but that of the empire. The empress, he said, 'should take her son in her arms and show herself to the people, pass through the streets, boulevards and suburbs, to give an example of heroic resolution'. The populace, he affirmed would applaud and echo 'what the Hungarians had cried out to her great ancestress, Maria Theresa, *"Moriamus pro rege nostro!"* '

Champagny and Regnier (president of the legislative assembly) backed up Boulay de Meurthe whole-heartedly. To the surprise of several present, Talleyrand, as cool and collected as the majority were heated, was of the same opinion; the empress's departure would play straight into royalist hands, making a change of régime inevitable. Savary, also supporting Talleyrand, mentions in his diary that: 'I spoke of the excellent spirit of that portion of the nation which is seldom taken into account, in spite of its untiring sacrifices.'

Cambacères who, like Marie Louise, had remained silent and looked and behaved like an exhausted old man, then called for a vote. It was overwhelmingly in favour of the empress remaining.

Clarke, however, was obdurate and, according to Savary, 'much excited'. He begged the council members to listen to reason. Paris, he insisted, was not the only centre of imperial power. 'So long as a village was left in which he' (the emperor) 'or his son was recognised, there all Frenchmen should rally, for that was their real capital. It was the duty of the empress and the king of Rome to go to the uninvaded provinces, there to summon all good men to their banner, and there die in defence of country and throne . . .'*

His eloquence was without effect. A second vote, always on Clarke's insistence, was called. Not a single member had changed his opinion. Marie Louise, still calm, anxious to remain and apparently unmoved by the menace of bodily harm, looked happy and was about to declare the meeting closed when Joseph, who had also maintained silence, suddenly rose to his feet. In his hand were two letters, those which Napoleon had written on February 8th and March 16th.†

Saint Amand, describing the effect their reading produced, says: 'When Joseph had finished the second letter, the members of the Council gazed at each other in stupefaction. Why had they been summoned if the emperor's orders were formal? Was this merely another mockery of a debate, of pretended deliberation of which the Imperial government had given so many examples? In that case it was easy to understand why the Duke of Feltre, who doubtless knew of these letters' existence, had urged so strongly that the Empress and her son should depart. Nevertheless, the members who disagreed still tried to prevent it. M. de Talleyrand repeated what he had said already. King Joseph then declared that it was impossible, without being guilty of rebellion, to disobey these precise orders. A third and last vote was taken and the departure inevitably determined; the Empress, who wished to remain, nevertheless announced that she and her son would leave at eight the next morning.'

Dismay and confusion was the result of this decision.

For Talleyrand it was the end of the Bonapartes. Remarking, 'Well, it's all over. Heavens, though, it's throwing the game away with all the trumps in one's hands,' he limped to his carriage, drove to his private hotel in the rue St Florentin, and there began to prepare to welcome allies and Bourbons alike; but before his carriage door was slammed, he whispered to Savary, 'You see what comes of the stupidity of a few ignorant men who are granted too much power.'

Though in despair, Marie Louise was incapable even of

* Extract from Savary's diaries.
† see pp. 166—7 and 174.

contemplating disobeying her husband's decree; Savary, Champagny and de Menéval, however – all implored her to change her mind.

'You are my lawful counsellors,' she said. 'I will not take it upon myself to issue an order opposing that of the Emperor and the vote of the Privy Council.'

A few minutes later a delegation from the unswervingly loyal national guard received the same answer to the same plea.

The same obstinacy, or lack of initiative, marked a conversation with Hortense, recorded in the latter's diaries:

' "I'm leaving, and you'd better do the same," the Empress said to me. "The War Minister assures me that Paris can not be defended."

' "I wonder, my sister," I replied, "if you realise you are losing your crown? I'm pleased to see you are making this sacrifice so light-heartedly."

'She approached me and said in a low voice, "You may be right but that is what 'they' have decided, and if the Emperor has any reproaches to make, they won't be made to me." '

Marie Louise's reactions, however, suggest that she was not making this 'sacrifice' as 'light-heartedly' as Hortense is anxious to make one believe. Immediately after the decision she rushed to her desk to pour out her misgivings to her husband: 'The Council has just ended its session and it's well after midnight, and after a long debate it has been decided that I must depart tomorrow morning at the latest. I must say frankly I am very much against this decision, I am sure it will have a terrible effect on the Parisians, and take away all the courage they would otherwise have guarded for the defence. The National Guard won't do anything now, and when you arrive to raise the siege, you'll find the capital already in enemy hands. But you have always said I must do what the Arch-Chancellor tells me and I will do so this time as well, because I don't want to expose my son to any danger . . .'

By dawn the carriages were assembled; ten huge Berlins. But Marie Louise could not bring herself to give the final order. She must have known instinctively that, once she left the palace, she would no longer be empress in anything but name, and that for only a very brief period of time. She had not slept and again at first light was busy writing to Napoleon: 'May God's will be done, but I am sure you will not be pleased. This will destroy the morale of the National Guard, and the enemy will be in Paris tomorrow. They say he' (the enemy) 'has not made any progress during the night, but has sent a column in the direction of Rambouillet; so apparently it's better to be captured by the Cossacks than stay calmly in Paris! However, everybody here has gone mad except me, and I hope that in a few days you will tell me that I was right not to have wanted to abandon the capital because of the presence of some 15,000 Cossacks who would never dare to venture into the streets in any case. I'm very upset about going because I know the consequences will be most unfortunate for you, but everybody said my son would be in danger, and with that I did not dare to resist especially after seeing the letter you wrote the King. So I commit myself to Providence, certain, however, that all will end disastrously . . .'

She was correct in her summing-up but, raised to blind obedience from childhood, how could a girl of only twenty-two years of age have been expected to assert herself, even when so passionately convinced of the fatal mistake she was committing? 'If the Emperor had reproaches to make, at least they would not be made to her!' Unfortunately for the Bonaparte empire, she was neither an Elizabeth nor a Maria Theresa.

By two o'clock in the afternoon the carriages were still waiting. Clarke was frantic. Earlier, Joseph had told Marie Louise that he would go up to the forward defences and let her have a resumé of the situation. He had not returned. Jerome, however, had demanded an audience and told her, rudely, that she was mad to think of leaving. Shortly afterwards a second deputation from the national guard spoke in the same vein.

Suddenly it was all too much for her. She collapsed on to a chair, and burst into loud sobs. The self-control of the previous evening which had so astonished the council had left her.

'Oh, my God,' she lamented, 'why can't somebody decide something and put an end to this agony?'

Then pulling herself together with a great effort, she sent for General Caffarelli, once more to be escort commander, and begged him to get the latest news from the war minister.

Clarke was categorical. If they did not leave immediately, the last escape route would be cut. Reluctantly, thinking of her son and cannibalistic stories concerning the Cossacks, Marie Louise gave the orders.

She was not the only one, however, to realise the fatality of this flight. The 'little king' made a terrible scene.

'I don't *want* to go to Rambouillet,' he screamed. 'It's a *horrid* château. Please, can't we stay here? I don't want to leave home.'

Madame de Montesquiou tried to reason with him. For once, her words had no effect, other than to increase his hysteria.

'I don't want to go,' he bawled again. 'As papa's not here, *I'm* the master!' Astonishing language for a child only just three years old. Madame de Montesquiou then tried to drag him downstairs. He wrapped his legs and arms round the banisters, clinging like a limpet. Finally, Monsieur Canisy, one of the equerries, managed to prise loose his grip, wrapped him in a blanket and carried him, kicking and bellowing, to the waiting carriage.

Chapter X

The mournful procession leaving the Tuileries was headed by the ten berlins. In them rode the empress and the 'little king', the duchess of Montebello, Madame de Luçay, doctors Corvisart and Bourdier, the principal members of the household – including Prince Aldobrandini, Baron de Bausset (palace prefect) and Baron de Menéval, Cambacères and members of the senate. Jerome and Joseph had stayed behind proclaiming noisily that they would die at the barricades rather than witness enemy boots defiling Paris's boulevards. The berlins were followed by heavy wagons containing, among other things, bullion, the crown jewels, silver, plate, glass, even furniture. This long column of vehicles was escorted by an imposing array of one thousand two hundred cavalrymen, hand-picked from *grenadiers à cheval, chasseurs,* dragoons and the *gendarmerie.*

Caffarelli, also convinced that flight spelt the end of the empire, says that: 'The cortège passed down the streets between serried masses of the people of Paris, and I saw many tear-stained faces'; while Saint Amand confirms that, 'This departure or, rather, disastrous flight made a most melancholy impression on the public, revealing as it did the full extent of the threat to Paris; and the gloom was even greater because hitherto government bulletins had spoken of only victories over the coalition forces . . .'

On March 29th Parisians had read in *Le Moniteur*: 'His Majesty the Emperor defeated General Witzengerode at St Dizier, taking two thousand prisoners, many cannon and baggage wagons. The enemy was pursued for some distance.'

There were no bulletins on March 30th, 31st or on April 1st. A proclamation of the czar's covered the front page on April 2nd.

And while the imperial government was winding towards Rambouillet, Chateaubriand noted: 'The head of the Russian columns, like the first ripple of the incoming tide on the shore, could be seen from Notre Dame's towers. I could understand what a Roman must have suffered when, from the Capitol, he saw Alaric's soldiers and the ancient Latin city at his feet, when I looked down on the Russian soldiers and the old city of the Gauls below me . . .'

Five hours after their arrival at Rambouillet, Catherine of Westphalia, Madame Mèri and Louis Bonaparte, ex-king of Holland, joined them. 'Louis,' (says Marie Louise) 'was in such a state of panic that he wanted to leave immediately for some fortress. I wouldn't hear of it; he was so demented that it was embarrassing.'

They were on the road early next morning – after another screaming fit on the part of the 'little king' – reaching Chartres without incident the same evening where, to Marie Louise's intense astonishment, she was rejoined by Joseph and Jerome. The former's presence, especially after his bombastic 'death or glory' declarations, revolted her. Their meeting was extremely frigid. Still without mishap, the journey continued on April 2nd, via Châteaudun and Vendôme, to Blois.

Though without incident, the last eight leagues to Blois were covered in supreme discomfort, in the almost record slow time of nine hours. Blinding rain had turned the road into a quagmire into which berlins and wagons alike sank axle deep. A spring broke on the empress's carriage. A wrong turning imposed the interminable process of turning the lumbering cortège about. Marie Louise kept thinking of those childhood flights from Vienna; only this time she was running away from her own people! With these imposed delays, darkness was falling by the time she found her lodgings in the Blois *préfecture*, a former bishop's palace.

Tired as she was, she wrote to Napoleon before going to bed. At Chartres she had received a scribbled word from the emperor telling her that Paris had fallen, and that he was concentrating what was left of the army at Fontainebleau. And at Vendôme, another note: 'My good Louise, I haven't had a letter from you. I fear you must be deeply affected by the loss of Paris. I beg you to be brave and watch over your health which is always so precious to me. Mine is good. Give the little King a kiss and love me always.'

Her reply ignored the tragedy of Paris's loss. His grief, that she could not doubt for a moment, aroused in her a desire to protect by distracting his mind to the object she knew was dearest to him: 'Your son embraces you' (she wrote) 'he was so wonderful on the journey. He is so cheerful, at such a happy age, I often envy him, he really is delightful and no trouble; he's such

185

a sweet amiable child that even people who have only just got to know him are enchanted by him.'

Marie Louise was not mistaken picturing Napoleon's distress on hearing of the allied entry into Paris and the garrison's surrender after a sharp, but brief, ill-planned, ill-led resistance; and it hurt him all the more that it was on Joseph's orders – his last act as 'lieutenant general of the empire' before his ignominious flight from the capital – that the white flag had been raised, giving Marshals Marmont and Mortier permission to negotiate the capitulation.

Foreseeing a general collapse and no longer able to put his trust in anyone, Napoleon had raced ahead of his army, accompanied by Caulaincourt, in a light carriage, after handing over to Berthier with orders to march without a halt straight for the capital. At half-past eleven, the night of the 30th (March), he had reached the posting stage of the *Cour de France*, a bare four leagues from Paris. Pacing up and down the road while the horses were being changed, he heard the sound of drumming hooves. A few seconds later, he made out the silhouettes of a considerable group of horsemen. Almost at once he recognised their leader. It was General Belliard, commander of Mortier's cavalry, who had broken through the enemy ring and was now riding hard to rejoin the emperor. Belliard has described this meeting:

' "What you, Belliard?" he (Napoleon) exclaimed. "What does this mean, you here with your cavalry? Where is the enemy?"

' "At the gates of Paris, sire!"

' "And the army?"

' "It is following me."

' "And who is guarding the capital? Where is the empress, my son?"

' "Paris has capitulated, Sire. The empress and your son are in security at Rambouillet."

'Napoleon was beside himself with fury. He railed against Joseph.

' "Joseph! That swine! That *Jean-foutre*! Clarke! That's what happens when I trust men who are gutless and without a scrap of commonsense in their make-up. If I'm not present myself, there's nothing but chaos, the most idiotic blunders. And Joseph! That dolt! I might have expected it. He lost me Spain, now he's losing me France!" '

186

Both Caulaincourt and Belliard had known Napoleon long enough to be well aware that there was no point in trying to break in on one of his tirades; but when he suddenly shouted for his carriage and announced his intention of driving straight into Paris, regardless of the situation, both were prepared to prevent him from carrying out this suicidal act, if necessary by force. Luckily, at this moment, other units of the remnants of Mortier's corps arrived so that, in his eagerness to find out the exact position, the emperor recovered something of his mental balance as he plied the senior officers with questions.

At last, realising that all was lost, he went back into the posting house followed by Caulaincourt and Belliard. The former tells how he spread his map on a wooden table and began to study it intensely, and how, after a long silence, he suddenly raised his head and shouted:

' "I've got them! I've got them! God has delivered them into my hands. But I must have a few days. Caulaincourt! You can give me these few days by negotiating. You will go to the emperor Alexander."

' "Sire," I (Caulaincourt) replied, "would it not be better to negotiate in all good faith and accept the Chatillon proposals, at least the main ones?"

' "No, no!" the Emperor answered. "No further humiliations! No shameful peace! This concerns France's greatness, her honour. This can only be settled by the sword. As for me I'm going to Fontainebleau to wait for you and the army, and to prepare to avenge France's momentary humiliation." '

At Fontainebleau Napoleon was encouraged in his belief by the soldiers' enthusiasm. Their shouts of '*Vive l'Empereur!*' had all the fervour of the eve of Austerlitz, and were mingled with cries of, '*A Paris! A Paris!*' His confidence was restored. Within a week he would be back in the Tuileries. Allied monarchs and commanders would be prisoners or in full flight; traitors facing trial.

This exultant mood lasted only a few hours. When the generals and marshals who had rallied at Fontainebleau were summoned to discuss the march on Paris, they rebelled unequivocally, refusing to contemplate such an operation. Again led by Ney, not only did they refuse to march, they demanded 'in the name of France' that Napoleon abdicate in his son's favour.

Even at this stage, if Napoleon had been prepared to arrest the ringleaders he might have saved his throne. There is every indication that there would have been no lack of volunteers for firing squads to deal with these upstart princes and dukes, thinking only of their titles and amassed wealth. But he was a tired man. One feels that in a way he was relieved by the *insurrection des grosses épaulettes*. Here was the excuse to claim that he had bowed to popular opinion rather than abandoned the party through cowardice, and to appeal to the sentimental side of the French nation to give unflinching loyalty to the regent and their three-year-old future emperor. As a result, the rebels were dismissed with scarcely a reproach.

At a further meeting the following day, the marshals renewed their threats and demands that France must be spared the horrors of civil war. Napoleon listened in silence, then looking round, fixing each in turn, said brusquely:

'All right, gentlemen. Since that is how matters stand, I abdicate.'

After calling for pen and paper, he wrote: 'The allied powers having declared that the Emperor Napoleon is the sole obstacle to the re-establishment of peace in Europe, the Emperor Napoleon, faithful to his oath, declares that he is ready to descend from the throne, to leave France, even to die, for the good of his country, inseparable from the rights of his son, from those of the Empress's Regency, and the maintenance of the laws of the Empire. At Fontainebleau, April 4th 1814.'

For both Napoleon and Marie Louise, tragic mistakes, misunderstandings, misfortune's cruellest blows, followed one another with a nightmarish, ever-accelerating rhythm during the next few days. Not only did these perversely unhappy factors complete the tottering empire's downfall, they also destroyed the bonds existing between husband and wife, wrecking the marriage as ruthlessly as they wrecked the embryonic dynasty. In these frantic days, the destinies of empire and matrimony were interlocked.

Napoleon longed for the comfort of his wife and son's companionship, but he had agreed to abdicate only on the assurance of his son's accession. For this he was forced to rely on allied good faith. If, therefore, he were to call his wife to his side, he feared that it might be thought that the abdication was no more than a tactical move to obtain a peace which, in turn, would provide him with the opportunity, behind the scenes, of preparing a war of revenge.

The immediate future must, therefore, be devoted to convincing the allies of his good faith and persuading the emperor Francis to back the continuation of the Napoleonic dynasty in the person of the infant Napoleon II, if necessary in face of British, Russian and Prussian opposition. With this in view, Napoleon had written on the 3rd, just before his stormy interview with the marshals, begging Marie Louise to send the strongest possible letter putting the situation to her father, and to entrust it to the hands of Champagny, duke of Cadore.*

She rose to the occasion. In fact, she exaggerated, pleading too much from weakness.

My very dear Papa,

Our situation is so miserable that you are the sole person to whom my son and I can turn. You, I am sure, are the only person who can help us. I am sure you will hear my prayers and not sacrifice the interest and well being of your grandson to England and Russia's cupidity. I know that the Duke of Vicenza has gone to Paris to negotiate and the Emperor Alexander refuses to receive him. I also know that at this critical moment the Emperor is prepared to make any sacrifice to obtain the peace so necessary for the happiness of all people. Paris would have been better defended if it had not been thought that it was being occupied with your connivance; we were convinced that you did not mean to abandon your grandson and your daughter. For this reason, my very dear Papa, I entrust you with our safety knowing that you will help us at this dreadful time. The Duke of Cadore will explain our situation even better than I could myself. My health is suffering severely from all these misfortunes, it deteriorates every day, and I'm sure you will not let me get to such a state that I prefer not to go on living. Once again, dear Papa, take pity on me. To you I entrust the fate of he who is most dear to me in this world, my son who is too young to understand our present woes, and who I hope to be able to tell one day that his actual happiness and good fortune are entirely due to your intervention . . .

* Champagny had been ambassador in Vienna, and the emperor Francis was godfather to one of his sons.

At the same time she longed to rejoin her husband. She mistrusted everyone in her entourage, with the exception of Dr Corvisart and the duchess of Montebello who, ironically, were the least trustworthy, the most hostile to the emperor.

It was not so far, a bare two hundred kilometres, from Blois to Fontainebleau, and at times she was tempted to call for a carriage and escort and take to the road. After all, she was the regent! But though the emperor was writing to her almost daily, there was no mention in his letters of their reunion. Fatally, for their mutual happiness, she might think, but never dared, to make an independent decision. She waited, praying for the order calling her to his side. It came eventually, but too late. Events were moving too fast to allow of procrastination or second thoughts.

Meanwhile, further disasters crowded in on Napoleon. Caulaincourt, accompanied by Berthier, Ney and Macdonald, was entrusted with the task of delivering the abdication act to the czar – the emperor Francis had not yet reached Paris, it was believed vaguely that he was 'somewhere in the east' – and to negotiate a definite statute for the regency and succession of Napoleon II. The delegation, joined en route by Marmont at Essonnes, had little difficulty in locating the czar who was a guest of Talleyrand. The czar, so Caulaincourt says, was in a most amiable mood, and even had a number of sympathetic remarks to make about Napoleon. On being told that Napoleon was willing to abdicate in favour of his son, and after bringing up a few 'minor' points, he said: 'I am not at all an advocate of the Bourbons. I don't know them. I shall put your propositions in front of my Allies, the King of Prussia and other Allied Ministers, and back them up. I am as anxious as you are to get everything settled.'

It was then decided that the next and, possibly, last session should be held at midday the following day. The meeting had gone better than Caulaincourt had dared to hope. It seemed as though the 'little king's' future was assured.

At eleven-thirty the next morning, just as the delegation was preparing to leave for their rendezvous with the czar, a messenger came to say that someone wished to speak most urgently, and in private, to the duke of Ragusa (Marmont). A few minutes later (according to Caulaincourt), Marmont returned, deadly pale.

Stammering, he told Caulaincourt, Ney and Macdonald that

his army corps, the 6th, led by its generals, had gone over to the allies during the night.

'My God,' he said, 'I would give my right arm to hear that this was not true.'

'Say your head,' snapped Ney, 'and it wouldn't be enough.'*

By this act of treachery the whole situation had changed radically. The 6th corps was composed mostly of veteran troops. They had fought well in front of Paris and had been exasperated when the 'cease fire' was ordered. Added to the forces concentrated at Fontainebleau they constituted a major threat to enemy-occupied Paris. Once they were neutralised the allies had nothing further to fear: Napoleon had lost his bargaining power. From now on the allies could dictate on a 'take it or leave it' basis. The czar, stable as a weathercock, was quick to react the moment the news was brought to him.

'After the defection of Essonnes, the Allied sovereigns no longer felt obliged to treat with Napoleon. So long as he had been at the head of fifty thousand men within a day's march of Paris, military conditions had outweighed intrigue. Now that Fontainebleau was no longer a threat, on account of Marmont's treachery, the whole aspect had changed, the time for being considerate had passed; abdication in favour of the regent and her son was no longer enough for a triumphant enemy, and the plenipotentiaries were told that Napoleon must renounce the throne, not only for himself, but also for his dynasty.'†

The czar tried to soften the blow. He mentioned, for the first time, that, in their generosity, the allies would be prepared to grant the late master of Europe the sovereignty of the island of Elba; and it was with this sop that, leaving Marmont, disconsolate, to rejoin his command, Caulaincourt, Ney and Macdonald reached Fontainebleau on the evening of the 5th.

Napoleon appeared strangely indifferent when the mission's

* Marmont could not really pretend to be shocked by the news. For several days he had been flirting with the allies and the Bourbons. He had been received by Talleyrand, and was discussing terms of surrender with Schwarzenberg. The senior generals of the army corps were well aware of these negotiations and the most senior, General Souham, was notoriously pro-Bourbon. There is no doubt that Souham, aware of Marmont's hesitation, took advantage of the marshal's absence to take the decisive step after opening a despatch, addressed 'Personal' to Marmont by Napoleon, calling him to attend a conference at Fontainebleau the following day.

† Imbère de Saint Amand. op. cit.

failure was reported. Like a man dazed, he shrugged his shoulders, making little or no comment about Marmont and the 6th corps, showing only a spark of interest at the mention of Elba.

This indifference may have been a blind for he spent the night studying his maps and trying to work out a last desperate plan to save the throne for his son. There were still a number of scattered garrisons who, he was sure, would remain loyal, would fight if called upon to do so; Soult, one of his best leaders, still had an army of between fifty and sixty thousand men intact in the south, round Toulouse, Augereau another fifteen thousand; another twenty thousand were scattered along the Rhine and at Fontainebleau itself there were his fanatically loyal veterans of the guard.

In the early morning he called another meeting of the marshals, proposing that they should retire immediately behind the Loire, there to prepare a lightning counter-attack. The proposition was received in dismayed silence, followed by an indignant chorus of protest. Even Caulaincourt was not prepared to support him. Tired, disgusted, he abandoned the struggle and signed a second act of abdication, more or less a copy of the first, but with this vital alteration: '. . . the Emperor Napoleon declares that he renounces *for himself and his house* the thrones of France and Italy . . .'

And yet, as Baron Fain, one of those present, says: 'If only Napoleon had walked out of the conference room into the adjoining hall crammed with junior officers, he would have found this crowd of young men eager to follow him! A few steps further, and he would have been received at the foot of the stairs by the cheers of his soldiers! Their enthusiasm would have restored his hopes! But Napoleon was the victim of his own régime; he imagined that he would have been degrading himself if he were to march without the high-ranking officers of his own creation . . .'

However, he did remark bitterly to Caulaincourt: 'I'm humiliated by the thought that men I have raised so high could fall so low. Anything that dishonours France is like a personal affront. I've identified myself with her to such a degree . . .'

Again his thoughts were with his wife and son.

The same day that he signed his unconditional abdication, he wrote:

Adam Albert von Neipperg

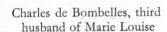

Charles de Bombelles, third
husband of Marie Louise

Marie Louise when Duchess of Parma

My good Louise,

I have received your letter and am happy to learn that your health is standing up under the strain. I was afraid that the distressing events of these days might have upset it. I'm most worried for you and for my son and, as you can imagine, a little for myself as well. My health is good. Kiss my son and write every day to your father, so that he knows where you are. Goodbye, dear Louise, my heart groans at the thought of your sorrow. All yours,

Nap.

Next day, however, under the impression that Marie Louise would be rejoining him as a result of the abdication, he sent a guard's cavalry officer, Colonel Galbois, to Blois with orders to deliver a much longer, more detailed letter personally to the Empress, as she still was in name:

My friend, I'm very pleased to see from your letter of the 7th that your health is better than might be expected. An armistice has been concluded and one of the Emperor of Russia's A.D.C.s will be reporting to you to escort you here; but I think it would be better if you halted at Orleans, as I'm on the point of departure. I'm waiting till Caulaincourt has made all the final arrangements with the Allies. Russia wants me to have the sovereignty of the Island of Elba, and I would take up residence there, and for you Tuscany, to be inherited after you by your son, and this would have meant we could be near to each other without your having to endure a bad climate which could do you considerable harm. But Schwarzenberg, in your father's name, is objecting to this. It would appear that your father is our most ferocious enemy. So I don't know what has been agreed upon finally. I'm sad that all I can do for you is to oblige you to share my ill fortune. I would indeed have taken leave of this life had I not thought that by so doing I would only be increasing your sorrows . . .

There follows a list of 'gratuities' to be distributed to Joseph, Jerome, his mother (a million francs apiece), and to Pauline and Elisa (six hundred thousand francs), followed in turn by some personal instructions concerning the household and, finally:

Goodbye, my good Louise, I really feel very sorry for you.
Write to your father asking for Tuscany for yourself, as for
me I'm quite happy with Elba.
Goodbye, my friend. Kiss your son.

(Unsigned)

During these critical days, Marie Louise was living in a complete
vacuum at Blois. Still retaining an implicit faith in her husband
and her father, she had not the slightest idea that she had become
an empress without a throne, that her empire was limited
to the periphery of the little town of Blois itself. Recovered
from the journey's fatigue, she made some attempt at revival
of court life, and went so far as to have a proclamation
printed, of which she was most proud* but which was never
distributed:

Frenchmen. Due to the fortunes of war the capital is in the
hands of foreigners. The Emperor, who has hastened to
defend it, is at the head of his victorious armies. It is from
the residence that I have chosen, and from the Emperor's
ministers, that will be issued the only orders you must obey.
Every city in enemy hands is no longer a free city. You will
remain faithful to your vows; you must listen to the voice
of a Princess entrusted to your loyal care, who glories in
being a Frenchwoman, and in sharing the destinies of the
sovereign chosen by yourselves. My son was not more sure of
your hearts even in the days of our prosperity. His rights,
his person, are under your protection.

As a result of having been kept in quasi-ignorance of the facts,
she was all the more appalled when she learned about the two
abdications from Colonel Galbois who, though officially only
the bearer of Napoleon's letter, almost certainly opened her eyes
to the true situation. Galbois himself says: 'I reached Blois early
and the Empress received me at once. She was greatly surprised
by the Emperor's abdication. She could not believe that the
Allied sovereigns meant to dethrone Napoleon.
' "My father," she insisted, "would not allow it; he told me
at least a dozen times when he placed me on the French throne

* Its wording is attributed to Cambacères.

194

that he would always maintain me there, and my father is an honest man."

'The Empress then asked to be left alone to think over the Emperor's letter. I then saw the King of Spain and the King of Westphalia. Joseph was deeply afflicted, but Jerome was very violently against Napoleon. Marie Louise then sent for me and said she wished to go to the Emperor. I told her this was impossible.

'Her Majesty then said sharply, "Why so, Colonel? You can do it! My place is at the Emperor's side when he is unhappy. I desire to go to him."

'I told the Empress how difficult it had been for me to reach Blois, and how I anticipated that the return journey would be even more hazardous. Indeed it was a most perilous journey. It was only with difficulty that the Empress was induced to change her mind, but at last she decided to write.

'I was able to reach the Emperor without being held up. He read Marie Louise's letter with the utmost eagerness and seemed much touched by it. The Empress had spoken, apparently, of the possibility of collecting one hundred and fifty thousand men. The Emperor read this passage aloud, then said to me:

' "Yes! Doubtless I could prolong the campaign and perhaps even in the end be victorious, but it would mean starting a civil war and that I refuse to do . . . Besides, I have signed my abdication and will not go back on my word." '

The shock was all the more brutal because of its suddenness but, as at the time of her youthful flights from the man who was now her husband, the tough streak dormant in Marie Louise showed itself; loyalty was her dominant emotion. Her husband was in distress, perhaps even in danger. Her rightful place, therefore, was by his side.

As Galbois himself pointed out, he refused to let the empress accompany him on his return to Fontainebleau because he considered the roads too unsafe. The threat to her person, however, did not deter her. If Galbois could risk the journey, she argued, then so could she. It was only when the Colonel mentioned that the king of Rome would also be involved in the hazards of the road that she asked – or rather ordered – Galbois to wait while she shut herself up in her room to try to make up her mind.

Once more, events which could have changed the course of history hung in the balance.

As soon as Marie Louise reached her bedroom she sent for Madame de Luçay, the lady of the wardrobe. The countess was loyal to the empire. She urged Marie Louise to hurry to Fontainebleau, stating categorically that in her opinion it was the empress's duty to rejoin her husband. At the critical moment, the duchess of Montebello knocked at the door and demanded to be let in. Immediately, the empress told Madame de Luçay to wait in an adjoining room from which, however, Madame de Luçay was able to hear only too well with what perfidious art the empress was induced to change her mind.

Unlike the lady of the wardrobe, the duchess of Montebello, together with so many other Napoleon-created dignitaries, was backing the hand of the Bourbons. Though a woman of irreproachable virtue, she had fallen completely under Dr Corvisart's influence and he, for some extraordinary reason delighting in his master's downfall, was in touch with both the czar and Schwarzenberg, happy to adopt the role of saboteur of any plan or project which might alleviate Napoleon's misery or strengthen his position. Knowing his influence at court, Metternich had requested him to ensure, if humanly possible, that the empress and the king of Rome did not rejoin the emperor. In the execution of this order, he found in the duchess a willing lieutenant and, since in turn the duchess's influence over Marie Louise was undiminished, Galbois – admittedly much to his relief – left Blois alone. Marie Louise, probably torn by remorse, gave way to a fit of near hysterics described as 'a practically convulsive state of nerves' and, Masson adds, a little unfairly one feels considering the circumstances: 'Her duty, her heart, called her to Fontainebleau; her personal interests, her *indolence* and her health retained her at Blois.'

By now Joseph and Jerome were thoroughly frightened. They could see themselves destitute exiles in the very near future. They may even have had occasional mental pictures of the scaffold or a firing squad. As neither was gifted with overmuch intelligence, they reacted with something of the blind stupidity one might expect of a trapped animal.

They had found out that a Russian A.D.C. was expected that morning to escort the empress either to Fontainebleau or to Paris, and decided to act before his arrival. It did not suit their plans that Marie Louise and the 'little king' should, for the moment, be either with the allies or Napoleon. As they saw it, she and her son provided them with a bargaining handle. What they planned was, therefore, more or less a kidnapping. With this in view, on the morning of the 8th they forced their way into the empress's apartments, booted and spurred, told the startled Marie Louise that Blois was likely to fall into enemy hands at any moment and that they must leave immediately for some – they were not even specific – place south of the Loire and there set up the seat of government to which, they insisted, the majority of the French people would rally. Something in their manner – fortunately for both Marie Louise and the brothers – alarmed the empress. Never having trusted them and always on the worst of terms with Jerome, it was probably instinctive. For once in her life she showed herself recalcitrant.

There are two rather contradictory eye-witness versions of this scene; those of Baron de Bausset – the same de Bausset who had welcomed the young empress four years ago on her arrival at Braunau – and of Marie Louise herself.

De Bausset in his memoirs states that the two kings wished to carry their sister-in-law off to some vague destination south of the Loire. He says that he heard voices raised and was then summoned by the empress who, after stressing her confidence in him, said: 'I count on your devotion . . . my two brothers (*sic*) have just told me that I must leave Blois at once and that if I resist they will force me and my son into the carriage.'

'May I ask Your Majesty,' I replied, 'what is your wish?'

'I wish to remain here and wait for the Emperor's orders.'

'In that case, Madame, I venture to assure Your Majesty that all the officers of your Household and of your guard will agree with me that we receive orders from you alone. I beg Your Majesty's permission to go and announce your wishes.'

De Bausset (always according to his memoirs) duly informed the guard officers, most of whom had little liking for the imperial brothers. Immediately they came clattering up the stairs declaiming their loyalty to the empress. Trying to calm Jerome's almost uncontrollable rage Joseph, tight-lipped, drawn, turned to de Bausset and stammered, referring to the officers:

'Repeat the words they used.'

'Their words would not make agreeable hearing,' I (de Bausset) replied. 'Besides, the uproar in the next room surely conveys their meaning to your majesties.'

'Hardly were the words out of my mouth,' he continues, 'than the doors were burst open and the officers came crowding in, expressing with enthusiasm the sentiments I had already mentioned.'

Marie Louise's version of this incident was rather different, as is obvious from this letter to her husband: 'King Joseph told me I must hurry away to hand myself over to the nearest Austrian corps. He told me that they (he and Jerome) would follow and that this was our only remaining hope of safety, and that there was no time to consult you and that in any case you might not approve. I replied that in my opinion such an action would be a betrayal on my part and that so long as I could still draw breath I would remain faithful to you, and that furthermore I was not at all sure that the Russians were not considerably nearer, and that I did not wish to abandon myself to *their* mercies. They said that I was talking nonsense and the King of Westphalia threatened to use force if necessary to get me to leave. After that I decided I would go as far as Rambouillet but no further. However, just as they were about to give orders for our departure, the officers of the Guard intervened saying they would not tolerate my being obliged to leave and that they were ready to be carved up into small pieces for you, your son and for me, that they knew the idea was to oblige me to give myself up to the Austrians, but without your orders or mine they refused to allow this, and that if your brothers were frightened, all they had to do was to get out as soon as possible. I managed to calm them down, and they left saying they were ready to die rather than desert your son. I then told the Kings that there was no question of my leaving, and that I was waiting for your orders. They were furious, but it left me indifferent. These tantrums cannot affect me. I am waiting for your orders and implore you to send them to me . . .'

Whichever may be the correct version, there is no ambiguity about the sequel.

Shortly after this scene, a Russian envoy, Count Shuvaloff, arrived, accompanied by Caulaincourt's brother-in-law, Baron de Saint Aignan, Napoleon's master of horse, mentioned sometimes, maliciously, as *un ami intime* of the duchess of Montebello.

Shuvaloff showed no respect for the so-called government assembled at Blois. He made it brutally clear that his orders must be obeyed without question, and that he had come to take possession of the persons of the empress and her son and to escort them to Rambouillet – there was no mention of Fontainebleau.

From this moment, and not at the time of the Leipzig catastrophe, one can make out the first chink in the armour of Marie Louise's almost blind love for, her rigid fidelity to, her husband.

The stress of the last few days had been almost unbearable, the rough awakening to reality a terrible deception, the scene with her brothers-in-law a mental shock subconsciously engendering a violent anti-Bonaparte, even unfairly anti-French reaction, imperceptible as a tiny shoot to begin with but flowering with the rapidity of a tropical weed.

She still thought that all she wanted was to hurry to Fontainebleau, but that same evening (April 8th) she called for de Bausset,'giving him a letter for her father who, she said, she 'hoped' was in Paris, and asking him to ride off with it straight away.

Since Shuvaloff's arrival, she had further reasons to feel disgusted with her adopted people.

The count's overbearing manner brought home to the Blois sycophants that the days of the imperial regime were not merely numbered but past. Oaths of loyalty were forgotten. There was a mad stampede for the *Mairie* where Shuvaloff was signing papers necessary for anyone wishing to return to Paris. It was a veritable *sauve qui peut* of the former imperial dignitaries who could not wait to throw themselves – some indeed literally – at the feet of the newly-established provisional government. It is hardly surprising then that there was a note of panic, combined with disdain, in the two letters which Marie Louise wrote to her father – one written before, the other after Shuvaloff's arrival – which she entrusted to de Bausset: 'My situation is really terrible; I'm really worried about my son's and my own safety; they say that Czernicheff is in the neighbourhood with three thousand Cossacks; he is on a secret mission which is, I am convinced, to take us prisoner. I beg of you, my dear Papa, if something dreadful happens, to allow us to take refuge in your estates with some of my household who have remained faithful to me in this moment of misery and who, I assure you, will not be a burden to you. All I long for is to be able to live peacefully somewhere in your estates and bring up my son. God knows I will warn him against the pitfalls of ambition . . .'

The second letter, slightly calmer, was, nevertheless, equally indicative: 'I send you Baron de Bausset who will be able to depict to you my terrible plight. Today I received Baron de Saint

199

Aignan and Count Shuvaloff who explained the Emperor's present position to me. I am not asking you to intervene on his behalf; it is for myself and my son, especially the latter. I am quite certain you would not wish the Island of Elba to be his unique heritage. I am sure you will defend his rights and see that a better future is reserved for him. My one desire is that you should see this unhappy child who is innocent of his father's errors. He does not deserve to share so sad a fate. I do not doubt that you will defend both him and me. Tomorrow I leave for Fontainebleau; all I ask is to be left in peace and not to be so tormented. I am very ill, and fear I am getting worse; I have terrible chest pains and am spitting blood. My anxiety has completely ruined my health and I am afraid to undertake a long journey. I commend my unhappy son to your care. I know he cannot count on France. I beg of you if possible, to obtain some other territory for him . . .'

For the first time Marie Louise refers to her husband in terms other than of adulation and deepest affection. She mentions the 'pitfalls of ambition', and even more surprising evidence of this lightning *volte face* is the reference to 'his father's errors', when, till that moment, she had always made it plain that in her eyes 'the emperor' was infallible. It is difficult to believe that this second letter could have been written within a few hours of that in which she had told Napoleon of her defiance of the brothers and assured him that 'as long as I can still draw breath I will remain faithful to you'. Puzzling, also, is the reference to her departure for Fontainebleau the following day. It appears in complete contradiction with her pleas to be allowed to find a quiet spot in her father's 'estates'. The fact is that at that moment she was both bewildered and frightened. Duty to her husband, perhaps even love, was still deeply rooted. Though she could not have meant that she was going direct to Fontainebleau after Napoleon's letter – 'It would be better if you halted at Orléans'* – there was no real doubt in her mind that Fontainebleau must be her eventual destination. She had no inkling that allies, Bourbons and ex-imperialists alike were determined to prevent this reunion at all costs, and that the letter she had given de Bausset would prove a valuable weapon in their hands. As a contemporary put it: 'Though she did not know it, this Good Friday (April 8th) was the empress's last day of freedom.'

* see p. 193.

This day, which must have seemed the longest in her life, closed on a last note of disillusionment.

The duchess of Montebello was furious when Shuvaloff told her that for the time being there was no question of her being allowed to return to Paris or of relinquishing her position as Marie Louise's *dame d'honneur*, so furious that she rounded on the empress, saying:

'How I'm longing for all this to be over and done with. All I want is to get back to my children and my lovely little house in the rue d'Enfer.'

Coming from the adored Montebello, it was like a slap across the face. Marie Louise replied brokenly, 'You've just said a very cruel thing to me, Duchess,' and burst into tears.

The much-reduced cortège set out early next morning for Orléans. Before leaving, the punctilious de Menéval burnt all the secret documents for which he was responsible, convinced that Fontainebleau was not, despite vague promises, their true destination. At the same time, determined to carry on the imperial tradition to the end, he left three thousand francs with the mayor as the emperor's gift to the poor.

Near Beauregency, the wagons transporting what was left of the imperial treasure were attacked by a 'hurra' of cossacks. The last two wagons had been almost entirely stripped of their contents before Shuvaloff himself, at a certain amount of personal risk, was able to exercise enough authority not only to persuade the cossacks to stop their looting but to replace what they had already loaded on to their horses.

Certain, after this incident, that they would have their throats cut or at least be raped, Marie Louise and her ladies sat shivering in their carriages until Orléans was reached at six in the evening. Marie Louise, who was again being lodged in the old bishop's palace, was, for the last time, received with the honours due to her as empress. From the city gates to the palace, the road was lined with troops, while the prefect of the Loire waited at the foot of the palace steps.*

In many ways, the days spent at Orléans were more harrowing

* De Menéval noted that the few citizens of Orléans who had collected in the streets watched the procession go by in a stony, significant silence. Only in the square itself was an occasional cry of '*Vive l'Empéreur!*' heard.

than those passed at Blois. Marie Louise was unable to maintain the stubborn courage in the face of adversity which at first had stood her in such good stead since the flight from Paris. She shut herself up in her apartments, was frequently in tears, and never stopped complaining about her health in between frenzied bouts of letter-writing. She was lost. More than ever she longed for someone – she was past caring who – to make up her mind for her.

This was Napoleon's last chance. Had he sent her a definite order to drive immediately to Fontainebleau, she would have obeyed promptly and joyously. But at this vital stage the emperor did not feel such a step morally justified. He could not, he felt, *order* his wife and son to share his misfortunes.

'Caesar can become an ordinary citizen,' he remarked to Caulaincourt, 'but it is not easy for his wife to renounce being Caesar's consort.'

Worse, such an order might expose them to actual danger since rumours of assassination plots circulated freely. On the other hand, as he said frequently on St Helena, he would have been overjoyed had she taken matters into her own hands and come to him on her own initiative. Yet it is difficult to see how he could have hoped for such a psychological miracle since even after he had himself appointed her regent he had insisted that her every gesture be dependent on his direct intervention.

Tragically, Marie Louise continued to pray that each letter would bring these longed-for orders. According to Savary, she complained bitterly to him: 'I really am to be pitied. Some tell me to leave' (for Fontainebleau) 'others to stay. I write to the Emperor and he doesn't even answer my questions; he just tells me to write to my father. Ah! My father! What can he have to say after the scandalous way he has allowed people to treat me. I'm abandoned and I put myself in the hands of Providence. I would have done better to have taken the veil. That would have been far better than coming to this country.

'Go to the Emperor? I can't go without my son. I'm responsible for him. On the other hand if the Emperor fears that an attempt is to be made on his life, as seems probable, and he will have to fly, if he were burdened with me it might well be the cause of his falling into his enemies' hands. I don't know what to do. I spend most of my time in tears.

'I understand the people of this country don't like me, but it's not my fault, and why did my father make me marry if he meant to behave like this?'

This outburst was, apparently, inspired by a letter she had just received from her father, brought by Champagny, duke of Cadore, who had at last run the Austrian emperor to earth at Chanceaux where he was hovering impotently in the background while Schwarzenberg and Metternich parleyed, in his name, with the czar and the king of Prussia. 'I've no complaints to make about my son-in-law.' (wrote Francis) 'On the contrary I'm deeply grateful to him for having made my daughter so happy. At the cost of my own blood I would like to see this happiness continue. Such are my paternal sentiments. As an Emperor, I must tread the path of duty. I have entered into an alliance with other sovereigns, and this alliance obliges me to align myself with their decisions. As yet I cannot say what they will be. I have sent Metternich to find out. Whatever they may be, I must abide by them and help in their execution, but I am deeply distressed by my son-in-law's misfortunes . . .'

This remarkable example of moral cowardice would have been condemnation enough of Francis's incapacity to exercise his role of monarch. In fact, his behaviour was even more despicable. At the same time that he had composed this hypocritical, crocodile-tear-jerking missive, he had written to Metternich: 'The important thing is to see that Napoleon is banished from France and, please God, the further the better. I don't approve of the choice of Elba as Napoleon's residence. It's *part of Tuscany, and this means part of my territory is being disposed of in favour of a foreigner*. I really cannot permit this sort of thing in future. Furthermore, Napoleon will be far too close to Europe . . .'

Duped by her father's pretended commiseration, Marie Louise bombarded him with letters, while further unfortunate incidents served to fan her newly acquired hatred of the French and fear for her own safety.

She now saw the French as shallow and treacherous, one and all imbued with evil designs on herself and her son. This nagging fear inspired her to write: 'My very dear Papa. I'm sending this letter by hand of one of my officers to implore you to give me permission to come to you. The Emperor is leaving for Elba and I am telling him that I cannot possibly go with him till I have seen you and listened to your advice. I beg you therefore to answer me. Every day my position becomes more critical and more alarming. *There is a plot afoot to force me to leave against my will.* I implore you to send me your answer as soon as possible, *because I'm nearly dead with fear . . .'*

She was also by now almost completely isolated. On Easter Monday (the 11th), after congratulating her on her promised accession to the duchy of Parma,* the few remaining members of her suite took leave of her as briefly as possible before hurrying to their carriages and heading for Paris. Cambacérès was not among them. He had avoided this painful farewell by the simple expedient of by-passing Orléans, going direct from Blois to the capital.

As a crowning insult, a certain Monsieur Dudon,† personal enemy of Napoleon, arrived in Orléans, accompanied by a band of thugs, armed with the provisional government's authority to seize what remained of the treasure and all objects of any value still in Marie Louise's hands.

According to Saint Amand: 'The Provisional Government needed money and decided on this legalised robbery on the pretence that the objects in question were State property, which was not the case . . . Nothing was respected, neither the plate which was the Empress's personal property, nor the diamond rings and snuff-boxes intended for presents. All Napoleon's clothing, even his handkerchiefs marked with an N, were seized. The Provisional Government's envoy was still not satisfied. He also seized the scanty service meant for the Empress and the King of Rome, not leaving one dish, so that it was necessary to borrow dishes and even china. General (*sic*) Shuvaloff, whose help was solicited, did nothing. As a final gesture Dudon demanded the pearl necklace, Napoleon's gift to his wife the evening their son was born. She was wearing it. Without a word, she undid the clasp, threw it on the ground and turned her back on him.'

Meanwhile, Dr Corvisart, terrified that if Marie Louise did decide to become empress of Elba he might be expected to accompany her, was playing successfully on her aggravated hypochondria. In an excessively long report on the actual state of her majesty's health, he wrote: 'The health of the Empress has been deteriorating markedly as a result of the Emperor's departure and the daily evolution of events. Frequent spasms are

* News of this had just filtered through from Paris.
† A government official, he had been imprisoned for fraud.

affecting the chest, in particular causing a shortage of breath, at times approaching suffocation, accompanied by disturbing expectorations, due to a painful spot situated in the middle of the chest both in front of and between the shoulders which, in turn, is due to the conformation of this region which has given me the most serious reasons for alarm ever since Her Majesty's physical condition and health have been confided to me.

'After this brief exposé to which I deem it unnecessary to add further medical details, I feel I would be gravely at fault if I did not state that in my opinion Her Majesty cannot undertake a long and tiring journey in her present state of nervous and physical debility, without risking bringing on an even more serious chest condition such as would be difficult, if not impossible to cure ... It is imperative that the Empress should for some definite period of time, be able to enjoy absolute physical rest and tranquillity in some suitable spot where she can follow a rigid course of treatment ...'

This report was sent to Napoleon while Corvisart was assuring the empress that the only watering-place which could do her any good in her alarming state was Aix-en-Savoie; that the Mediterranean sun would prove almost as deadly as a bullet in the heart, and that this stigma applied to *all* Italian spas. He was even able to coin a convenient catch phrase deeply impressing his willing dupe: 'Aix spells salvation: Elba, death.'

Napoleon was just as much taken in by the doctor's eloquence as was Marie Louise, and even wrote by return courier:

My good Louise. I'm so glad Corvisart is giving you courage. Tell him that his noble behaviour more than justifies my confidence in him. Tell him to send me word of your health as often as possible, and try to get to Aix, as he advises, as soon as possible. Keep well. Try to preserve your health for the sake of your husband and son who both need you. I will write to you from Elba where I will be making preparations to greet you ...'

Corvisart's report finally decided Marie Louise. She redoubled her exhortations begging her father to receive her, but promised Napoleon, somewhat half-heartedly, to hurry to Elba *after* she had seen her father and taken the cure.

That evening Francis's long-awaited reply arrived, carried by two high-ranking Austrian noblemen, Prince Esterhazy and Prince Wenzel of Lichtenstein. She was a little disappointed that the letter Esterhazy handed her was from Metternich, but it brought the news she wanted to hear. Metternich assured her that the emperor, his master, was overjoyed at the thought of seeing his beloved daughter once more and of meeting his grandson for the first time. He then went on to say, almost casually, that perhaps the best arrangement under the circumstances would be for her to return to Austria with her son and then make up her mind whether she wished to reside in her own, or Napoleon's estates. 'The Emperor Francis' (the letter continued) 'will be able to enjoy the happiness of helping to dry those tears which you have had only too great reason to shed, Madame. Your Majesty will be at peace and be able to decide your own future freely . . .'

The arrival of the Austrian envoys and Metternich's letter coincided with that of a message from Napoleon, brought by Madame de Montesquiou's son Anatole, former A.D.C. of the French emperor and, like his mother, a staunch imperialist. This message confirmed the 'arrangements' made by the allied powers for their future: 'Elba is being given to me, and for you and your son Parma, Plaisance (Piacenza) and Guastalla. You will thus have a Court of your own and a delightful country to retire to when your stay in my island of Elba begins to weary you, and I begin to bore you, which must inevitably happen as I grow old and you still remain young. Metternich is in Paris. I don't know where your father is. You should arrange to see him en route . . .'

As well as of Metternich's letter, the two Austrian princes were also bearers of the strictest instructions to escort the empress to Rambouillet where, they said, her father would be waiting for her. She was profoundly shocked when, still wishing, perhaps, to show that she was mistress in her own home, she pretended to hesitate, saying that before leaving Orléans she really ought to wait for her husband's permission to do so, she received an undisguisedly brutal reply from Esterhazy to the effect that she had no choice in the matter. She must have realised her true position from that moment, for that night she wrote miserably to Fontainebleau: 'I told them' (the princes) 'that I couldn't leave without your consent and they said they couldn't wait and that even if I wished to leave with you before seeing my father they had instructions to prevent me doing so. I saw then that I had no other course than to obey and submit with a good grace though the thought of leaving without seeing you fills me with despair . . . Please don't be angry with me my dear friend, it's not my fault, and I love you so much that my heart is breaking; I'm so frightened that you may think this is all a plot between my father and myself . . .'

Now that the final step was to be forced on her, she was more vacillating than ever, regretting her insistence on seeing her father, terrified by this dawning revelation of its probable consequences and of her lost liberty, tormented at the same time by a feeling of semi-justifiable guilt. As if to purge her conscience, with growing hysteria she continued: 'I want to share your misfortunes, I want to look after you, console you, soften your grief. Your son who does not understand all this is happy, poor little boy; only he and you can make my life bearable. I am taking him with me and feel sure he will touch my father's heart and I will be able to bring him back to you, because I want to be with you; the more people try to separate us, the more I long to be near you and look after you . . .'

Her sudden despair, prophetic repentance for the as yet unformed future were too late. The following morning, the still further reduced cortege left Orléans, travelling all day and all night till Rambouillet was reached the following midday, the 13th.

Napoleon must have had a sudden premonition of disaster. Making up his mind after so much hesitation, so many hopes based on Marie Louise's non-existent will, he sent a detachment of the old guard under General Cambronne – later to win immortality by his use of the word *Merde* at Waterloo – to Orléans to bring back the empress and the king of Rome. Cambronne arrived a few hours too late. Marie Louise and her son, virtually prisoners, were already heading for Rambouillet.

Chapter XI

The morning of the 11th, Baron de Bausset* presented himself at Fontainebleau. He had just arrived from Paris where, learning that the emperor Francis was still hesitant about setting foot in the capital, he had managed to obtain an interview with Prince Metternich. The latter had confided in him that Napoleon was to be allowed to retire to Elba, retaining his title of Emperor, and Marie Louise was to be given the duchy of Parma.

'Never perhaps did he' (Napoleon) 'seem greater,' the baron wrote in his memoirs. 'I spoke to him about Elba. He knew already that he was to be given this petty sovereignty. He even went into a few geographical details and statistics. "The air is healthy," he said, "and the people kindly. I shall not be too badly off, and I hope Marie Louise will find it comfortable." He knew all about the obstacles to their meeting in Fontainebleau, but hoped that once in possession of the Duchy of Parma, the Empress and her son would be permitted to live with him in Elba.'

Just before leaving, the baron recalls that Napoleon was reviewing recent events and uttered extremely significant words, all the more so in view of the drama of the following day: ' "See what fate is! At the battle of Arcis-sur-Aube, I did all I could to court a glorious death incessantly. Bullets rained about me; my clothes were ripped by them, but not one touched me. For me to die by my own hand would be cowardice. Suicide is contrary to my principles, to the position I occupy on the world's stage. I am a man condemned to live." '

Next day Caulaincourt, Ney and Macdonald, who had taken Napoleon's second abdication to Paris, arrived back with a copy of the peace treaty. In the circumstances, its terms were generous. There was official confirmation regarding Elba and Parma, and the fact that Napoleon was to be allowed to maintain a small

* From his memoirs, de Bausset seems to wish to give the impression that he was one of the devoted few. His actions prove, on the contrary, that he was a fervid on-the-fence sitter.

standing army of some 1,500 men, and confirmation – on paper at any rate – of generous pensions allotted to all the members of the imperial family, which sums included three hundred thousand francs per annum to Madame Mère and, surprisingly, a million to the ex-empress Josephine. In addition to two millions a year to Napoleon himself, a further two millions were placed at the emperor's disposal for gifts, a sort of legacy to be granted during the testator's lifetime.

Yet to Napoleon it spelled the end. He could not translate the document before him as an apparently open-handed gesture indicating the path of honourable retirement: to him at that moment of unrelieved bitterness it was the supreme humiliation. Elba after Europe; a bare thousand men after the *Grande Armée*; a vague promise of succession to an obscure Italian duchy for his son who had been born king of Rome. Even with the aura of glory dissipated, he could perhaps have settled down to domesticity, a semi-bourgeois family existence, but news had just reached him that Cambronne had arrived too late. His wife, his son, were hurrying to place themselves in the power of the father-in-law who had turned against him, betrayed the blood ties which should have been sacred. Napoleon the realist saw all too clearly that hopes of a family reunion were now more than slender, even though to the outer world and even to himself the pretence that this separation was only temporary would be kept up for more than a year.

As if this were not enough, Ney and Berthier rushed back to Paris, for 'personal' reasons they said. The deposed emperor was not deceived; they could not wait to re-affirm their protestations of loyalty and devotion to the provisional government.

The wave of desertion was infectious. By evening, both Constant and the supposedly devoted oriental, Rustom the Mameluke, had slunk away. To Caulaincourt, who stayed with him, last symbol of loyalty, he kept repeating, 'My life is unbearable.'

After an evening meal which he scarcely touched, and a few sips of brandy, he wrote a hurried letter to Marie Louise which he handed to Caulaincourt at three o'clock in the morning before saying that he was going to try to sleep:

My good Louise, I have had your letter and approve your departure for Rambouillet as your father will be joining you there. It is perhaps the only consolation available to you at this moment of our misfortunes. I've been waiting impatiently for this moment for the last eight days. Your father has been led astray and has done us great harm, but he will be a good father for you and your son. Caulaincourt has arrived. I sent you yesterday a copy of the arrangements, signed by him, regarding your son's future. Farewell, my sweet Louise. You are the one I love most in the world. And my misfortunes only hurt me because they hurt you, too. All your life, love and cherish the most tender of husbands. Give your son a kiss. Farewell my Louise. All yours, Napoleon.*

Disgusted, Napoleon had made up his mind to take his own life. Before setting off on his hazardous journey from Smorgoni to Paris, he had hung a small dose of poison round his neck. From that time he had been in the habit of keeping it by him constantly. His *valet de chambre*, Hubert, said that he saw the emperor get up, pour something into a glass, add a little water, then swallow the mixture and go back to bed.

Shortly afterwards Hubert was awakened by the sound of alternate retching and groans. Terrified, he rushed off to look for Dr Yvan, the same who had helped Corvisart at the time of the 'little king's' birth. As Yvan arrived, Napoleon murmured something about 'a stronger dose'. Guessing what had happened, Yvan forced an emetic down the emperor's throat and then, as Caulaincourt came into the room, lost his head and fled, saying there was nothing further he could do.†

His first reaction had, however, been efficacious. After being violently sick, Napoleon stopped groaning. The pains ceased.

'Even death betrays me,' he said weakly to Caulaincourt, repeating, 'I am condemned to live.'

Marie Louise knew nothing of this drama, but her fears increased as they arrived at Rambouillet. The château gardens swarmed with Russian troops. One would have said it resembled a heavily guarded prison rather than a royal palace. When, thoroughly alarmed, she demanded to be shown immediately into her father's

* This letter was never delivered but was found in Caulaincourt's archives.
† Hubert mentions that at the time he heard Yvan say, 'You would make me a poisoner, an assassin in the pay of your enemies. No! I will not do it!'

presence, she was told roughly by Prince Esterhazy that her father would not arrive for at least three days and that while waiting she had better remain in the palace as he 'could not be responsible for the actions of the Russian soldiers'.

Now, at last, Marie Louise understood that she was a prisoner, and again regretted her lack of initiative in not defying all restraint and setting out for Fontainebleau.

During the three interminable days she waited, she was the victim of a plot which in the annals of history has few equals for sheer, blatant, cynical immorality. Having separated Marie Louise physically from her husband, and since this separation was considered vital in the interests of peace, the Powers – acting, so it is claimed, on Metternich's advice, prompted by Dr Corvisart – approved a plan to make the separation not only physical but sentimental, to destroy the bonds of love and affection still uniting the unfortunate couple.

The principal instrument was, once more, the spiteful duchess of Montebello who, with details supplied by Dr Corvisart, filled Marie Louise's ears with the most lurid stories of her husband's 'love life'.

'Without the slightest compunction she did not hesitate to reveal all the Emperor's infidelities. What an evil pleasure she must have taken, the Lady of Honour, who claimed to be speaking "with the utmost frankness" in telling these intimate stories, revealing the existence of illegitimate children. And, in order to finish off this cruel work, she called as witness the valet, Constant,* whose ready tongue gave a sort of intimate note to his outpourings, above all when talking of the bedroom, and also de Bausset who, on his return from Fontainebleau pretended to have proof that the Emperor was suffering from a "gallant ailment".'†

It says a great deal for Marie Louise that these stories made little impression. Probably she did not believe them, and even if she had done, she belonged to a generation whose marital infidelity was taken more or less for granted. These attacks, however, wore her down physically for they were interspersed by equally violent counter-attacks by Napoleon's still staunch admirers, the countesses de Montesquiou and de Luçay, and Baron de Menéval, to such an extent that 'she spent most of her

* An added refinement, sponsored by Talleyrand.
† Raymonde Bessard: op. cit.

time in her room and there, her head buried in her hands, she abandoned herself to the bitterness of her thoughts and shed abundant tears'.

Exactly three days later the emperor Francis, accompanied by Metternich, arrived, having made the journey from Paris in a light open carriage and with an escort of only two troops of dragoons. The meeting between father and daughter was more melodramatic than dramatic. With an admirable sense of theatre Marie Louise placed herself at the foot of the staircase, with Madame de Montesquiou carrying the former 'little king' now, for want of a better title, known vaguely as the 'prince of Parma', in her arms two paces behind her.

'At the sight of the Emperor Francis, Marie Louise burst into loud sobs, possibly genuine, and, seizing her son from his governess's arms, thrust him into those of his grandfather.* This was a reproach which the Emperor of Austria must well have understood when, for the first time, he pressed to his heart the grandson he had never seen, and now beheld the circumstances so agonising for the unhappy mother.'†

Weak and sentimental, Francis was probably impressed by the pathos of the moment and, acutely introspective, by a sense of personal, as distinct from patriotic, guilt. A long talk, at which not even Metternich assisted, then followed between father and daughter. Its length, and the fact that both gave the impression of being emotionally exhausted when it was over, suggest that Marie Louise did not hesitate to speak her mind freely and to allow herself the relief of recrimination. However, as a result of this long and obviously painful interview, Francis was able to persuade his daughter to return with him to Austria as quickly as possible, rest, recover from the unbearable strain of the past few months and then decide 'freely' her best course of action. Having done this, he settled down to write to Napoleon the same day:

Monsieur, my brother and dear son-in-law, the tender solicitude I have for my daughter the Empress obliged me to arrange a meeting with her here. I have been here only a

* The child was not, apparently, impressed. On being taken away by Madame de Montesquiou, he whispered, 'Mamam' Quiou, he's not very pretty, is he?'

† Imbère de Saint Amand, op. cit.

few hours, but am already convinced that her health has deteriorated grievously since I last saw her, I therefore decided to ask her to return for a few months to the bosom of her family. She is in great need of rest and peace, and Your Majesty has given me in the past so many a proof of his genuine devotion that I am persuaded he will approve of my decision. Once having regained her health, my daughter will take possession of her territories, and this as a matter of course will bring her nearer to Your Majesty's residence. It is, I am sure, superfluous for me to assure Your Majesty that his son will be considered as one of my family and during the time he spends on my estates, he will enjoy all the attentions which will be lavished on his mother. *Recevez, Monsieur mon frère, l'assurance de ma considération très distinguée.'*

This letter was signed:

From Your Majesty's affectionate brother and father-in-law, Francis.

In view of Francis's earlier voiced objections to the fact that Elba was too close to Europe for the sake of Europe's peace of mind, this letter appears at first sight a monumental example of hypocrisy. On the other hand, Francis is a clear pre-psycho-analysis-era example of schizophrenia. As a man, he still loved his daughter and admired his son-in-law; as a monarch – in name at any rate – he was obliged, as a result of Metternich's brain-washing, to consider the emperor Napoleon as a national enemy. He was not seeking petty revenge for past humiliations but justification in the eyes of God who had called him to such a high position. For this he is, perhaps, a man to be admired for the introspective acceptance of his own inadequacy and moral cowardice, and at the same time infinitely to be pitied. Genuinely fond of children, he must have felt profound remorse as he contemplated his grandson, knowing that he was going to submit to the general demand that this child of the detested (and feared) Bonaparte be removed from the international scene. Madame de Montesquiou noted that, after staring at the little boy, he muttered, 'After all, my blood runs in his veins.' And even if this slightly melodramatic utterance is a figment of the countess's imagination, the thought must have been pounding in his brain.

Metternich had every reason to be satisfied. Of her own free will, the ex-empress had consented to return to Vienna with her son. From his point of view, the son was more important than the wife. Though only three years old, he was the incarnation of the Napoleonic legend, of the future of Bonapartism and, as such, Metternich was determined that, once in Vienna, he would remain for ever in Austrian quarantine even if the mother was able to stray from the Habsburg fold.

Gloating over his victory, convinced that his diplomacy had been the foundation of triumph on the battlefield, he indulged in an inexplicable and unjustifiable act of refined cruelty at Marie Louise's expense. As if anxious to emphasise her humiliation, he was able to persuade Francis to insist that she receive visits from both the czar and the king of Prussia. Francis obeyed meekly, but that he was ashamed of himself can be judged by the fact that having told Marie Louise of his decision, he added hastily that he himself would not be present as he was obliged to hurry back to Paris to make final arrangements for the return to Vienna.

Alexander behaved with great tact. Savary asserts that 'he' (the czar) 'must have seen from her face which had been bathed in tears for the last twenty days, the effect which his presence produced on her'; and de Bausset records: 'He' (the czar) 'was so amiable, so pleasant, that one could have been tempted to believe that nothing untoward had happened in Paris. After breakfast, he asked the Empress if he might see her son. Then turning to me – for I had had the honour of meeting him at Erfurt – he asked if I would kindly take him to the "little King"; those were his own words. When he saw the boy, the Emperor kissed him, played with him, and looked at him intently. He even said soothingly to the distraught Marie Louise, "Of course, no one will stop you, even though it may be a mistake for you to go to Elba." '

Three days later occurred the king of Prussia's visit, even more dreaded than had been that of the czar. Protestingly, Marie Louise had written to her father: 'I am afraid that he' (the king of Prussia) 'will not behave as nobly as the Emperor Alexander, and you can imagine how unpleasant it will be for me to hear what he will have to say.'

Slightly embarrassed, this unwelcome caller stayed only a very short time. After his hurried departure, Marie Louise remarked coldly that she had felt 'stifled' by his 'clumsy attempts to be polite'. She reported both these interviews to Napoleon and, as proof that the slander campaign had been without effect, also wrote:

My father was very sweet and good to me, but this was all spoiled by the fact that he dealt me the most terrible blow imaginable by stopping me seeing you, rejoining you, and he does not mean to allow me to make the journey' (to Elba) 'with you. It was all very well for me to say that it was my duty to follow you, he said that he did not wish it and that he wanted me to spend three months in Austria and that after this I could go to Parma and from there to see you. I really feel this will kill me, and I pray that you will be able to be happy without me, for I can never be happy without you. I will write to you every day and will never stop thinking about you!

Your faithful friend, Louise.

When, on April 23rd, Marie Louise and her son, accompanied by a suite of seventy-two, including the duchess of Montebello, Madame de Montesquiou, General Caffarelli, Barons de Bausset and de Menéval and, inevitably, Dr Corvisart, set out on the long journey from Rambouillet to Vienna, Russian troops had been replaced by an Austrian contingent commanded by General Karl Kinski. The duchess was furious that the provisional government had insisted on her staying with the ex-empress, but Madame de Montesquiou, who worshipped the king of Rome, willingly accepted the temporary exile in a spirit of exalted martyrdom, and near-primitive possessiveness. As Octave Aubry says: '. . . she was one of those people whose sense of duty was exalted by misfortune. She adored her pupil. She had brought him up, for her he was like the last child born in approaching old age. She was ready to sacrifice everything for him – parents, family, friends – and to live in exile amongst spies in enemy employ.'

The journey was an unhurried affair. Marie Louise was miserably unhappy. It was not as Hortense, jealous and inclined to be spiteful, has suggested, because she grieved at no longer being empress, the first lady of Europe. Far more objective than Hortense, Caulaincourt noted: '. . . She' (Marie Louise) 'was always deeply attached to the Emperor. She was sorry for him and much more worried about him than the catastrophe which had precipitated her from the first throne of the world . . .' She regretted, morbidly, not having gone to her husband and, though repeating she had never been popular, was distraught at the thought of her late subjects' uncertain future. At Vesoul, she noted: 'I received the Austrian staff. The sight of them made me feel ill; I could see the light of triumph in their eyes; I felt I could read in them that they were delighted to realise how sorrowful I felt at leaving poor France . . .'; and on May 2nd, the day she crossed the frontier into Switzerland: 'I prayed for the happiness of poor France. May she soon come to regret the loss of someone who was deeply attached to her and weeps over her fate and the loss of friends obligatorily left behind.'

For his part, de Menéval noted: 'Since crossing over into Switzerland, her sadness has redoubled, her nights are troubled by chronic insomnia, and most of the time her cheeks are wet with tears.'

Even though just over three years old, the young Napoleon realised that something was wrong. 'I know I'm not a king any more,' he said very sadly to Madame de Montesquiou, 'because I haven't got any pages.' And, on another occasion, even more sadly, 'Why don't I ever see my papa these days?'

Yet, as she approached Austria slowly via Schaffhaus and Zurich, dallying to make excursions on Lake Constance, Marie Louise grew calmer: 'Her memories of France dimmed. Her "German" past, from which she had been absent for only four years, gradually caught up with her and slowly wrapped her round.'

It must, indeed, have seemed at times as if the French interlude were but a dream – half roseate, half nightmare. At Innsbruck, the cheerful Tyroleans welcomed her as though she were returning in triumph rather than as a fugitive. The town was hung with streamers, brilliantly illuminated; enthusiasm attained such a pitch that the horses were unharnessed and her carriage pulled through the streets by the tough mountaineers, shouting and singing. This strange aura of continuity must have enveloped her still further when she was met at Moelk by Count von Trautmannsdorff who, just four years and four weeks ago, had handed her – timid, tearful, proxy bride – to the waiting, intensely curious French reception committee.

A bare four leagues from Vienna, Marie Louise was surprised to find the empress, Maria Ludovica herself, accompanied by the former governess, Countess Lazanski, waiting to escort her 'home'. They greeted each other with ritual embraces. Maria Ludovica tried hard to be agreeable. She could afford to be. Able lieutenant of Metternich, she had exerted every ounce of her influence over her vacillating husband to persuade him that it was his duty to join the hallali to destroy his daughter and son-in-law; Marie Louise's physical presence on the outskirts of Vienna was visual proof of success.

Instinctively, Marie Louise seemed to have realised this and, though she was more than happy to see Madame Lazanski, there was an inevitable coldness - manifesting itself by her much-reproached 'gaucherie' during the drive; a 'gaucherie' which Maria Ludovica was quick to criticise in the most adverse terms. The atmosphere in the following carriage in which rode the duchess of Montebello and Madame Lazanski was even more strained: the duchess in the worst of tempers at finding herself so far from home, Madame Lazanski unable to forget that the duchess had been largely responsible for her summary dismissal at Munich.

At eight o'clock in the evening the cortège entered the outskirts of Vienna and headed for the Schoenbrunn. There were crowds waving, cheering, a solid phalanx massed round the palace railings and entrance to the drive.

'They seemed,' records de Menéval, 'more anxious to get a glimpse of "the little Napoleon" than of Iphigenia returning alive from the Minotaur's embrace'; while a police officer actually mentioned in his report that the crowd was carried away by the little prince's charm and good looks.

On the palace steps the cohort of relatives – brothers, sisters, cousins, aunts, uncles – almost smothered the weary Marie Louise with their embraces and risked drowning her in their happy tears 'as if she'd just escaped, by miracle, with her life from some terrible danger'.*

This over-fussy welcome completed Marie Louise's dismay, due largely to nervous strain and physical exhaustion. There took place in her one of those sudden and totally unpredictable changes of heart, due to too-often-repressed emotion. She had been quietly contented as she neared the Austrian frontier,

* de Menéval.

217

touched by the reception at Innsbruck. But now, back again in the Schoenbrunn, the full meaning of the abdication, of her own position, struck her once more.

Her one emotional outlet remained her private diary, and she wrote: 'I return to you, my beloved country, but with what bitterness. Why has this happened to me? Why am I delivered up to every humiliation, to all the reproaches of my heart? Why didn't the people of Paris, like the Tyroleans, unharness the horses of my carriage? Ah, what a heart-rending fate is mine; to slip from the Emperor's care and depart from unhappy France! God only knows my grief! Alas for my fatal weakness caught up in this maelstrom of betrayal and intrigue . . .'

The disillusion was reciprocal. The euphoria of both the family and the Austrian court at refinding their lost archduchess did not last long. As a girl, her awkwardness passed comparatively unnoticed as she made few appearances in public; but now that she was still a figure of some international importance and the object of almost animal curiosity, adverse remarks, to Maria Ludovica's delight, made themselves heard in all grades of society.

Typical was that of Countess Potocka: 'The good taste in which she was dressed made her appear a little less ugly. But her expression didn't change. Never did an agreeable smile or a warm glance light up those wooden features.' While Metternich noted grimly: 'Prince (*sic*) Trautmannsdorff complained to me today about the Empress Marie Louise's haughtiness. People are remarking that generally she behaves and talks as if the Emperor Napoleon were still ruling France.'

One can read in the note the hint of a but-you-wait-and-see menace which, indeed, the chancellor was soon to put into effect.

It was to prove a last spiritual convulsion in this sense. Suddenly she felt French, thought French, only wanted the company of her small French entourage: a violent convulsion which, however, was not to last more than a few fleeting weeks.

Once Napoleon had announced that he was 'condemned to live', he set about trying to organise his life as emperor of Elba with the same systematic thoroughness he had devoted to his position as emperor of France, virtually of Europe. Aware of his terrible error in hoping that Marie Louise would decide to join him on her own initiative, he tried to persuade himself nevertheless that her health had deteriorated to such an extent that a cure was indeed necessary, and that once this precious health were recovered her first move would be to hurry, with their son, to Elba.

To reassure himself that this was the case, he continued writing, almost daily, as if the world-shattering events of the past four months had not affected them basically, and their reunion was a matter of course. He showed annoyance over the fact that his wife had been obliged to receive the enemy monarchs: '. . . I am very angry that they had so little consideration for you in your state of health as to oblige you to receive visits which must have gone against the dictates of your heart . . .' (April 19th).

And an hour later, the same day: '. . . I do pity you being obliged to receive such a visit but, as he' (Alexander) 'is very tactful, I hope that he did not say anything that you found hurtful. But I pity you still more being obliged to receive the King of Prussia who is quite capable of saying the most offensive things without really meaning them . . .'

There was yet another letter written the same day (April 19th), eve of the departure for Elba, as though the unfortunate exile knew that in fact the flight from French soil spelled the end, even of their dreams of an anonymous domestic peace: 'Montesquiou has given me your letter. I'm very upset to learn of the poor state of your health, try to be brave and take care of yourself for my sake and your son. Go straight for a cure and try to avoid Vienna, if possible . . .'

As a PS, he added: 'If what I'm told is true, the behaviour of Aldobrandini and Beauharnais is a disgrace and dishonours them. Tell me what really happened; I can hardly believe such infamy.'*

The first letter from Elba was written on May 4th, from Portoferraio, and is profoundly pathetic in its obstinate, yet obviously unfelt, pseudo-optimism regarding the future:

My good Louise, I was four days at sea in a dead calm. I wasn't ill at all. I have arrived in Elba which is very pretty. The accommodation is very poor; but I will get it vastly improved in the next few weeks. I haven't had any news of you. I grieve about this every day. My health is excellent.

* Both the former grand equerry and grand master had, in fact, refused flatly to follow Marie Louise, so anxious were they to find suitable positions with the new régime.

Goodbye, my friend, you are far from me, but my heart is always with my Louise. A tender kiss for my son. All yours, Nap.

Another letter followed, written May 9th, extolling the virtues of the island as a health resort, after which no other letters of the emperor are available until July 3rd.

My good Louise, I received your letters No. 8 and 11, dated June 8th, the others are lost. The news you give me of your health and that of my son, makes me very happy. I think you ought to go to Tuscany as soon as possible, where there are 'waters' as good and of the same quality as those of Aix in Savoy. This move would be very advantageous. I would hear from you more often, you would be nearer Parma, and you could have your son with you and you wouldn't be the cause of anyone worrying. Your journey to Aix would be most inconvenient. If this letter reaches you, only go for a short time, rather go for your health's sake to Tuscany. My health is good, my love for you remains unchanged, and I long to see you more than ever. Goodbye, my good friend. A tender kiss to my son. All yours, Nap.

'The others are lost'! Already Napoleon may have suspected that the losses were not entirely accidental but, in any case, his next letter, dated August 18th, three days after his birthday, is a cry of anger and despair, containing also the merest hint or, rather, fear already engendered by certain rumours that the once disconsolate wife had now found other distractions. In the complete collection of his letters to his wife, this one is numbered 317; no. 318, written ten days later, is the last of his letters which survive:

My good Louise, I write to you so often, *and I imagine you do the same to me*; and yet I haven't received a single one from you since several days before your departure for Vienna. I have no news of my son. This is stupid and atrocious. Madame (Napoleon's mother) is here and is very well; she is comfortably lodged. I am well. Your apartments are ready and I expect you to be here in the month of '7bre' for the *vendange*. Nobody has any right to stand in your way. I've written about this. Come then! I await you impatiently. You know how I feel about you. Princess Pauline will be here towards the middle of '7bre'. It will soon be your name day. I hope you have a happy day. Complain about the way they are behaving, preventing my wife and child from writing to me. Such behaviour is despicable. *Adio, mio bene,*

Nap.

What Napoleon did not realise was that between the dates of the despatch of these two letters, July 3rd and August 18th, the unpredictable, emotionally distraught Marie Louise had had yet another – by far the most violent she was ever to undergo in her lifetime – change of heart. So violent that, within a few days, after so many broken-hearted protestations over the cruelty of the separation and of slavish devotion to an unlucky but adored husband, she would be writing petulantly to the duchess of Montebello in Paris about the emperor's attempt to get her to Elba: 'I'm afraid all his letters will influence the Court in Vienna,* and this will mean I may be kept away' (from Parma) 'for some time: however, I have given them' (Metternich and Talleyrand) 'my most sacred word of honour that I haven't the slightest intention of going either now or ever to the Island of Elba (for you know better than anyone that I have no desire to do so), but the Emperor is really so irresponsible, so feather-brained . . .'

---

* Proof that they were subject to censorship before being handed on to her.

Chapter XII

Marie Louise had been told so often that Dr Corvisart was the best doctor in Europe that she clung to his report as to a sacred testament, and insisted on going to Aix, and only Aix, for the prescribed cure. For once she was prepared to defy everyone. She had Napoleon's letter disapproving of the choice; her father had told her that it was inconvenient, had warned her that this was Metternich's opinion and also that of the French provisional government. Of a sudden she was impregnated with a weak character's occasional unshakeable obstinacy. It was *her* health which was at stake and, thrown in the balance with this precious health, the world's, Europe's, her country's interests were without weight.

This determination to submit to Corvisart's judgment was reinforced by the fact that she was still under the influence of her revived nostalgia for France, the country she had come so near to hating in the last months, whose people she had stigmatised as fickle and unstable but for whom she now felt, in a spirit of contradiction, an almost unbearable retrospective love.

Her unexpected francophilia was gaining for her an increasing unpopularity. Within a few weeks, condemnation of *La Française*, as she was called sarcastically, was no longer limited to a small francophobic minority, but almost universal. As might have been expected, Maria Ludovica was one of her most vehement detractors. To Francis, still in Paris, she wrote venomously: 'Really one would think that the French were again masters of our palace' (Schoenbrunn) 'and your country. All the time one hears the word "Emperor" which exasperates even though it is of little significance as he is now a creature of no importance, and who *at last* has been rendered harmless.'

A member of the palace staff was heard to complain: 'Her Serene Highness has only portraits of her husband in her bedroom, and not one of her august father . . .'; while archduke John proclaimed angrily: 'She's completely gallicised. She seems to despise us Germans.' The criticisms were justified. 'She received Napoleon's letters and always replied immediately. She spoke of him with deep nostalgia. She was never without her bracelet inset with Napoleon's portrait. One day she showed it to everyone at a reception, saying, "It's all I have left of a husband I loved and with whom I lived in the most perfect harmony." '*

It was a terrible blow, therefore, when suddenly both Corvisart and the duchess of Montebello decided that they were unable to bear life in Vienna any longer, and insisted on returning immediately to Paris. There were scenes, entreaties, tears: all without effect. The duchess and the doctor, complete egoists, were untouched by Marie Louise's distress. Their own interests lay in France. The fact that they owed everything – wealth, position beyond what could have been the most ambitious of youthful dreams – to the dethroned imperial couple was of no importance to them.

With their departure about mid-May, Schoenbrunn's little French colony, with the exception of those in menial roles, was reduced to three: Madame de Montesquiou, the countess of Brignoles and Baron de Menéval – all of impeccable character, yet dull companions for the increasingly unbalanced ex-empress.

Though outwardly disapproving, Metternich was not disturbed by Marie Louise's apparently rabid francophilia. So long as she and her son remained prisoners behind the Schoenbrunn's gilded bars, they were harmless; and the more unpopular she made herself, the more effectively she blunted the only remaining weapon in her armoury, namely pity. Within a fortnight of her arrival, even in her family circle, she could count on only one genuine sympathiser, and that the most surprising of all.

On hearing of Napoleon's defeat and abdication, the seventy-four-year-old queen of Naples, Maria Carolina, sister of Marie Antoinette and Marie Louise's own grandmother, came hurrying to Vienna to claim her throne from which she had been ejected by Napoleon to make way for his brother-in-law and sister, Joachim and Caroline Murat. Few people had as much reason to hate the Bonapartes as Maria Carolina. It is said that when she heard of the Austrian defeat at Marengo, she had an apoplectic fit which came near to ending her life.

After a long and hazardous journey† from Sicily, she installed

* Octave Aubry: op. cit.
† Rabidly Anglophobe – she was certain the English wished to make her a prisoner, why one does not know – she had crossed to the North African coast, eventually reaching Vienna via Cairo, the Bosphorus and Athens, rather than risk being 'interrupted' by a British warship.

herself in Hoetzendorf, whose château gardens adjoined Schoenbrunn. But though determined to regain Naples, the elderly Maria Carolina had very confirmed ideas as to the sanctity of marriage and was disgusted to find that her grand-daughter was the central figure of a plot whose object was to ensure that she be held, not temporarily but permanently, separated from her husband. She took a great interest in the little 'prince of Parma' and was often expansive with de Menéval whose simple, disinterested loyalty greatly appealed to her.

'This princess,' says de Menéval, 'who had been Napoleon's declared enemy during the time of his prosperity and whose opinion could certainly not be suspected of partiality, professed nevertheless a great admiration for his qualities. She said that he had formerly given her many reasons to complain, but now with the coming of his misfortunes she had forgotten all. She could not restrain her indignation at the conspiracies designed at detaching her grandchild from the ties which should be both her duty and glory, and thus deprive the Emperor of the sweetest consolation he could receive after the terrible blows his pride must have suffered. She added that if their reunion were forbidden, Marie Louise should make a rope of her sheets, let herself down by this means from her window, and escape in disguise. "That is what I should do in her place," said she, "for when one is married it is for life!" '

The baron, however, saw fit to add: 'But such a bold act, which would have had an attraction for the daring spirit of the old Queen, agreed neither with Marie Louise's character nor with her ideas of decorum. Besides, she was just beginning to feel rather happy at the thought of going to Parma, where she would be her own mistress, free to come and go as she chose.'

De Menéval was a shrewd judge of human nature. He guessed that the ex-empress's passionate nostalgia was not as deep-rooted as she herself would like to imagine and that behind her violent francophilia it was the husband for whom she fretted rather than the nation. At heart she had always been Austrian, as her pleasure at the welcome prepared for her at Innsbruck had shown. The real reason for her fits of melancholia, her obsession with imaginary, petty ills, was not so much that she missed Parisian gaiety or the language of Voltaire, but the absence of a husband's embraces; and since that husband happened to be French, nation and individual became one and undivided in the turmoil of her emotions.

Marie Louise was twenty-three years of age. She was born an

archduchess; for four years she had been an empress, consort of the world's most powerful monarch. Yet she had never known the meaning of the word 'liberty'; never known what it meant to be able to 'come and go as she chose'. Not only had, first, her parents then her husband exercised complete control over her movements, they had sought – and largely succeeded in so doing – to dominate her mind, thereby imposing a moral serfdom with, certainly for Napoleon, calamitous results – as exemplified by her fatal lack of initiative at the time of the debate as to whether or not she should leave besieged Paris and, later, her inability to *order* on her own initiative the move from Blois to Fontainebleau. One cannot _be surprised that the thought of genuine individual liberty should find itself wrapped in an aura of infinite appeal. To this awakening desire to assert herself can also be attributed the rare obstinacy regarding Aix.

Temporarily, Metternich was content to adopt a velvet glove technique in dealing with the problem. He wrote to the emperor Francis suggesting that there was no real danger in giving in to this whim, provided the 'prince of Parma' was retained in Vienna as an unofficial hostage; that the ex-empress travelled under an assumed name and was accompanied by one or more trusted individuals charged with responsibility for her actions, and he proposed that these provisos should be submitted to the French provisional government. After which, taking it for granted that the matter was settled, he left Francis the delicate task of informing his daughter that her journey depended on her promise to travel without her son.

Fully aware of these facts, Maria Carolina provoked a sharp drama with her granddaughter. During one of her frequent visits, the 'prince of Parma', breaking in on an adult conversation asked: 'When am I going to see my dear papa again?'

The old queen looked at him sombrely before replying: 'You'll never see your papa again.'

This cruel answer, which made the little boy burst into tears, was uttered deliberately with the intention of shaking Marie Louise out of her complacent acceptance of her fate. Momentarily, it had the desired result. Marie Louise leapt to her feet, seized her son in her arms, hugged him and kept repeating furiously: 'You *will* see him. I promise you, you *will* see him!'

A few days later she realised how hard it would be to keep her promise.

On June 15th she left Vienna to meet her father at Siegarts-kirchen on his return from Paris. The meeting took place in the same room in which, in 1805, Napoleon had received the Austrian delegation bringing him the keys of Vienna. After his long journey, the Austrian emperor was tired and irritable. Marie Louise jittery, sure as usual that she was ailing, immediately brought up the subject of Aix, after their formal greeting. Francis, unwilling to commit himself, said that the journey 'might' be possible but only if she agreed to leave her son behind. This Marie Louise refused to do, whereupon Francis is supposed to have said (vague repetition of Metternich's words): 'As my daughter, you are all I hold dearest in the world. As a sovereign, I don't even know you.'

At last, on their return to Vienna, Marie Louise was presented with an ultimatum. She must make up her mind: 'yes' or 'no'. Permission was granted for her to reside six or seven weeks in Aix in order to effect a cure. She could leave at the end of the current month (June), but there was no question of her son accompanying her. She accepted the terms with bad grace. It was not only her obsession with her health which prompted her to do so. She was beginning to worry about her future.

The longer she remained in Vienna – 'this prison' as she was now referring to the city in her letters to the duchess of Monte-bello – the more she realised the hatred and fear Napoleon's name was capable of inspiring, which sentiments inevitably reflected on her and, more particularly, on her son. Many of the allied statesmen and rulers who would be gathering in the Austrian capital in a few months' time for the famous congress showed signs of being opposed to her accession to the duchy of Parma, and had already stated that even if this should, exception-ally, be permitted, there could be no question of her son's rights of succession.

These rumours terrified her. She was haunted by the thought of spending the rest of her life, a disinherited poor relation, semi-prisoner, depending on her father's notoriously parsimon-ious charity. And already most of the two millions saved from the French wreck were spent! Her only chance, she began to see with a certain shrewdness, was to co-operate by showing an exemplary docility which might possibly dispel suspicions that she was capable of incorporating a future danger, however shadowy, to the old order's restored peace. At this stage, also, she began to think seriously of the considerable disadvantages of her fate being linked with that of the Elban exile; and though capable of isolated acts of physical or moral courage, she most definitely was not of the fibre of martyrs.

But such thoughts were still amorphous. To Madame de Montebello she wrote plaintively: 'My son is just as sweet and gay as when you last saw him. You have no idea how cruelly the thought of leaving him torments me . . .'

And in archduke John's diary one reads: 'She' (Marie Louise) 'is still very attached to Napoleon. It's only natural.'

On June 29th, travelling under the pseudonym of the duchess of Colorno, accompanied by de Menéval and the countess of Brignoles, riding in a carriage still embossed with the imperial arms of France, Marie Louise left Vienna after an emotional leave-taking with her son beneath Madame de Montesquiou's disapproving gaze.

The journey was carried out in short stages and, en route, the ex-empress was allowed to visit a number of ex-imperial dignitaries; proof that Metternich's view as to her inability to be a present or future trouble-maker had been generally accepted.

In Munich she was greeted by Prince Eugène de Beauharnais and his wife. At the dinner given that night in her honour, she met a plump young girl, brimming over with high spirits – Caroline Augusta, princess royal of Bavaria – who only a few years later was to become Francis's fourth wife and Marie Louise's second step-mother; a step-mother many years younger than her step-children. At Baden she was entertained by Louis Bonaparte, ex-king of Holland; at Payerne she was the guest of Jerome and Catherine, and at Allaman of Joseph.

Now that the imperial adventure was over, the ex-empress of the French had got beyond the stage of detesting, even fearing, these untrustworthy brothers-in-law. The permanent intrigue of those closely-guarded days no longer made sense. Even the Blois drama was forgotten. Ex-kings and an ex-viceroy reminded her of a past glory, a slightly roseate dream, while, for their part, these deposed dignitaries could hardly believe in their good fortune at being allowed to retain honorary titles and most of their wealth in comfortable retirement. Louis XVIII was indeed remarkably free from any desire for 'revenge' or the need to 'make examples'.

Apart from missing her son, Marie Louise was really enjoying a journey, and that for the first time in her life – she could console herself, also, with the thought that the child could not be in better hands than those of the doting Madame de Montesquiou. She was en route for Aix, convinced that Aix did indeed spell 'health', and where the beloved Louise Montebello and Dr Corvisart would be waiting to greet her. It was such a pleasant change not to be under anybody's orders or following a strict timetable. There was no fixed itinerary. If she felt like a halt, she ordered a halt. If she wished to stop to admire the view, she could do so, and there was nobody to nag her with reminders that they were already behind schedule.

On reaching the vicinity of Geneva, she decided that there was no hurry and took the impromptu decision to visit the Chamonix valley. This detour lasted six days, and de Menéval noted:

'It was impossible to tire the Duchess of Colorno and her courage at times amounted to folly. It was evident that she was seeking excitement in order to divert her mind from other subjects. She displayed, too, a good temper and endurance which astonished even the guides. Her whole time was spent walking or riding on a mule, and as a result of this exercise her health improved visibly.'

The *ad hoc* tour ended on July 16th, and on the 17th the little party set out on the journey's final stage from Geneva to Aix.

'Just as she' (Marie Louise) 'was about to enter the town, she met a man on horseback wearing the uniform of an Austrian general, who bowed profoundly then turned to escort her. Doubtless she would have been greatly surprised had anyone told her at that moment the part this man was to play in her life. He was forty-two years of age, nineteen years older than she. He had but one eye; a black bandage hid the scar which had deprived him of the other. It was General Count von Neipperg who had acted as chamberlain to Marie Louise at the time of her stay in Prague in 1812 shortly after the Dresden conference. She had not really noticed him then, and never seen him since.'

He had, according to de Menéval, a good figure, fair curly hair and a ruddy complexion 'which, however, lacked the freshness of youth', and he adds that the sight of this uniformed figure, accompanied by an A.D.C. 'produced a disagreeable impression in the mind of Marie Louise which she made no attempt to conceal'; and that, after the general had introduced himself, 'Adam Albert von Neipperg, Your Highness's devoted servant', without answering she threw herself back in her corner and sulked.

She had been used to being controlled so long, she was no longer able to be tricked. The suave general had been appointed to spy on her. Her intoxicating, newly-found freedom was over.

In the two years that had passed since their meeting in Prague, which Marie Louise barely remembered, von Neipperg's life had unfolded at the same hectic rhythm. Recalled to the army after the successful conclusion of his Stockholm mission, he distinguished himself on the battlefields of Reichenbach, Stolpen and Leipzig. His brilliant handling of his cavalry division and his personal bravery at Leipzig earned him promotion to lieutenant field marshal, and the honour of carrying the victory despatch to Vienna. Reverting, with the cessation of hostilities, to his diplomatic role, he was in Naples in January 1814 where he was able to persuade Murat, in return for the promise of Austrian backing for his claim to Naples, to betray his master and benefactor and contribute a neapolitan contingent to the allied army. This mission successfully concluded he returned to Vienna from where Metternich, who had the gift of choosing the right man, promptly sent him to Mantua, this time to Prince Eugène de Beauharnais, with a letter from the latter's father-in-law, the king of Bavaria, suggesting that since Napoleon was obviously finished, the best line of action would be to follow Murat's example.

Eugène, of a more sterling moral fibre than the innkeeper's son, was indignant. He insisted that even if Napoleon abdicated it was his duty to defend the rights of the regent and the prince imperial. Neipperg redoubled his arguments against the advisability of such a step. Eugène hesitated, then seemed as if he had nevertheless decided to fight romantically for the lost imperial cause, when news came that Marie Louise had given herself up, with her son, to the Austrians. There was, therefore, no longer a regent or a prince imperial to defend.

Resuming command of his division, then at Pavia, Neipperg was speculating as to his future when he received secret instructions from Prince Schwarzenberg ordering him to report, and attach himself, to the suite of the archduchess Marie Louise, travelling under the pseudonym of the duchess of Colorno, on her arrival at the town of Aix in Savoy, where she would be remaining for several weeks, in order to take the waters.

'Count von Neipperg', the instructions elaborated, 'will endeavour to dissuade the Duchess of Colorno, as tactfully as possible, from attempting to undertake a journey to the island of Elba, a journey which would deeply pain the paternal heart of His Majesty who formulates the tenderest wishes for the happiness of his much-loved daughter. He must not fail, therefore, to try *by any means whatsoever* to dissuade her from such a project, and to do all in his power to gain time for precise instructions from His Majesty to arrive, and, if the worst comes to the worst and all his attempts prove vain, he will follow the Duchess to the island of Elba. As the passports which have been delivered to Madame the Archduchess and her suite are valid only for the journey from Vienna to Aix and the return, and new passports would be necessary for any variation of this itinerary, the fact could well be exploited to prevent such a journey. The police officer Siebert who will be handing these instructions to Count von Neipperg will be attached to him during the sojourn at Aix.'

Neipperg is said to have been both annoyed and disappointed on receiving these instructions. He had been hoping for an ambassador's nomination as it seemed that the war was definitely over. This spy-cum-gaoler role was, he felt, beneath his dignity. At the same time, he was amused, particularly by the phrase, '. . . *by any means whatsoever* . . .' Mentioning it to his wife, he said casually, 'I'll guarantee she'll be my mistress within six months.'

The elderly Prince Esterhazy had been cast originally for this role; but Schwarzenberg, whose bulk was one of Marie Louise's favourite subjects for jibes and sarcasm, was, like Metternich, a talented amateur psychologist. He is supposed to have had a down-to-earth conversation with Dr Corvisart, in the course of which the doctor assured him that most of the ex-empress's ills, both real and imaginary, were due to sexual starvation since her carnal appetite was as keenly developed as that of her father. The answer to the problem, as Schwarzenberg saw it, was, therefore, comparatively simple. Instead of the ageing and slightly infirm Esterhazy, Austria's most notorious Don Juan should be the official curator of her highness's person. And in drafting his instructions, Schwarzenberg felt convinced that a man of the world of Neipperg's calibre would not fail to grasp the significance of the key phrase, '. . . *by any means whatsoever* . . .'

Always thorough, Neipperg personally supervised the preparations for welcoming Marie Louise in her hired villa, a charming house, the property of a Monsieur Chevalley, overlooking town and lake and commanding a superb view of the high alpine peaks capped by eternal snows. Josephine and her daughter Hortense had stayed there in previous years. It might be said that it served as a refuge for deposed queens and empresses.

Neipperg took a pride in ensuring that it should please this latest exiled monarch. He checked credentials and capabilities of the staff engaged; especially that of the cooks. He was present while the piano was being tuned and, expert pianist, tried it himself before pronouncing himself satisfied. The flower arrangements were the result of his personal supervision.

Marie Louise was, indeed, most agreeably surprised on her arrival but, though pleased, still felt deeply resentful of von Neipperg's presence.

For the first week, his was an unenviable position. Again on French soil, the ex-empress was, to begin with, very much *La Française*. Her personal servants wore the imperial livery. All the guests as well as the entourage, with the exception of Neipperg, were French. Corvisart, now a baron, and Madame de Montebello had kept their promises and were present at the rendezvous. With them were Talma, the great but now elderly actor, and Isabey the portraitist, to remind her still more keenly of the empire's heyday. Neipperg was the odd man out, the foreigner, and made to feel it. The interviews Marie Louise accorded him were brief, dealing strictly with the running of the house. Her manner was 'polite, but scarcely amiable'.

For the time being Neipperg was content to wait, to efface himself. He made no attempt to interfere or assert even a minimum of authority. Always pleasant, even-tempered, exquisitely-mannered, he was invariably on the spot if wanted. After de Menéval's departure on the nineteenth (July) for a few weeks' leave in Paris to visit his pregnant wife, Marie Louise, very gradually to begin with, came to find that she was relying on the one-eyed general for the smooth running of her household and daily existence which meant so much to her, even to the extent of 'allowing' him to take her for a morning row on the lake and, in the evenings, 'allowing' him to accompany her while she treated her guests to her amateur talent as a *prima donna*. Much to Madame de Montebello's annoyance – she hated any form of outdoor amusement – these rowing expeditions, alternating with hours in the saddle, took up more and more of Marie Louise's time.

There were frequent garden parties, dinners and musical evenings during which Marie Louise appeared to be enjoying herself so much that Neipperg felt justified in writing cautiously to the Austrian Emperor: 'The Empress frequently mentions the Emperor Napoleon; yet she assures me that concern for her son takes precedence over all other considerations and has decided her – although she wishes to share her husband's lot – to give up the idea of the journey to Elba so as to be able to devote herself entirely to her son's education . . .'

As August 15th approached, however, there were signs of gathering nervous depression. There was a major reason for this emotional relapse. The fifteenth was Napoleon's birthday, a day on which for the past ten years fêtes as grandiose as any known in European history had been given throughout imperial France.

'August 15th 1813 – August 15th 1814! At this time last year France, still exulting over the victories of Lutzen and Bautzen, was expecting a speedy and glorious peace. Regent of the great Empire, Marie Louise seated on her throne in the Tuileries, the imperial mantle on her shoulders, her head encircled by the most brilliant of the crown diamonds, had received the high officials who came to offer their homage. Afterwards she had assisted at a solemn high mass and *Te Deum* in the palace chapel. In the evening she had been received with cries of joy and wild enthusiasm when she made her appearance on the balcony of the Hall of Marshals... What a difference August 15th 1814. Instead of the great capital, an obscure little town; instead of the Tuileries, a humble white house; instead of the title empress of the French and queen of Italy, that of duchess of Colorno . . .

'The former Empress may never have been ambitious, but such contrasts could not fail to cast over her a sombre and melancholy veil.'*

Always anxious to find someone to whom she could confide her problems, it was to de Menéval, still in Paris, she wrote:

* Frédéric Masson, op. cit.

How can I be gay on this of all days when I am obliged to spend it so far from the two persons dearest to me? Forgive me these sad reflections; but the friendship you have always shown encourages me to make them, providing you promise to tell me if I weary you. Begging you to believe in my most sincere friendship. Your Affectionate Louise.

On the other hand, despite the sadness which, on the actual day, was undoubtedly genuine but which like most of her moods was only fleeting, she had already written to her father: 'Count von Neipperg is most helpful and is doing everything he can to make my stay in Aix agreeable. He is a most worthy person and his manner pleases me . . .'

And to the suspicious duchess of Montebello who had returned somewhat huffily to Paris and suspected that Marie Louise was not altogether indifferent to her imposed watchdog and who, through sheer jealousy because of the still considerable material benefits brought her by Marie Louise's devotion, saw fit to warn that Monsieur de Neipperg, as she insisted on calling him, was a 'thoroughly dangerous person', she wrote soothingly: 'Do, I beg of you, continue with your sermons. You know I love to hear them, and don't have any fears about the little evening promenades; you must know that I never indulge in the fantasies with which you reproach me, and my heart which is like a rock as regards a sentiment which so far it ignores, will remain calm. No! It is made only for friendship and yours takes first place; the rest belongs to my son . . .'

The latter half of August was an increasingly difficult time for Marie Louise, hemmed in by problems whose solutions could not be long delayed. To begin with, although she might still not be prepared to admit it, she was in love with von Neipperg, and bewildered by the fact.* She was waiting, also, with great anxiety, for confirmation of her official title as duchess of Parma, dreading, as she waited, lest a general revisal of policy might cheat her out of this much-longed-for possession. In addition, as the imposing

* In some ways it would appear that she wished to remain faithful yet, after eight months, the memories of the husband as a flesh and blood man were fading. Von Neipperg enjoyed the fatal advantage of being present; before her eyes, his voice in her ear. And again, though stories of Napoleon's infidelity had never worried her unduly, she was piqued when she learned that he had been visited in Elba by Marie Walewska and their son: piqued, possibly, because she was subconsciously looking for an excuse for herself.

cohort of foreign monarchs and statesmen gathered in Vienna, she was unwilling to return to the Austrian capital, still feeling a basic resentment against all those who had deprived her of husband, glory and wealth. She was both unwilling to meet them and afraid that she would be looked on as a circus exhibit, a sort of relic of the fallen empire, to be stared at with a mixture of pity and satisfaction.

The French government, however, was becoming restless at her continued presence on French soil, haunted always by the bogey of a revival of Bonapartism. This fear had prompted Talleyrand, as early as August 9th, to send a message to Metternich: 'When you were last in Paris, my dear Prince, you told the King' (Louis XVIII) 'you did not approve the journey which Madame the Archduchess Marie Louise had made to Aix. Because the waters were beneficial to her health, the King shut his eyes to the inconveniences of the journey. But you, my dear Prince, felt it might give occasion, if not to intrigue, to a good deal of gossip. You know what the tittle-tattle of a thermal resort amounts to, and what mischief idle chatter may engender. Joseph Bonaparte, who lives near Aix, has behaved foolishly, which he might not have done but for her presence. All this is of little importance, and the King is not disturbed by it; but rumours have reached Paris and have started gossip within the Diplomatic Corps. People fancy that they discover secret machinations at the root of matters which are in fact perfectly innocent. I would suggest, therefore, my dear Prince, that since Madame the Archduchess has probably completed her cure, it would suit us both if her stay in Aix were not prolonged. Do not misunderstand, however, the motives causing me to make such a suggestion. Adieu, my dear Prince; think kindly of me, and believe in my sincere attachment to yourself.'

The result of this note was that Marie Louise was told she must leave the villa Chevalley at the beginning of September but as a sop, would be allowed to prolong her absence from Austria by a further tour of Switzerland. Her request that she be allowed to proceed direct to Parma was rejected. 'Everything that I can do to make you and your son happy, I will, be assured of that' (wrote the Emperor Francis). 'As far as you are concerned personally, I must beg of you to keep your promises and that being the case to come back and, as long as the Congress lasts, not to go to Parma, because by so doing prematurely you could

do the greatest harm to your own cause and that of your son . . .
your presence close to us during the Congress can be of much
greater importance to you than you realise and so I must ask you
to have confidence in your father in such matters . . .'

At the end of this letter was a note: 'I gather you are satisfied
with Neipperg: I thought you would be . . .'

During this same period, Napoleon precipitated matters by his
understandable apprehensions and impatience.

Already he guessed that his letters to his wife were being
intercepted, as were hers to him. How else could this long
silence be interpreted after their mutual vows to write to each
other daily? In addition, realising that Marie Walewska's visit
had been a great mistake, he bombarded Marie Louise with
letters, none of which was delivered to her. Then, losing his
head, as weeks passed and no reply was forthcoming, he committed a fatal error.

On August 20th, he sent for Captain Hurault de Sorbée,
Captain of the Guard, who had married Mlle Katzener, the
Femme Rouge who, imagining him to be an assassin, had tried to
prevent his entry into Marie Louise's bedroom the night of the
return from Russia in December 1812. Madame Hurault was with
Marie Louise at Aix, an excuse for Napoleon to grant the captain
prolonged leave, and a more than legitimate excuse, in the eyes
of the authorities, for such a journey. Napoleon, however, was
quite frank as to the real reason. He gave the captain a letter
which he had to swear to deliver, secretly, to the ex-empress. The
letter, he explained, was an *order* to Marie Louise to rejoin him
at Portoferraio, as soon as was humanly possible. He had waited
long enough. The brig, *L'Inconstant*, which would take Hurault
to Genoa would remain in that harbour till September 10th. If
any difficulties were put in the way of their flight, then it was
Hurault's duty more or less to kidnap the empress and get her
to Genoa and aboard *L'Inconstant*.

The captain, a brave man and a loyal Bonapartist, promised to
carry out this mission. He was accustomed to obey and not to
'reason why'. It is difficult to see, on the other hand, how Napoleon
could possibly have imagined that such a hare-brained scheme
had the slightest chance of success, even if Marie Louise were
willing to take the risks involved.

On arriving at Aix, Hurault, with a total lack of finesse and making no attempt to pretend that his visit was for purely family reasons, immediately demanded an interview with the duchess of Colorno, insisting at the same time, that no one else should be present.

Marie Louise was aghast at the letter's contents. It was also a rude shock. Its tone was apparently so brusque,* so quasi-accusing, and the directions it contained of such military bluntness that she was overcome by a wave of revolt. It was true that she was still not the free agent that she longed to be but, clinging desperately to the dream of Parma, she had half-persuaded herself that this longed-for 'freedom' was just round the corner. Now she was being recalled to the Napoleonic yoke, and with such brutality that tender memories were effaced by those of eternal submission to the exactions and exigencies of the all-powerful imperial will. Nor did Hurault's attitude help. Unlike Neipperg, he was no diplomat. Feeling that he was the emperor's mouthpiece, he adopted a hectoring manner, treating the letter as an ultimatum, and demanding immediate compliance.

Furious, but controlling herself, Marie Louise informed Hurault that she must have time to think it over and make the necessary plans, intimated that the interview was at an end and told him to report back to her later that evening.

Her first action, as soon as the captain had unwillingly taken his leave, was to send for Neipperg, show him the letter, repeat Hurault's words, express her own indignation over the whole matter and place herself under 'Count von Neipperg's protection'. Neipperg acted quickly. The Aix *gendarmerie*, informed of Hurault's presence, were easily persuaded to take the captain into custody and charge him with an attempt to kidnap. From Aix, he was sent under escort to Paris where he was soon released without being brought to trial. He was not, however, allowed to return to Elba.

The shock to Marie Louise's system produced by this letter was so great that it shattered her last illusions of fidelity, throwing her into Neipperg's arms. Never again would she pretend, even to herself, that she wished to share her husband's exile. Instead, she began to complain bitterly of the 'emperor's lack of balance', of his 'thoughtlessness and selfishness'. With an almost naïve inconsistency, she was to deny or ignore the hundreds of letters

* The original, unfortunately, has been lost.

236

professing her great love for Napoleon she had showered on friends and family alike for the last few years, insisting, rather, that 'none but the most superficial sentiments had ever existed between herself, victim of political intrigue, and the Emperor'. Some writers like to suggest – though since no direct or circumstantial evidence to the fact is on record, this cannot be affirmed – that it was this night, following on Hurault's arrest, that Marie Louise and von Neipperg became lovers.*

In any case, a few days after this blind attempt of Napoleon, Marie Louise and Neipperg, now travelling in her carriage, set off for a protracted Swiss tour before returning to Vienna. On September 9th they spent the night at Lausanne, reaching Berne on the 11th. From there, with Madame de Brignoles, a doubtful *chaperone*, she set off on a nine-day tour to the neighbouring beauty spots, accompanied by von Neipperg.

Menéval, back from Paris, and de Bausset stayed behind in Berne. 'Monsieur de Menéval and I' (de Bausset noted in his diary) 'had seen enough snow in Russia. We were not particularly anxious to wander over these mountains all covered with it.'

News which upset Marie Louise deeply waited for her on her return to Berne after visits to Grindelwald, Lauterbrunn and the Righi. Her grandmother, Maria Carolina, had been found dead in her bedroom in Hoetzendorf. Though she had not followed the dramatic advice to escape from Vienna by swarming down an improvised sheet rope – and now certainly had no desire to do so – she remembered that the old lady had been the only one to show her any real sympathy. Profoundly distressed and emotionally on edge, she shut herself up, moping, in her bedroom and was only roused from her apathy by the news that a highly eccentric traveller wished to see her.

It was the princess of Wales – another Caroline – a woman then forty-six years old, whose turbulent matrimonial entanglements with George, Prince of Wales, prince regent in 1811, had been for some time one of gossip's favourite topics. The princess was in the early stages of a lengthy tour-cum-pilgrimage to the Holy

* Andre Castelot in his '*L'Aiglon*' is more categoric: '. . . Neipperg had his reward a few days later, the 27th September to be exact, during an excursion on the return journey. The ex-Empress and her "guardian angel", caught in a violent storm were obliged to spend the night at the *auberge* of the *Soleil d'Or* near William Tell's chapel. That night, the over-amorous, languishing Marie Louise gave herself to Neipperg. . .'

Land which was to include Italy, Greece and Syria; but she was unable to resist making a detour in order to meet 'Napoleon's wife', and was even contemplating a descent on Elba.

De Menéval described her appearance, diplomatically, as 'highly original'. She wore 'a white muslin gown and a large white muslin veil covering her head, shoulders and breast. This was surmounted by a diadem of a single row of diamonds. She looked rather like a priestess of ancient Greece.'

Her conversation at the dinner arranged for the 23rd was singularly uninhibited for those days. She entered into great details about her world-famous relationship with her husband.

'Your Majesty will hardly believe it,' she said, 'that I was not allowed to be present in the Queen's drawing room while the sovereigns of Russia and Prussia were there, because my husband refused to meet me either in public or in private. I complained to the Queen, and I even wrote my husband a most beautiful letter to which I signed myself the most faithful and submissive of wives' (the princess smiled maliciously while pronouncing these last words) 'but he did not deign to answer . . .'*

Of her daughter, Princess Charlotte, she commented: 'Apart from myself she is the most quarrelsome person I know . . .'

After dinner, Caroline suggested a little music and that she and Marie Louise should sing a duet while von Neipperg accompanied. A trifle hesitant, Marie Louise agreed, whereupon Caroline made an astonishing choice; the duet *La ci darem il mano*, for the Don and Zerlina, from the first act of Mozart's *Don Giovanni*. Zerlina's music suited Marie Louise's light, sweet soprano to perfection. What, however, was really remarkable was the fact that the role of the Don, for baritone but often sung by a lyric bass, suited Caroline who, according to de Bausset, produced such a resonant, rather cavernous contralto that there seemed nothing incongruous in the words, *'Vedi! Non c'e lontano. Partiam ben mio da qui'*, or the blending of the two voices in the finale.

Refreshed by this encounter, Marie Louise decided to leave Berne the next day, but was in no hurry to get back to the realities of Vienna. There was a stop at Zurich and a visit to the ruined castle on the right bank of the Aar river, birthplace of Rudolph of Habsburg. While wandering through the ruins, 'the ingenious Neipperg suddenly and with an exclamation of triumph

* E. M. Oddie, op. cit.

picked up a piece of flat, pointed iron in which he was pleased to recognise a fragment of Rudolph's lance. The Empress was so completely taken in by this deception that, on her return to Vienna, fragments of the fictitious relic were set in gold rings which Rudolph's descendant presented to the General' (Neipperg), 'Madame de Brignoles, Menéval and Baron de Bausset.'[*] One does not know whether acceptance of the relic, as such, can be attributed to Marie Louise's naivety or love's traditional blindness.

Still unhurried, Marie Louise re-entered Austria by the Braunau frontier post, finally arriving in Vienna the evening of October 4th, the feast of St Francis of Assisi and her father's name day.

The little 'prince of Parma' was there to greet her, though the greeting was not all she had hoped for: 'I found my son had grown a lot,' (she wrote to the duchess of Montebello). 'His hair is right down to his shoulders in long curls and you know what a lovely colour it is, and his mourning suit' (for his great grandmother) 'looks marvellous on him. I had it made with long sleeves so he wouldn't catch cold. He speaks very well and spends hours alone with me in my room. My *amour propre* received a great jolt the day I arrived. I'd been thinking a lot about how he would greet me. I came in and he let himself be kissed. Then General Neipperg came in, and there he was resplendent in hussar uniform which fascinated my son who ran to him and didn't take any notice of anyone else. I admit I was very put out.'

However, a greater shock awaited her.

The Vatican had come to the conclusion that Napoleon's marriage with Josephine had not been correctly annulled, and that his marriage with Marie Louise was, therefore, non-existent. But since the former empress Josephine had died, it was suggested that Napoleon and Marie Louise should regularise the situation by another religious ceremony. The document presented to Marie Louise ended: 'Posterity will praise the most honest and generous of sovereigns for having sacrificed his daughter for the good of his people, but if we have been deceived in our good faith by the Monster' (Napoleon), 'posterity will also ask us why we have allowed the scandal to continue by recognising the innocent victim as the wife of one who, from a Catholic point of view, she could only marry with dispensation, now that the Monster is a widower and free to contract a new alliance.'

Horrified though she was at the idea that she was considered

* Max Billard: *Marriage Ventures of Marie Louise.*

the 'Monster's' concubine and her son a bastard, she was even more appalled at the possibility of a new marriage with Napoleon. She would not, she affirmed hysterically, contemplate it for a second.

Tragically, for Napoleon, the Vatican's bombshell, like Cambronne, was too late. Two months ago Marie Louise would have welcomed the Vatican's ruling, seizing upon it as a valid excuse to push her father, mouthpiece of Metternich and the allies, to give his consent to that reunion which, she had stated so often both verbally and in writing, was her one hope of happiness. In the meanwhile, however, she had fallen in love with Adam von Neipperg.

Neipperg had been convinced that his temporary attachment to Marie Louise's staff would automatically end with the return to Vienna, and had asked to resume his command of his division. He had taken it for granted that any sentimental interludes would be as inconsequential as his appointment. Marie Louise, on the contrary, thought differently. At his hint that his services were no longer required, she was panic-stricken. She had none of the eighteenth- and early nineteenth-century levity where affairs of the heart were concerned. She implored him not to leave her. He was, she insisted, the only person in whom she had any confidence; her only friend and adviser in a coldly hostile world.

For once her wishes and those of Metternich and – despite his not entirely hypocritical piety – her father coincided. Both were delighted to see her dominated, mentally and physically, by a loyal Austrian, thus destroying once and for all the nightmare of a reunited Bonaparte family.

Neipperg's feelings were mixed. He was certainly ambitious, but at the same time too much an epicurean, too intellectual perhaps, for yearning for power to become a lust. He had already risen to considerable heights: field marshal, renowned diplomat. Demagogically, his name was as much on the man-in-the-street's lips as a dashing light cavalry leader as that of Murat; while his amorous adventures made equally popular legend. Yet, noted Don Juan, he was not, like Casanova, a ruthless cynic. There was in him a strong chevalieresque streak. He was touched by Marie Louise's helplessness and eager trust. He knew that in her own mind she was not exaggerating when she assured him that he was her only real friend. The emperor Francis's slavish subservience to Metternich, common gossip in Vienna, revolted him.

Though the ex-empress of France might be exacting in her physical demands, her devotion was certainly touching; and flattering. After all, she was an archduchess, his own emperor's eldest child who, of her own free will, had made herself his responsibility. So, when she begged him not to leave her, and when her pleas were subtly echoed both by the chancellor and Francis, he made no further reference to Pavia.

Chapter XIII

The congress of Vienna, greatest gathering of monarchs and statesmen ever known in European history, opened on September 26th.

For an international conference whose object was the re-establishment and permanent reinforcement of traditional order, it soon proved to be a ponderous, even slightly frivolous affair in which entertainment threatened to take precedence over the exigencies of the conference table, to such an extent that the old prince de Ligne was inspired to make his classic remark: '*Le Congrès danse, mais il ne marche pas.*'

For supporters of traditionalism, the divine right sovereigns, Napoleon's downfall marked not only the end of an enemy who had defeated them both singly and unitedly on the battlefield more often than they cared to remember, who had bound them to his will reducing many to vassal status, dominating continental Europe, a resuscitated greater Charlemagne, but also of the even more dangerous, because spiritual, precepts of the French revolution.

It was, therefore, a victory which called for rejoicing on a hitherto unprecedented scale. Wives and daughters of prominent men spent vast fortunes on their *toilettes*. Money was poured out on the most fantastic *soirées* and receptions. The most exquisite gourmet meals were served *chez Monsieur de Talleyrand*. Countess Zichy, imitating fables of the 'mysterious East', gave a chess party with human pieces. The czar's morning ablutions, for which an enormous block of ice to be provided, became one of those spectacles which had to be seen. Reviving mediaeval pageantry, a mock tournament was staged in what is today known as the Spanish Riding School: 'Opposite the monarchs, in a tier of boxes placed in front of the musicians, were sedately ranged the twenty-four ladies of the twenty-four knights about to do combat in the lists. They were beautiful, animated, clad in red velvet robes against which the lustre of their jewels sparkled to great effect. The gems worn by Princess Esterhazy, born Princesse de la Tour et Taxis (*sic*), were valued at more than six million francs. The spectacle was magnificent. The twenty-four knights, superbly costumed and mounted, entered to a fanfare of trumpets. Riding forward, they made their reverence to the sovereigns without dismounting; then, turning, made a similar homage to the ladies whose colours and scarves they wore . . .' Baron de la Tour noted: 'This fête was quite beautiful, and the splendour of the ladies exceeded anything yet seen. One could have said they were clothed with diamonds and precious stones rather than adorned with them . . .'*

Another evening there was a performance of a comedy by Etienne, *Le Pacha de Surène*, acted by an amateur cast including Prince Anton Radziwill, Count Ferdinand von Waldstein, Princess Teresa Esterhazy and the Princesses Maria and Sophie of Lichtenstein. After the final curtain, a series of *tableaux vivants* were presented for the benefit of the aristocratic would-be comedians, who had not been included in the play, wishing to display their plastic – if silent – talent. De Bausset was most impressed by one of these *tableaux* entitled *The Tent of Darius*, inspired by a Lebrun painting, in which Count von Schoenfeld represented Darius and Countess Zichy, Statura. 'The scene was at the same time heroic and voluptuous,' says de Bausset. 'The facial expressions, the attitudes of the figures in this living picture were all suitable to their age, their condition and their situation.'

Nor were the great professionals of the art world neglected. Beethoven was there to conduct his seventh symphony and performances of *Fidelio*. Looked upon as a rival of Schiller, the Lutheran-turned-Roman Catholic, the Abbé Werner, made the round of the salons reciting extracts from his *Cunégonde*, a tragedy in twelve acts. Ballet was represented by the beautiful Italian ballerina, Vigano; the drama starred first the German *Mademoiselle*, Schultz, and later her even more successful rival *Mademoiselle*, Stephanie, from Paris.

'In fact, the Viennese forced their epicurean philosophy of life and manners upon their guests; and these, remembering perhaps the old instruction to do at Rome as the Romans did, behaved at Vienna after the manner of the Viennese.'†

It was during this time, while congress revelled, that Napoleon

* Imbère de Saint Amand, op. cit.
† Algernon Cecil: *Metternich*.

243

made another desperate, but less foolhardy, attempt to bridge the abyss gaping between him and his wife and son. On October 10th, he wrote to Marie Louise's uncle, his old friend the grand duke of Wurzburg (now the grand duke of Tuscany) who had witnessed his marriage and was one of the former 'little king's' godfathers. It was a pathetic appeal, tragic in its humility: 'My brother and very dear uncle. Having received no news from my wife since August 10th, nor from my son for six months, I am entrusting this letter to the Chevalier de Colonna. I beg Your Royal Highness to let me know whether I may send you a letter every week for the Empress, and if you will forward me her replies and those of the Countess de Montesquiou, my son's governess. If this could be done it would indeed be a great consolation to me. I flatter myself that in spite of the events which have changed the hearts of so many persons, Your Royal Highness still preserves some sentiments of friendship for me . . .'

In spite of all the favours Napoleon had lavished on him in the past, the grand duke did not have either the compassion or the common politeness to reply. He handed the letter, without comment, to the emperor Francis. Francis kept it four days, then passed it on to Marie Louise who, in turn, seems to have mentioned it to de Menéval: 'It had been shown to the sovereigns without any doubt,' de Menéval commented, 'for it was with that intention that the Emperor Francis required his daughter to hand over all letters received from her husband. The Empress did not reply to this epistle as she did not receive permission to do so.' The Baron does not add – perhaps at that stage he did not realise – that she had no wish to do so.

The blank silence greeting this appeal did much to contribute to Napoleon's determination to embark on his last gamble.

Behind the congress's façade of abandoned gaiety, a number of deputies were more interested in the work in hand than the apogée of good living and luxury. Leader of this party was Talleyrand, determined to extinguish the last embers of Bonapartism even though he still continued to cling to his Napoleonic title of prince of Benevento. His reports to Louis XVIII show frequent signs of impatience – 'his' (Metternich's) 'great art is to make us lose our time, for he believes that he gains by it' – particularly when Metternich, surprisingly enough, defended Murat's doubtful rights to the throne of Naples, a partisanship which Talleyrand did not hesitate to put down to the Austrian chancellor's passion for Caroline Bonaparte. However, if he saw fit to give way over the question of the Murats, feeling that Murat, brilliant as he might be at leading a cavalry charge, was so inept a politician he would inevitably bring about his own destruction, Talleyrand was an even more bitter opponent of Parma being handed over to Marie Louise, with rights of succession for her son. Such an act, he insisted, was to provide an incubator for future Bonapartist plots.

Article V of the Fontainebleau treaty had laid down that the duchies of Parma, Guastalla and Piacenza were guaranteed to Marie Louise and her son. Talleyrand himself was one of the signatories. The prince of Benevento, however, was not the sort of man who allowed his policy to be affected by such trifles as signatures and treaties. From the moment the subject was brought up for discussion, he threw himself wholeheartedly in with the Spanish faction.

The Spanish delegate, the marquis of Labrador, seconded by Talleyrand, claimed that the duchies should revert to the Infanta Maria Luisa of Spain, Queen of Etruria, and that, as compensation, Marie Louise should be given certain estates, nominally the property of the king of Bavaria, bringing in an annual revenue of 400,000 florins; and, in addition, the miniature principality of Lucca which, however, would have to revert to the grand duke of Tuscany on her death. Talleyrand himself summed up the proposals in a despatch to Louis XVIII, dated February 15/18th 1815: 'As to the territorial arrangements in Italy, the commission charged with preparing the plan have proposed to give Parma, Piacenza and Guastalla to the Queen of Etruria; the Legations to the Holy See; the Prendes, Piambino and Elba, on reversion, to the Grand Duke of Tuscany. The Archduchess Marie Louise would have certain fiefs formerly held by the old German Empire . . . they are situated in Bohemia and would yield an income of four hundred thousand florins. This scheme was presented by us. It has the double advantage, not merely of diminishing the number of petty sovereignties in Italy but, what is still more essential, of keeping the Archduchess's son out of the way and depriving him of all expectation of ever reigning . . . But, knowing that his' (the emperor Francis) 'daughter is determined to have an independent establishment, he has proposed that she shall have Lucca, and has charged his Minister to negotiate the affair with her.'

At this point, Neipperg proved invaluable. Metternich was as little troubled by scruples as was Talleyrand. The new scheme struck him as admirable. It was also approved by the chief British delegate, Lord Castlereagh, and the king of Prussia. Francis certainly felt guilty at once again betraying his daughter's interests and dishonouring his signature, yet he would not consider opposing his chancellor's decision.

Neipperg, outraged at the thought of what was to him a stain on Austrian honour and thinking, also, that his own future might, under certain circumstances, be wrapped up with Parma, urged Marie Louise to protest, to refuse the petty offer made her under the guise of compensation. Because she was in love, to everyone's great surprise she protested most vigorously. Caught off balance by this unpredicted opposition, an alternative scheme was put forward by France and Spain to depose Murat in return for Marie Louise's accession to Parma. This, however, ran foul of Metternich's plans.

Matters had reached an apparent deadlock when Neipperg had the genial idea that Marie Louise should make a personal appeal to the czar.

Alexander was flattered and at once promised his help. An incurable romantic rather than a Casanova, he saw himself as an imperial knight errant, the champion of ladies in distress. In this role, he had visited Josephine at Malmaison and Marie Louise at Rambouillet. Now he saw another chance to be known, above all, as a chivalrous prince. On the personal side, there was also an ingrained hatred of the French and the Bourbons. He had even been heard to hint that he preferred Napoleon to Louis XVIII and to suggest that perhaps he had made an error in not insisting on the rights of the king of Rome. Looking on him as the founder of allied victory, impressed by Russia's military power, the delegates bowed to his pleas, or rather insistence, that article V of the treaty of Fontainebleau be honoured.

Talleyrand fought them doggedly. Alexander, however, exercised the greater influence and at last, since there were other, more important, issues to be discussed and settled, a compromise was reached. The ex-empress of France could take possession of the duchy of Parma, provided she agreed to two conditions: the first, that her son would not inherit the duchy; the second, that he would not accompany her but remain under tutorship in Vienna. On these two points the delegates were unanimous.

Von Neipperg, charged with the task of informing her of these conditions, was able to persuade her to accept them without undue difficulty; especially when she realised that they would be taking up residence in Parma together. It was a question of sacrificing herself for her son, Neipperg argued. If she refused the duchy of Parma, under the terms offered, what would happen to him? He reminded her that she was almost penniless. As matters stood she had no sources of income whatever, and Austria was still poor. Since fear of Napoleon was so much alive in Europe she could never hope to obtain any form of political independence for her son, but at least she could, as duchess of Parma, a wealthy state, assure him a considerable material independence.

Her acceptance took the form of a letter to her father: 'I will not hide from you, my dear father, that it grieves me deeply to have to agree to these changes regarding my son's future, which I certainly did not expect, especially after the immense personal sacrifices I have agreed to in the past for the sake of Europe's tranquillity . . .'

There is a brief passage of near defiance when she adds: 'It is my duty as a mother, and my firm resolution to see, not only fixed, but established in my lifetime the basis of my son's future establishment . . .'

But she ended submissively, on Neipperg's suggestion: 'It will break my heart going to Parma separated, by your gracious decision, from my son; but, better than anyone else, you know what is best for me and for him, and so in this as in everything I will follow your paternal advice blindly . . .'

Both de Menéval and Madame de Montesquiou were horrified. They now despised their ex-empress more deeply than ever before. It was bad enough that, after being Napoleon's wife, she made little attempt to hide the fact that she had a lover while her husband was a lonely exile, but that now she proposed to abandon her son, her only child, placed her beyond contempt. De Menéval had the courage to remonstrate with her. She told him sullenly that he did not understand, that she was doing the best she could for 'Napoleon's son', and that the situation was probably only temporary as her father had promised 'to do everything possible in their interests'.

'The child hasn't even a name,' de Menéval continued. 'Nobody knows what to call him these days.'*

Marie Louise confined her reply to a vague statement regarding 'financial benefits' and 'financial independence'.

Madame de Montesquiou knew that arguments, pleas, were useless. She maintained an austere silence. When, however, she received a letter from her husband, begging her to return to Paris, she replied: 'My dear friend, please don't tell me it's my duty to return to France; as I have told you already, were I to do so, I would live with a guilty conscience for the rest of my life. If this child had a mother, well and good, I would place him in her arms and be happy. But this is not the case. She is a creature more totally indifferent to his fate than the least of the strangers in his service.'

There follows a reference to the remaining French members of Marie Louise's entourage: 'Without me they would not know what was to become of them and the poor child would suffer still more. We are a forlorn flock weeping often round this sad cradle . . .'

Though this letter is in rather a melodramatic vein, there was no doubt that the young Napoleon deserved to be pitied. Fatherless, thanks to political intrigue, his mother was by now so infatuated that all her flamboyant declarations concerning maternal love and duty were so many empty phrases. At this stage Marie Louise would, Faust-like, have sold her soul to the Devil if Neipperg had suggested it.

By the New Year of 1815, Napoleon realised that his dream of a peaceful life on his miniature island was a chimera.

Difficulties, deceptions, backed by vague threats, multiplied almost daily. He now knew for a certainty that he would never be allowed to see either his wife or his son again. In fact, not one of the conditions to which he had agreed and which, basically, had governed his final decision to abdicate, were being honoured by the allies. The two million francs annual pension promised under the terms of the treaty of Fontainebleau had not been paid. He had every reason to suspect that they never would be. He was

* It was very true. No longer king of Rome, he was referred to for a brief while as prince of Parma. Once deprived of this ephemeral title, he was generally spoken of vaguely as *le petit Monsieur*.

approaching bankruptcy. Furthermore, he was informed of the trend of opinion, openly discussed at the Vienna congress, that Elba was too close to Europe for Europe's peace of mind, and the proposals that he should be removed, by force if necessary, to one of the Azores or St Helena; that others, more extremist, were suggesting that even this was not enough, that peace would only be assured from the day of his death, if need be, from an assassin's knife or bullet. This latter threat was, indeed, so sharply defined that both day and night guards on his residence were doubled and orders issued to coastal forts to fire on any ship approaching the shore that might be suspect. At the same time, stirring barely-dimmed memories, rumours poured in from France, that already, a bare six months after the restoration, Louis XVIII and his régime were detested, and that in all grades of society people talked nostalgically of their 'emperor', offering up prayers for his return.

Fears, loneliness, material difficulties, false hopes, decided him finally to risk everything. Ageing in mind though still only middle-aged in years, and with no really valid advisers, he lapsed into the fatal trap of what is popularly known as 'wishful thinking', deforming hope into reality.

'France having welcomed him with open arms, Europe, disgusted with the Bourbons, would not hesitate to recognise him. England, satisfied by the fact that France was once again limited to the pre-Revolution boundaries, would not refute him. The Austrian emperor would be happy to re-find a son-in-law and see his daughter once more on Europe's most dazzling throne. Finally he, Napoleon, would reassure the legitimate kings that they had nothing to fear from him and that he would be even more "constitutional" than the Bourbons . . .'*

In this mood he made his preparations. On Saturday, February 25th, he attended a fête in Portoferraio given by his sister Pauline who, with his mother, had insisted on sharing his exile. It is reported that he was unusually gay, stayed later than was his custom at such functions, then ordered Generals Druont and Bertrand to accompany him home. Both generals knew what was in the emperor's mind but, so Bertrand says, could hardly believe their ears when they were told, 'We start tomorrow.'

*   *   *

* Jacques Bainville: op. cit.

The evening of March 6th the Austrian empress, Maria Ludovica, already affording observers justifiable cause to predict that she would not be much longer with them, gave a gala. The highlight was another series of the *tableaux vivants* which were proving such a success. 'The principal scene, the gem of the evening, represented a meeting between Maximilian I with Mary of Burgundy, after the picture by the Viennese artist, Petter. The most beautiful women of the Court, the duchesse de Sagan, the countess Fuchs, the duchesse de Dino, etc. excited, one after the other, the admiration of the spectators who sought to identify in each succeeding *tableau* the fair representatives of the various parts. The air of revelry had, to a certain extent, set etiquette at defiance.

'The audience marvelled at the beauty of the performers and an atmosphere of seductive mirth seemed to fill the great halls of the palace . . .'*

The same evening, Metternich was presiding over a meeting, in his palace, of the council of five, which lasted till four in the morning of the 7th.

At six, he had only just got to sleep when his valet came into his bedroom with an urgent despatch from Genoa. Metternich left the despatch unopened on his bedside table and tried to go to sleep again, but at roughly seven-thirty, wide awake, decided to open it. Its contents made him jump out of bed and hurry across to the emperor Francis. 'The English commissioner Campbell† has just come into the port' (Genoa) 'to find out if anyone had seen Napoleon in Genoa, after his disappearance from Elba. The reply being negative, the British frigate put to sea again without delaying.'

Francis, according to Metternich, received the news calmly.

He said: 'Napoleon seems bent on running the gravest risks, that is his business. Ours is to give the world that peace which he has troubled for so many years. Please inform the Emperor of Russia and the King of Prussia straightaway and tell them I am ready to order my army to march on France. I am sure the two sovereigns will wish to follow my example.'

*   *   *

* Max Billard: *The Marriage Ventures of Marie Louise.* Nash, 1910.
† Colonel Campbell had been appointed by the allies to take up residence in Elba to keep watch and report on Napoleon's activities.

The news produced a brief moment of near panic, followed almost immediately by satisfaction. The 'Monster' had played into the allies' hands. He had proved, beyond a doubt, that his very being threw a menacing shadow across the world and that, like a wild beast, a mad dog, he must be destroyed: there could be no further question of mercy, of dealings based on the tenets of normal, civilised diplomatic procedure. Those who had warned against the danger of Elba's proximity to the mainland, who had urged banishment to St Helena or the Azores, were able to adopt a triumphant 'I told you so' attitude. To such an extent that one is tempted to wonder whether the incessant goading, the sad record of broken promises, the retention of wife and son, were not all part of a deliberate plot to bring about this very situation in which scruples could, with outward legality, be banished.

Certainly nobody could have seized upon the occasion with greater determination and alacrity than the delegates – of these, Talleyrand being by far the most virulent – to draw up the document declaring Napoleon an 'outlaw', to which they hastened to put their signatures. 'By returning to France with the purpose of stirring up strife he' (Napoleon) 'has deprived himself of the protection of international law and has manifested clearly to the universe that, with him, there can be neither truce nor peace. Consequently, the Powers declare that Napoleon Bonaparte has placed himself beyond the bounds of normal civil and social relationships, and will be handed over to public vengeance.'

'Now that he has escaped, he must be hanged!' Alexis de Noailles, one of the French delegates shouted excitedly.

To which the king of Prussia replied gloomily, 'You've got to catch him before you hang him.'

A number of people, as always, fancied they saw in Napoleon's escape some sinister machinations on the part of 'perfidious Albion'; but this age-old cry did not last long in view of violent British reaction, the British army being the first to complete its re-mobilisation. For once, in fact the only time in her quarrelsome history, Europe stood united.

Again Neipperg had the task of imparting the news to Marie Louise.

While on one of their solitary morning walks he told her that Napoleon had run the blockade, was on French soil and advancing, across the Alps, on Paris. As usual, he showed himself an able diplomat, for her first positive action was to write a letter,

251

probably at his dictation, to her father: 'At this moment, when a further crisis threatens Europe's tranquillity, and further misfortunes menace me, I cannot hope for a more sure asylum, a more certain protection, than that which I demand for myself and my son from your paternal affection. It is in your arms, my very dear father, that I take refuge with the one who is the most dear to me in this world. Into your hands, under your paternal care, I entrust our fate. I could not place it under a more sacred aegis. We will not seek any other direction than yours. You will deign to order, with your usual gentleness, all our coming and going.'

This done, she issued a statement to the effect that she had no part in the emperor's plans and placed herself under the protection of the allied powers. In diplomatic jargon, she was reiterating her uncle's, the archduke John's, words: 'I feel very sorry for you, my poor Louise, but the best thing that could happen both for you and for us would be for him to break his damn' neck!'

It was several months since love had turned to indifference, a desire to forget, to ignore the past, and this indifference now flamed to near hatred, for Napoleon's ill-considered return meant that she was to be separated from her lover, a separation whose prospect drove her almost frantic since it would entail exposure of that precious life to the perils of battle.

In Naples, Murat had been kept well informed of the congress's bitter opposition to everything that smacked of Bonapartism. He knew that he enjoyed Metternich's protection, but was afraid that even the chancellor's influence could not prevail permanently against the united front of the rest of the allies. Nor, clinging to his precious throne, was he happy. Though vain, stupid, weakly ambitious, he was not a born Judas. The trappings of majesty could not entirely stifle the voice of his conscience or obscure the memory of his betrayal. It is possible that there were times when he was tempted to admit that the retribution hanging over his head was not unjustified. As a result, when he heard the news of the landing at Cannes, he welcomed it as a heaven-sent opportunity to wipe out the stain on his honour.

Without attempting to weigh up the situation, without even waiting to ascertain whether his action would be welcomed by the man in whose esteem he hoped to re-establish himself, he left

Naples at the head of 50,000 men, after writing to Napoleon: 'I learn with inexpressible joy that Your Majesty has landed on the shores of Europe. I should have been glad to receive some instruction to co-ordinate my movements in Italy with yours in France,' and marched north in order, as he thought, to create a diversion which would draw off the bulk of the Austrian army from France, thus facilitating the imperial advance on Paris.

It was a pity, both for him and Napoleon, that he acted so typically impulsively instead of waiting for 'some instruction'. His act of war became known just as Napoleon was bombarding Vienna and London with protestations of his pacific intentions, with his solemn assurances that all he wished to do was to devote himself to France's internal prosperity and live on the friendliest terms with his neighbours. The allies would have in all probability refused to listen to him in any case, but Murat provided them with a perfect excuse for not doing so, for rejecting his peaceful declarations as false and hypocritical. Later, Napoleon was to say: 'Twice Murat was responsible for the Empire's downfall. The first time by abandoning it, the second time by coming to its aid.'

Though the Austrians had a very low opinion of the Neapolitan troops, Murat's name as a military leader was still redoubtable. For this reason it was decided to send the one man looked upon as his rival against him. Towards the end of March, therefore, von Neipperg reassumed command of his cavalry division and moved to join the main body of the Austrian army under General Bianchi near Tolentino.

Marie Louise was inconsolable. The role of grass widow did not suit her. She was so much in love that she could not find any solace in her son. Even the adored duchess of Montebello, whose company in the past had compensated to some extent for Napoleon's absences, was many hundreds of miles away.

As usual, she spent hours writing long letters, while Neipperg, even on campaign, was able to find time to compose lengthy epistles often attaining eight to ten pages. Both became agitated if the correspondence's rhythm broke down. From Sinegalia, on May 2nd, Neipperg wrote: 'I have received no news from Your Imperial Majesty since the 17th of last month. This makes me very anxious, as I gathered from the last news Your Majesty was good enough to send me regarding your health that it was not quite what it should be. I tremble when I think of anything disagreeable happening to Your Majesty, whose extreme kindness

253

and angelic nature merits nothing but happiness, and I pray God daily, even in the heat of battle, for the well being of Your Majesty. Your Majesty does not tell me whether you ride much, and if so, with whom.

'I shall always be delighted to hear even the smallest detail as to life at Schoenbrunn at the present time. I have not seen a pianoforte since I left Schoenbrunn; music, like everything else, is now laid aside . . . Firing has broken out at my outposts. I am going to join them on Cortez, my favourite charger.'

The firing he mentioned was the prelude to the battle of Tolentino, a battle fought with great ferocity. A furious cavalry charge, headed by von Neipperg, was the decisive action giving the Austrians victory. The Neapolitans broke and ran before the onslaught of close on two thousand horsemen. Murat himself left the battlefield, raced back to Naples from where, abandoning Caroline, he escaped to the island of Ischia and thence, after a hazardous three-day journey, landed on the coast of France, also near Cannes, hoping to take refuge with his brother-in-law. A vain hope: Napoleon, wild with rage at his disastrous folly, refused to receive him.

Eighteen days later Neipperg, at the head of two cavalry regiments forming the Austrian army vanguard, entered Naples.

Hero of this short successful campaign, he expected to be able to return to Vienna. Instead, he was ordered, with his division, to the south of France, to take up his appointment as military governor of the provinces of Herault, Gard and Ardèche.

Generally speaking, Neipperg is most unpopular with French writers. Few can refrain from making highly uncomplimentary remarks about him. Even anti-Bonapartists find it impossible to forgive him for having made a *cocu* out of Napoleon; but of his brief – till December of that year – exercise of power, Max Billard says: 'It was now that his energy, tolerance and moderation enabled him to solve problems more difficult for a soldier than mere acts of heroism. Although he was in command of an army of Catholics, he protected the Protestants from the tyranny of the rival Church, and succeeded in reconciling the hitherto unreconcilable parties. He displayed so much moderation and justice in his dealings with the people that, in token of their gratitude, and prompted by a unanimous impulse, they erected floral triumphal arches in his honour . . .'

Carrying out this task, Neipperg was obliged to dominate his impatience to rejoin Marie Louise. But he was not worried that he might be supplanted, for shortly after Tolentino he had received a long letter from her, ending: '. . . my son sends you all sorts of affectionate messages. He is always asking about you and about Cortez who, he is fully convinced, made the journey sitting by you in your carriage. Please keep on giving me advice, I feel no one can do so as well as you. I count on you absolutely, however difficult the circumstances, because I know you always tell me the truth. Be assured, too, of all my gratitude and friendship . . .'

Napoleon's reappearance on the European stage also marked the end of Marie Louise's miniature French court within the court of Schoenbrunn, and with the departure of its last figurants departed the last vestiges of French influence in her life.

The ex-empress ceased to be *La Française*. Spiritually she reverted to the land of her birth. From then on she would be totally Austrian, with no regrets, no nostalgia for that other life with all its brilliant, though transient, glory.

Madame de Montesquiou was the first to leave.

Typical war-time rumours were circulating that there was a plot to kidnap the little Napoleon and smuggle him into France. A preliminary step to safeguard against this reunion of father and son was the prompt removal of the child from the Schoenbrunn to the more easily guarded Hofburg. Even there he was not considered to be in total security since Madame de Montesquiou was known to be such a fanatical Bonapartist.

March 20th, two days after he and his entourage had taken up residence in the grey, rather gloomy Hofburg, was the little boy's fourth birthday. According to Madame de Montesquiou, he was dressed and had just finished saying his prayers when there was a knock on the door and the grand chamberlain, Count d'Urbain, entered. The countess, imagining he had come to present official birthday congratulations, was surprised when he said, ignoring the child: 'Madame, I wish to speak to you in private.'

The moment the child and his under-governess had left the room, the count announced abruptly: 'The Emperor, my master, has ordered me to tell you that due to the political situation, he is obliged to make certain changes regarding his grandson's education. He wishes to thank you for all you have done for him and requests you to leave for Paris immediately.'

Although staggered by the suddenness of the blow, she managed to say calmly that, if such were the case, she wished to hand the child into the emperor's *personal* care. Surprised by her attitude, d'Urbain said that he must 'discuss the matter' and left the room. He was back within a few minutes, this time with a letter in the emperor's own handwriting:

Madame, Countess of Montesquiou. Circumstances oblige me to order a change regarding the persons responsible for my grandson's education. I do not wish to let this occasion go by without expressing to you my deepest gratitude for all the care you have given him since his birth. Accept this gratitude and also this little souvenir that, Madame Countess of Montesquiou, I have asked my Chamberlain to offer to you.

Your affectionate: Francis

'This little souvenir,' says Madame de Montesquiou, 'was a superb sapphire necklace. My first reaction was one of extreme indignation. I told him' (Count d'Urbain) 'that I refused to accept any gift from the Austrian emperor. He put it on the table. I asked him to take it back to the emperor, and say that I did not accept any reward for having done my duty. Count d'Urbain said that he could not do this and that, moreover, one could not refuse the emperor's gifts. Then suddenly he began to mutter excuses that perhaps it had not been presented in a proper case. I was disgusted, realising, too, that this imbecile was incapable of understanding my feelings . . .'

At that moment, the countess goes on, the door opened and Marie Louise came in. She looked 'cold but slightly embarrassed', though at the same time obviously delighted by the news that at last she was getting rid of the person who had been such a deadly enemy of the adored Montebello, and who lately had made herself even more unpopular by not hesitating to make her stern, puritanical disapproval of the 'ex-empress's' liaison with 'the one-eyed general' abundantly clear.

'So, Madame,' said the countess, 'I suppose you will always believe the unpleasant things my enemies say about me.'

'They say a great many,' was the cold reply.

Madame de Montesquiou goes on: 'I then said that I wished the Emperor's leading medical advisers, as well as the child's normal doctor and the Empress's surgeon, to be called in, that the child should be carefully examined, and that a certificate should be handed to me that the child was in perfect health . . .'

The determined Madame de Montesquiou had her way, not only as regards the certificate but also on her insistence that she spend the rest of the day with the little boy, put him to bed in the normal way and that he should not be told of these 'changes' till after her departure. That evening 'I went over to the little bed where my charge was sleeping. I got down on my knees and prayed for him. I prayed above all that his name should never be made use of for the stirring up of strife. I kissed him several times, then tore myself away after attaching a little crucifix he'd often asked me to give him to his bed curtain . . .'*

De Menéval did not have to be asked to leave. He was anxious to be with Napoleon again, though dreading the inevitable explanation as to how matters stood with Marie Louise. Feeling that he was harmless, the Austrian authorities gave him the necessary travel documents immediately. Before leaving, however, he had a brief interview with the empress (as he insisted on calling her) and took his farewell of the little Napoleon, now generally known as Franz, the use of the name Napoleon having been forbidden officially.

Marie Louise, says the baron, seemed 'very moved' but quite determined as regards the attitude she meant to adopt. She told him frankly that she hoped Napoleon would not expect her return. 'I feel that all relations between France and myself are at an end,' she said. 'But I will always remember with affection my adopted land. Assure the Emperor of my good wishes. I hope he will understand my unhappy position. I will never consent to a divorce, but I flatter myself that he will agree to a friendly separation and will not conceive any resentment on that account. Such a separation has become inevitable. It will not, however, alter my sentiments of gratitude and esteem.'

The baron was then presented with a gold snuff-box inlaid with the empress's monogram in diamonds.

* The countess had to pay for her forthrightness. On leaving the Hofburg, she was escorted to a small, two-room apartment with her son Anatole, who had arrived in Vienna with a message from Napoleon that same day, where they were kept under 'house arrest' for ten weeks.

The prim discourse has a hypocritical ring, and the statement regarding divorce would seem, on the surface, surprising until one remembers that her marriage to Napoleon was considered invalid by the Vatican. Mere words, therefore, cost her nothing.

The farewell to the former 'little king' is described in an emotional vein. Having witnessed the child's heartbreak on learning of his beloved 'Mama Quiou's' departure, de Menéval pitied him profoundly. He touches on his 'wistful appearance', and continues: 'He had a serious, even melancholy air. He had lost that gaiety and loquacity which everyone found so charming. When I entered, he gave no sign of welcome. I went up to him, took him by the hand and asked if he had a message for his father who I would soon be seeing. He withdrew his hand, looking at me sadly, and walked over to a window. After a few words with his entourage, I followed him to where he was apart, all by himself, staring at us. As I stooped towards him to say farewell, he drew me to the window and whispered with the most touching expression: "Monsieur Méva, tell him that I still love him very much" . . .'

Chapter XIV

Within a few hours of being re-installed in the Tuileries, Napoleon was writing to Marie Louise, begging her to hurry back to Paris with her son, and to the emperor Francis to respect the sanctity of marriage and family ties.

A first message was transmitted through Count Bubna, then Austrian commander in Torino: 'Come and join me with your son. I hope to hold you in my arms again before the end of March.'

This was followed by a more formal letter from Paris: 'My good Louise, I am master of all France. The people, the army, are mad with joy. The soi-disant King has fled to England. I expect you here with my son, sometime in April. Goodbye, my friend . . .'

A few days later: 'My good Louise. I've written to you several times. I am adored and master of all I survey. Only you and my son are missing. Come straight away to Strasburg. The bearer of this letter will tell you everything about the spirit in France today.'

To reinforce this call, there was an appeal to the emperor Francis: '. . . I know fully the principles guiding Your Majesty. I know so well the value you attach to family ties, not to be happily confident that you will be only too eager, whatever your cabinet and politicians may say, to help the reunion of a husband with his wife, of a son with his father . . .'

Despite stony silence and a statement from Metternich to the French envoy, Montron, that 'Europe will *never* negotiate with the usurper or any of his family' Napoleon persisted in his deluded optimism. Even his talks with de Menéval, on the latter's arrival from Vienna, could not rid him of the delusion that family bonds which he himself held so sacred would triumph in the end.

To begin with, as in the early days of the 1814 campaign, it seemed that there might be some justification for this optimism.

The first week in May, a meeting took place at Basle between a secret emissary of Metternich's, Baron Ottenfels, and Fleury de Chaboulon, acting on Napoleon's behalf, to discuss the possibility of the French emperor's abdication following on the solemn promise of the allies to recognise the child Franz as the 'legitimate' future Napoleon II, and the interim regency of Marie Louise.

Napoleon, definitely marked by the cancer of the stomach which was to prove fatal, disappointed by the mire of political intrigue engulfing him in Paris, and the allies' continued and bitter hostility which, too optimistically, he had hoped would be dissipated by the *fait accompli*, looked upon this solution as his salvation.

Baron Ottenfels, in a message which gave the impression of being addressed to the French people rather than to Napoleon in person, stated: 'I am authorised to make a formal declaration to the effect that the Allied sovereigns have renounced their intention of restoring the Bourbons on the throne and consent to give you the young prince Napoleon. But first the Emperor must be deposed. After this, the Allies will take the necessary steps; they are powerful, generous minded and humane, and you may depend upon it that Napoleon will be treated with the regard due to his rank, his marriage and his misfortune . . .'

There was something in this document's tone which aroused the emperor's suspicions. He hedged. 'These gentlemen are beginning to get soft,' he remarked. 'Give me another month and I'll have nothing to fear from them.'

Three nights later, that of May 14–15th, another of his envoys, Baron Stressard, on his way back to Paris from Vienna, was stopped at Linz and politely forced to make a wide detour via Munich where, to his astonishment, he was interviewed by Prince Eugène de Beauharnais who assured him that: 'Prince Wrede, who had just arrived from Vienna, was now authorised to state that if Napoleon abdicated before the first shot was fired, his dynasty would be recognised by Austria who had every hope that she could persuade the Allies to follow her example, but on condition that he, Napoleon, gave himself up to his father-in-law who offered to house him in any place of his choice, within his estates . . .'

Like a wary animal, Napoleon sensed a trap. After the treaty of Fontainebleau he had too little confidence in allied promises, including those of his father-in-law, to place himself meekly in their hands, a willing lamb for the sacrifice. Whether or not the offer were genuine will never be known. In view of the proclamation placing Napoleon 'outside the protection of normal inter-

national law', it is open to doubt whether, even had he wished to
do so, Francis would have been strong enough to keep his
daughter's husband from the clutches of his more baleful enemies.
At the same time, the hypothesis of a trap, either to lay hands on
the emperor's person or enflame discord within France itself,
cannot be ignored.

A third aspect, however, which these two declarations seemed
to have brushed aside, was Marie Louise's possible refusal of the
regency, obsessed as she was at this time by paradisiacal dreams
of her little duchy, and of Neipperg, and her growing retrospective
detestation of the French people – with the exception always of
Madame de Montebello – whom she referred to frequently as
'disloyal, shameless, Godless', adding, 'I am determined never,
at any price, to set foot in France again!'

To all these feelers, Napoleon's final reply, undoubtedly very
much to his regret, was 'No.' The result of this 'No' was Waterloo.

It could hardly have been otherwise. Mutual trust was non-
existent.

While these semi-secret negotiations were in progress, the vexed
Parma question came up for debate before the Vienna congress
on May 27th.

The proceedings were heated. The king of Prussia, Talleyrand
representing Louis XVIII, Metternich himself, fervently sup-
ported the Spanish claim, basing their arguments on the fact that
by his escape from Elba, Napoleon had automatically rendered
the treaty of Fontainebleau null and void. Once more, but for
the czar's mulishly obstinate chivalry, Marie Louise's dreams
would have been dissipated. As it was, the Russian emperor – to
whom, acting on Neipperg's written advice, Marie Louise had
paid another tearful visit imploring his protection – feeling more
than ever the champion of all ladies in distress, was so dramatic
in his repeated assertions that the question was not one of
politics but of honour, that his opponents gave way. It was
stipulated, however, that the duchess of Parma should not enter
her estates till the 'emergency' had been resolved – in other
words, till after Napoleon's defeat – and no mention of her son
was made beyond an oblique reference that 'the reversion of the
duchies would be studied at a later date'.

The czar, however, still persisting in his championing of

Marie Louise's cause, persuaded both Metternich and the Prussian king to sign a secret clause promising to back young Franz's claims on his mother's death. Metternich signed for the sake of form. He had taken into account Marie Louise's youth, reckoning that where such long-term questions were concerned the future had a habit of looking after itself. Prussia's monarch, less subtle of mind, appended his signature, not feeling himself strong enough to oppose the two giants.

The matter settled, Marie Louise issued her first declaration to her future subjects:

'We, Empress Marie Louise, Archduchess of Austria, Duchess of Parma, Piacenza and Guastalla, make known to all subjects and inhabitants of our Estates of Parma that, having taken into consideration the many circumstances rendering our presence impossible in the above mentioned Estates, we have begged our well beloved father, Emperor and King, to administer them temporarily in our name. We wish and conjure our faithful subjects of Parma, Piacenza and Guastalla to obey all orders and dispositions that his Imperial Majesty will deign to make known to them, because such is our pleasure.'

The final sentence was a diplomatic untruth. Marie Louise was most displeased at being kept from her 'Estates'. She was only comforted by the word 'temporarily', consoling herself with the thought that, in any case, she did not wish to make her official entry into Parma unaccompanied by Adam von Neipperg. For both these reasons she now prayed fervently for the speedy defeat of the man who, a few months ago, she had professed to love faithfully, gratefully, ardently.

To try to kill time, Marie Louise accompanied her stepmother to Baden, leaving Vienna at the beginning of June. It was there they received the news of Waterloo, followed soon after by that of Napoleon's flight and surrender to the English. Europe rejoiced. The reigning families, especially, felt as though they had just escaped from a twenty-year epidemic of the plague.

Maria Ludovica informed the emperor Francis: 'When I received your letter I was with our dear Louise who thanked God that, for the sake of the world's peace of mind and because it means she can soon go to Parma, he' (Napoleon) 'is in captivity.'

There is, however, another version of the duchess of Parma's reactions which we owe to the baroness Montet who heard the news as she arrived in Baden, and hurried to tell her friend Elisa, the Marquise de Scarampi, Franz's governess, who had taken over the ungrateful post of successor to 'Mama Quiou'.*

The baroness says she was a bit surprised as 'Elisa received us with transports of joy which, considering her position, I found really a little extravagant. She was jumping about, singing, dancing, so overjoyed was she by the good news. When she calmed down a little, I asked her if Marie Louise had been informed. "I'm going to write it down for her," she replied, "because the Empress never receives anyone before eleven o'clock." She sat down at her desk and wrote a note to the princess. We awaited the reply with impatience and a lively curiosity; and here it is, word for word: "Thank you. I already know about this. I think I'd like to ride to Merkenstein; do you think the weather is good enough to risk it?" '

In spite of her often quoted naivety, it would seem that Marie Louise had learned how to administer a snub.

On the contrary, her letter to her father was coldly explicit: 'Nobody could be happier than I am at the satisfactory issue of the war. I have learnt, too, with joy, that the King' (Louis XVIII) 'has re-entered his capital. This reassures me over the question of stupid rumours which are circulating, for you know, my very dear papa, how anxious I am to spend my life near you and at Parma. Do you not think that this might be the right moment to get the English and French cabinets to agree to the secret clauses assuring my son's succession to the duchies? . . . my son kisses your hand, and begs me to say he will do everything he can to grow up a good boy. He reads French very well and a little Italian. I've promised him when he knows this language really well to ask you, in his name, for an Austrian regiment, it is all he wants, and if you will grant him this, I hope that my little François (sic) will, with time, show himself worthy of it . . .'

The 'stupid rumours' were those referring to the Bourbons' extreme unpopularity and the revival of the idea that the regency and Napoleon II would be preferable to the eighteenth Louis.

* Elisa had been Countess Mitrovsky when she succeeded Madame de Montesquiou, but shortly afterwards married the Marquis de Scarampi.

The very thought filled her with panic. How could she, regent in Paris, possibly get her lover accepted as a member of her household? He, an Austrian, a foreigner, in a re-born imperial Court!

She needed reassurance.

Her father was in Paris when she wrote to him in August: 'I beg of you to remember what you said just before you left, that is to say that, never, under any circumstances whatsoever, would it be possible for me to return to France. I've just heard that the King's party is very strong, and I'm delighted . . .'

'You may be sure' (Francis replied soothingly) 'that I won't make you come to Paris. I wouldn't want even my worst enemy to rule, let alone live, here . . .'

Nevertheless, a slight feeling of remorse may have stirred within her when Metternich sent a casual note to say that Napoleon was on his way to permanent exile in the open prison that was St Helena, a remorse she felt necessary to commit to paper: 'My very dear papa. I hope we will have a lasting peace now that Napoleon is en route for St Helena, and will never again be able to trouble it. I hope he will be treated with kindness and clemency, and I beg you, very dear papa, to ensure it. It is the only request I dare to put forward, and it is the last time I will occupy myself with his future; I owe him a certain gratitude for the calm indifference in which he allowed me to live instead of making me unhappy . . .'

The letter was dated August 15th – Napoleon's birthday.

France's ex-empress could not congratulate herself on her behaviour since leaving France just over sixteen months ago. The most charitable of biographers could hardly deny that she had been guilty of the grossest ingratitude combined with abject betrayal. Under the stress, the outside pressure to which she had been subjected almost continually, combined with Neipperg's notorious talent in the art of seduction, she might be forgiven for accepting the one-eyed general as her lover. What is more difficult to whitewash is her repudiation of Napoleon who, in many ways, could scarcely have been a kinder, more tender and devoted husband and father; her cynical disregard of her own words, her vows of eternal love poured out in a flood to friends, relations, family, during her four years as empress, only to be followed by equally ardent prayers for this same, apparently once-adored husband's defeat and ruin. In this she was betraying not only her husband but her son. To gratify her longing for her peaceful Italian estates, she was quite happy to see her son's life wrecked before it had even begun, indifferent that the child who had been born king of Rome should end his days an obscure German princeling without estates, an embarrassment to the Austrian court, virtually and permanently a semi-prisoner.* Her only excuse – if it can be ranked as an excuse – was her genuine worship of von Neipperg.

Love for Napoleon had been forced on her. It had been born of the incredible relief at the discovery that the 'ogre', the master, was in fact a warm, affectionate and passionate individual who, as a lover, awakened her to the subconscious realisation of her congenital sensuality. Adam von Neipperg, on the other hand, appeared as the man of her own choosing, and their love a spontaneous eruption divorced from political expediency and parental authority. Nor should it be forgotten that whereas Napoleon and Marie Louise – apart from marriage's purely physical aspect – had nothing in common, she and Adam von Neipperg shared a dozen pleasures, and in particular their love of music.

Fortunately for the memories that she was to leave behind her, in 1815 Marie Louise had still not arrived at her *mezzo camino de la vita*. She was only twenty-four, and was to live another thirty-two years. In 1815, though her betrayal had undoubtedly served the allied cause, there were many among the allies themselves who despised her, and for a multitude in France her name was anathema. However, when she died in 1847, she was mourned not only by most of those in whose company she moved as parent or friend, but by those whom she had ruled so benevolently.

Marie Louise and her stepmother returned to Vienna in mid-September. At this stage she could have evoked the fact that the 'emergency' was ended and set out for Parma. She preferred, however, to wait for von Neipperg and remain near her son

---

* Her behaviour seems all the more sordid when compared with that of Jerome's wife, Catherine of Westphalia. After Napoleon's abdication, every effort was made to force her into a divorce. She refused categorically. 'Forced by political reasons to espouse the King, my husband,' she wrote to her father, 'I bear for my husband all the united sentiments of love, tenderness and esteem. . .'

till the inevitable separation – a separation which she envisaged at times tearfully but with enough resignation never to be tempted to resign from the sovereignty of those promised 'Estates'.

For the last few months she took an interest in the soon-to-be-abandoned child's education, which she was now so determined must be one hundred per cent Austrian, as she stressed in answer to a query on the subject from the duchess of Montebello with whom she was still keeping up a close correspondence: 'You ask me what I mean by, *I want him brought up in the traditions of my country*. I'll explain it. I want him to be in every way a German prince, loyal and courageous. I wish him when he attains manhood to serve his new country. It will be his accomplishments, his spirit, his chivalry, which will make his name, for that which he has by birth is not, unfortunately, very reputable . . .'

With this in mind, and encouraged by her father, Marie Louise considered it time that Franz should be severed from his exclusively feminine entourage and handed over to the formative care of a tutor. Her mind was finally made up for her by Metternich who not only took the final decision, but himself appointed the tutor without consulting the mother.

His choice fell on Count Maurice Dietrichstein-Proskau-Leslie.

'A tall thin man; fussy in manner, melancholy of face. Younger brother of Prince Dietrichstein, he belonged to the high nobility. He had fought under Mack in 1798 against the French. Retired with the rank of major, very wealthy, he had devoted himself to the arts. His home was one of the most refined in Vienna. He gave magnificent concerts; Beethoven was often there.'

His ideas regarding Franz's upbringing coincided with those expressed by Marie Louise in her letter to the duchess. 'It will be necessary,' (he himself wrote to Marie Louise) 'to exclude everything that could remind the prince of his life up to the present moment. One guards a clear enough memory of one's childhood, that is to say of the age at which the prince now finds himself, that one may fear that, in view of what he is being told these days, the time will come when he will think sadly of the life he might have been able to lead. Above all, one must avoid giving him exaggerated ideas regarding the qualities of that race to whom he no longer belongs, ideas which might stay with him in his years of maturity.

'It seems to me that the prince, for whose education I am to have the honour of being responsible, ought to be considered as of pure Austrian descent and educated German fashion.

'Such an education deserves most careful study. Many of his precociously sensitive tendencies should be moderated, many of the ideas implanted in his mind should gradually be effaced, without making him suffer or wounding his self pride more than is strictly necessary.'

Marie Louise agreed wholeheartedly; with the exception of Madame Marchand, the night nurse, the female staff were given notice to leave within the month. Even Madame Marchand, *Chanchan* as Franz called her, did not long survive the purge. Accused of Bonapartist chatter, she too left Vienna on February 25th 1816, her place being taken by an under-tutor, Captain Foresti. Shortly afterwards, a third tutor was added, Mathias von Collin, a specialist in Teutonic history. The de-Bonapartism team was complete.

On December 12th, Marie Louise's birthday and almost three years to the day since Napoleon's tumultuous return from Russia, a weary, mud-bespattered traveller arrived at the Schoenbrunn. It was Adam von Neipperg. He had covered the distance from Venice to Vienna in three days.

The year 1816 marked a further turning-point in Marie Louise's existence. It was the beginning of a period of almost total happiness, the only truly happy period of her life, which was to last for thirteen years, till von Neipperg's death on February 22nd 1829.

On his return to Vienna, von Neipperg found himself very much *persona grata* in court circles. Marie Louise was almost hysterical with delight to see him back. She was determined, if humanly possible, that they would never be separated again. There had been rumours of the highest diplomatic posts being offered the victor of Tolentino, but again Marie Louise produced one of her rare streaks of mulish obstinacy combined with deliberate spells of nervous exhaustion, to batter her father into making a formal promise that von Neipperg should be at her side when she went to take up residence in Parma.

In this Metternich was her ally. Von Neipperg's defeat of Murat had had an extraordinary effect on the Viennese. The one-eyed field marshal was the popular hero of the day. The very aura of romance enveloping Murat – the dashing, devil-may-care, handsome, happy warrior in his brilliant uniforms, galloping on every battlefield of Europe at the head of his dreaded cavalry – not only with the French but with France's enemies, only seemed to enhance his own reputation as the man who had destroyed this myth of invincibility. So great, in fact, was his popularity that Metternich was very happy to think of him a comfortable distance from the capital. The chancellor did not relish the idea of a possible rival, and he knew that nothing was more fickle than the sentiments of the masses, no memory more short-lived. Von Neipperg installed in Parma, it would be a question of 'out of sight, out of mind'.

At Metternich's residence, the Belvedere Palace, von Neipperg was received on December 14th with the gushing affability that in another might have fringed on the obsequious. He had been appointed, the chancellor told him, grand chamberlain to the duchess of Parma and would also, on arrival in Parma, assume the title of commander-in-chief and the functions of both ministers of Foreign and Home Affairs. The following day Francis, passing a diplomatic veil over a mere count's liaison with his daughter and conveniently relegating his normally stern moral code to the background, addressed him as 'my very dear son' and made him a knight of the Golden Fleece and privy councillor of the Austrian empire.

Neipperg guessed that, with a little deft manoeuvring, he could set himself up as Metternich's rival. He was not interested. Appreciating life for its own sake, he had already seen too much of political intrigue's sordid machinations to wish to be further involved. Furthermore, by now – though possibly not truly in love – he had become genuinely fond of Marie Louise; was touched by the trust and devotion she made no attempt to conceal. His life had been over-full and he was past forty, and now he had no other ties.* Parma, he could see with a certain calculating practicality, offered him an unusual combination of peace and authority on a scale he had never dreamed of.

Blindly infatuated, Marie Louise abandoned discretion. One would have said that she was proud of having an accredited lover. Her uncles' disapproving airs, her sisters' pained expressions, left her supremely indifferent. She insisted, and unexpectedly got

* His wife, Teresa, had died on April 30th 1815.

268

her way, that von Neipperg should take up residence at the Schoenbrunn till the day fixed for their departure.

With the advent of 1816, the Napoleonic epoch seemed to belong definitely to the pages of history. The principal figure had disappeared from the scene into lonely, distant captivity. The Bonaparte family was settling down to thankful obscurity, retaining titles and wealth enough to provide shelter from material cares.

Caroline, a far from grief-stricken widow, still enjoyed Metternich's protection. Jerome and Catherine had taken up residence as ordinary citizens of Trieste. Another young Napoleon, son of Louis and Hortense, was only eight years old; not even the most prophetic could have imagined that one day he would rule France as Napoleon III. Two of the great military figures, Marshal Ney, prince of Moscova, and Marshal Murat, king of Naples, had fallen before firing squads. Others, notably Marshals Davout, Soult and Macdonald, were busy ingratiating themselves with the Bourbon Louis. Austria's empress, Maria Ludovica, one of Napoleon's bitterest opponents, whose influence behind the scenes had so greatly contributed to Francis's final decision to ignore treaties with France and declare war on his daughter and son-in-law, had only a few months to live. The very spirit of malevolence, it was as though, dying of tuberculosis sharply aggravated by her husband's uncontrollable sensuality, she awaited her end with grim tranquillity having accomplished her life's ambition and witnessed the 'Corsican's' downfall.

Only one person clung tenaciously to the Napoleonic legend; the four-year-old ex-king of Rome, ex-prince of Parma, ex-Napoleon II,* now simply 'Franz'. In spite of his age, the little boy displayed a will-power, a strength of character, worthy of his father. Whatever ideas his mother, grandfather or tutors might have, Franz made it clear that he did not consider himself German. To Dietrichstein's horror, he would insist on talking about 'When I was king' and on wearing French clothes.

* On June 22nd, Napoleon had abdicated for the third time. 'My political life is ended and I proclaim my son under the name Napoleon II as Emperor of the French,' It was purely a matter of form, legalising Napoleon's departure. Even so, this 'on paper' reign lasted 15 days, till July 7th, when Louis XVIII reoccupied the Tuileries.

Dietrichstein countered by impounding all his French toys – especially those which happened to be marked with an N, bees or an eagle – any book mentioning France or referring to French history, and the decorations bestowed on him at birth, the grand cross of the legion of honour and the iron crown of Italy. The French language was declared taboo, supreme hardship since till then 'Franz' had spoken only French. Scene after scene followed, with Franz bellowing, 'I *don't* want to be German. I want to be French!'; scenes ending frequently with a beating administered – with the emperor Francis's permission – by the outraged, exasperated Dietrichstein.

Marie Louise worried – but not overmuch – about her son's future. She took it for granted that he should be submitted to a 'male' discipline, and was able to persuade herself that in an exclusively German environment it would not be long before the process of de-gallicisation were completed. For the sake of form, tinged with a moment's sadness, she wrote to Dietrichstein: 'This separation will upset me as much as anything that has happened in recent years. However,' (she continues complacently) 'it's all for my son's good, so I mustn't really complain. Provided he grows up virtuous and amiable that is all that is needed to make me happy, and I know that entrusted to your care he cannot fail to do so.'

At last, on March 7th, after a few tears that soon dried, she left Vienna, heading south for Italy, von Neipperg, in his official capacity as chamberlain, beside her in her carriage.

A week previously, she had written to the duchess of Montebello: 'I think I would die of grief but for the fact that I count on seeing him' (Franz) 'again in a few months.'

In actual fact, more than two years were to go by before she would see her son. Even then she made the journey half-grudgingly. Not only was she enchanted by her miniature world over which she and her lover ruled so benignly that she could not leave it without extreme reluctance, but in going she was tearing herself away from a very dearly loved being: a daughter, her first child by Adam von Neipperg, christened Albertine Maria.

That day, March 7th, it must also have seemed to Metternich that one of his policy's few loose ends had been neatly tied up. From the moment of taking over the direction of his country's destiny, he had exploited the young Marie Louise as a political instrument, a pawn in his power game, not once according her the slightest consideration due to the least of human creatures. In marrying her to a man she had been brought up to fear and hate, he gained the precious time to rebuild from national ruin and re-arm. When the hour came to launch out in the 'war of revenge', he had no compunction in tumbling the young empress from the throne on which he had set her. The imperial edifice destroyed, he then set out to wreck the marriage instigated by himself and with such success that, this early March day, Marie Louise was on her way to her vassal duchy, a prisoner of her own infatuation; the once 'little king' was a prisoner, his gallic leanings being whipped out of him; the former 'ogre', a slowly dying man, on a wind-tormented, South Atlantic rock.

Not only had Bonapartism been destroyed – Metternich was not worried by the impotent minority who occasionally uttered cries of '*Vive l'Empereur*', waved tricolours, read and distributed crudely nostalgic imperial doggerel – but Austria had been restored to her 'rightful' place as leader of continental Europe; and that with a minimum loss of life. In the 1813, 1814 and 1815 campaigns, Russians, Prussians and British had done most of the fighting, though Austria claimed the prestige due to the fact that an Austrian – Prince Schwarzenberg – had been allied supreme commander. Indeed, what further proof could be demanded of Austria's dominant position than that it was at Vienna allied monarchs and leading statesmen had gathered to impose the Europe of coming generations.

There is no doubt that Clement Metternich was one of Europe's most masterly statesmen. He was also a great Austrian; a great patriot. His Macchiavellianism was directed to his country's, not his personal, glory. His was not a parochial mind; his horizons were spread. Yet, though he invariably looked to a future beyond the immediate, his vision, at the supreme moment of Napoleon's first abdication was – tragically for Austria – bounded by spite, by hatred of Napoleon as a man. It was a hatred that never died, not even when Napoleon lay buried in St Helena's Geranium valley, which flared up, searing, in the fanatical outburst: 'Once and for all! Excluded from all thrones!' when there was talk of Franz, *l'Aiglon*, becoming newly-independent Greece's first king.

Blinded by animosity, the chancellor did not pause to weigh up the enormous advantages that a France, ruled first by an Austrian regent, then by a half-Austrian emperor, could not fail

271

to represent for Austria, maintaining her in a diarchy no one would have dared to challenge. Still less was he able to foresee that, thirty-three years later, another Napoleon, offspring of Louis' and Hortense's unhappy marriage, would revive imperial glories, embark in turn on his 'war of revenge' whose seed would flower on the battlefields of Magenta and Solferino, which in turn would set in motion Austria's fatal downhill slide, never to be arrested.

In the meantime, Marie Louise and Neipperg were hurrying towards the Venetian frontier which they crossed on April 12th. It was Marie Louise's first journey south, and she was seeing this new landscape at one of the year's most lovely moments.

The soft countryside, the profusion of spring flowers, a serenely blue sky, enchanted her. She thrust the past resolutely from her mind. There was only the idyllic present.

The visit to Venice was an unqualified success. Marie Louise forgot about ailments as, inexorably, she made the round of churches, art galleries and museums. She would have liked to have stayed longer but news arrived that the empress Maria Ludovica, then in Verona in the mistaken, prevalent belief that sunshine was the panacea for all lung troubles, was dying.

Neipperg by her side, she hurried to Verona, remaining there for the few days left to Francis's third wife. Of these last days Marie Louise, who was incapable of lasting malice – except, paradoxically, where the husband she had once loved was concerned – wrote to Madame de Montebello: 'Even if I hadn't had any affection for her previously, I would have now, for she is so resigned, so gentle, so angelic that even the most indifferent of beings could not fail to be touched . . .'

On April 17th, after the empress's death and while her body was being driven north to Vienna for the state funeral – after which, in its bronze coffin, it would repose in the Capucin church crypt beside that of the great Maria Theresa and her husband – the journey to Parma was resumed.

Marie Louise entered her estates two days later, crossing the Po by a bridge of boats near the town of Casalmaggiore, and spending that evening and the night in the château of Colorno, a bare seventeen kilometres from the city of Parma itself. Colorno charmed her – it was under the assumed title of duchess of

Colorno, it may be remembered, that two years previously she had made the journey to Aix, had seen von Neipperg riding up to her carriage.

The château which, sadly, today has been taken over by the government as a mental home, was often spoken of as a miniature Versailles. Built by order of the Farnese, it had been considerably embellished by the Anjou Bourbons: 'They say that when the regent's daughter, Charlotte d'Aglae of Orléans, visited Colorno, she said that if she had had a similar park in her duchy of Modena she would not be weeping for Paris and Versailles. Everywhere (in the château) conformed to French taste and was of extreme luxury. One could imagine nothing more sumptuous than the magnificence of its marbles, its tapestries, its furnishing and pictures. Marie Louise was enchanted . . .'*

Not rising till late, the young duchess made her formal entry into Parma beneath a glorious early-spring sun at three o'clock in the afternoon of the following day, the 20th.

In full field marshal's dress uniform, von Neipperg, superbly mounted, rode beside her carriage. She herself was radiant, and her happiness infectious. The crowds, which to begin with had gathered sullenly to stare at yet another Austrian-imposed foreign ruler, began to wave, then to cheer, in a spirit of genuine welcome. By the time the procession reached the Duomo, famous for its collection of Coreggios, where the bishop was waiting to receive her at the foot of the steps before the singing of the *Te Deum* preceding the new ruler's occupation of the ducal palace, enthusiasm had reached such a pitch that acclamations rivalled the clamour of Parma's sixty churches' madly pealing bells.

'The enthusiasm of my reception' (she wrote to Francis) 'only made me all the more determined to do everything in my power to make the country happy.'

It was significant, and typical of the new Marie Louise that, on von Neipperg's advice, her first official decree was to cut short the official celebrations and request that the money thus saved be distributed to the poor.

* Raymonde Bessard, op. cit.

Epilogue

One is tempted to believe that there was something of the occult in Marie Louise's passionate determination to become duchess of Parma, an objective she pursued with a rare singleness of purpose. She must have known that Parma was synonymous with happiness. She was not mistaken. The twelve years and ten months separating her entry into the city from von Neipperg's death, was the only joyful interlude in her life.

It seems strange that – if only in moments of retrospection – she should not have felt herself diminished by her rôle of ruler of a tiny duchy after that of first lady of the world's most powerful empire. But with her the mind dominated; moral outweighed material considerations. Apart from her sensual response to Napoleon's rough but ardent love-making and her blind schoolgirlish passion for the duchess of Montebello, she was uneasy with the French; incapable of being other than gauche in their court circles, equally incapable of forging a sentimental link with the French people.

In Parma she cherished the feeling of being virtually at home. She was Austrian; Austrian ruler of an Austrian state. The fact that the Parmesans were foreigners as the French had been was of no consequence. They were a subject race but of the great Austrian family. She felt for them much of that very genuine love that inspired many a colonial governor in the days of the *Pax Britannica* in his dealings with those he administered in the name of the king emperor. She wanted to help them, to make their life agreeable, to encourage them to bask in the warmth of her heartfelt benevolence.

In this she was most ably abetted by von Neipperg who saw clearly that under normal circumstances, with the exception of a few fanatical nationalists, a contented people with no positive grievances could be counted upon to remain peaceful. Thus the complete harmony of the ideals of both virtual and nominal rulers brought a spell of peace and prosperity to the Parmesans, marked contrast with the miseries of the inhabitants of Austria's other Italian states. It was entirely due to Neipperg's judicious handling of affairs that when the first insurrections broke out in 1820, not a single incident was reported from Parma.

The following year the duchy of Modena was the scene of a bloody revolution bloodily suppressed by the late empress Maria Ludovica's brother, Ferdinand – who Marie Louise had hoped to marry to save her from Napoleon's clutches* – known ever afterwards as 'The Butcher of Modena'. Subsequent trials of surviving ringleaders disclosed the presence of prospective trouble makers in Parma, but when these individuals were arrested they were treated with a clemency unknown in those days. Only one death sentence was pronounced, immediately commuted by Neipperg to a term of imprisonment. Metternich was furious, but Parma remained at peace.

Marie Louise's feelings were admirably summed up in a letter to her old *ayah*, Madame de Colloredo – 'I have a beautiful country, a delightful household and worthy people . . . all my care and attention is devoted to the best means of relieving the miseries of this people whom I wish to make happy . . .'

Her private life, however, though serenely happy, was far from uncomplicated.

Early in 1817, she had to admit that her increase in girth could no longer be explained away in court circles as the result of excessive gourmandise. On the pretext that her delicate constitution demanded a prolonged rest from affairs of state, she retired to her country home at Colorno. Though the nightmarish circumstances of the young Napoleon's birth had made her terrified at the prospect of a second pregnancy while empress of France, she was enchanted by the thought of this child of Neipperg's which was born with no attendant complications on 1st May 1817; a daughter christened Albertine Marie. This happy, though unconventional, event caused a certain amount of amusement in court circles but 'after nine days it was forgotten'†. Marie Louise and Neipperg adored their offspring and it was the latter who had the genial idea that the little girl's family name should be Montenovo, Italian translation of Neipperg.

* see page 36.
† According to Raymonde Bessard, 'It (the child's birth) gave rise to much gossip. But with their natural charm and indulgence, the Italians did not reproach their sovereign, on the contrary she became all the more dear to them because of this proof of her human frailty. . .'

In her state of euphoria, Marie Louise seems to have forgotten the forlorn ex-king of Rome in Vienna, but his existence was brought back to her notice abruptly the following year when she received an official document to the effect that on her death Parma would pass to the ex-queen of Etruria's son, Charles Louis. As for the ex-king of Rome, Francis – with Metternich's blessing – had decreed that the name Napoleon was to be dropped in favour of Francis Charles (popularly abbreviated to Franz), that he would be given the title of duke of Reichstadt, addressed as Serene Highness, and rank after the princes of the imperial family and the archdukes.

Marie Louise took this arbitrary disinheritance of her son calmly as can be seen from her letter to Victoria de Crenneville – 'My son's fate has been decided. As you know, I have never wished either thrones or vast territories for him. All I pray is that he may become the richest and most agreeable *individual* in Austria . . .'

She might then have dismissed the matter complacently, but it was the family-minded Neipperg who insisted that it was her duty to make the journey to Vienna, a journey which she made eventually – and most unwillingly – in the late summer of 1818. The meeting with her son gave her a temporary sense of guilt and deeply moved her.

Even though the Austrian court had been enlivened by Francis's fourth wife, the youthful Charlotte of Bavaria, known after her marriage in November 1816 as the empress Caroline-Augusta, who made a great fuss of the little boy invariably addressing him as Franzchen, Marie Louise could not close her eyes to the fact that the child's life, spent almost entirely in the company of his three conscientious, but humourless, tutors, was bleak in the extreme. She promised that she would come to see him more often, but conveniently for her own peace of mind was able to persuade herself that his misfortunes were entirely due to the sins of his father. Another visit to Vienna was planned for the following year. It never took place, for on August 8th 1819, her second child by Neipperg, a son, William, was born.

But she was back in the summer of 1820 accompanied by von Neipperg and his son Gustav, about the same age as Franz. The two-month interlude was a great success. Gustav and Franz played happily together. Francis, ignoring Neipperg's non-imperial blood and the irregularity of his relationship with an

276

imperial archduchess, received the couple regularly at the palace treating Neipperg, of whom he was genuinely fond, as one of the family.

Next year, May 5th 1821, Napoleon's miserable existence as an exile came to an end. Although perfectly aware of Marie Louise's infidelity, he himself maintained a show of loyalty to the very last. As she blamed the father for the son's misfortunes, so he insisted that she had been the victim of coercion bordering on sheer physical restraint, going as far as to commit to paper the gallant untruth – *J'ai toujours eu à me louer de ma très chere épouse, Marie Louise; je lui conserve jusqu'au dernier moment les plus tendres sentiments*. And amongst his innumerable legacies he bequeathed her his heart which the Corsican doctor Antommarchi was ordered to deliver to her in person. One wonders whether in a morbidly sentimental way he was not trying to kindle some feelings of remorse.

Marie Louise was in her box at the opera enjoying a performance of Rossini's *Il Barbiere di Siviglia* when news of her husband's death reached her. She was honest enough not to put on a false show of grief. She wrote both to the duchess of Montebello and Victoria de Crenneville that her husband had 'never been unkind' but made it quite clear that she was shedding no tears for him. There arose, however, the delicate question of mourning – the defunct was, after all, legally the duchess of Parma's consort – a question neatly solved by Neipperg who himself composed the notice which appeared in the Parma Gazette of July 24th:-

Because of the death of our august sovereign's most serene husband – which occurred on the island of St Helena May 5th – Her Majesty, the gentlemen and ladies of the court, the members of her household, will be in mourning tomorrow July 25th till October 24th inclusive. The mourning will be divided into three classes; from July 25th to September 4th, first class mourning; from September 5th to October 2nd, second class mourning; from October 3rd to October 24th, third class mourning.

This 'solution' met with Vienna's unanimous approval.

There was one major reason why Marie Louise did not regret her husband's death. From the beginning she had been happy enough to be von Neipperg's mistress, yet she longed for the cloak of legality especially since the birth of their children. She wanted marriage as a further proof of her love for this man so much her social inferior, and also, one suspects, remembering his past Don Juan reputation – not unmerited – as the tie to bind him to her irrevocably.

At that time in Italy, Baron de Menéval has stated in his memoirs, getting married presented no technical difficulties. It was enough for a couple to inform a priest of their desire to be united in holy wedlock, make their confession, receive absolution, for the ensuing ceremony to be legal without the presence of witnesses.

Taking advantage of this, Marie Louise and Neipperg were married secretly in September 1821 by the bishop of Guastalla, after the birth of a second daughter on August 15th – ironically the date of Napoleon's birth – who, however, died when only three months old.

For the next eight years, Parma could be described as a model state. Rulers and subjects alike were happy. Public money instead of finding its way into private pockets was spent on such things as bridges over the Taro and Trebbia rivers, a hospice for orphans, a home for old people, hospitals, and to the delight of the music-loving Parmesans, a magnificent new opera house.

Visiting Parma during this period Lamartine wrote – 'The princess (Marie Louise) considerably more at her ease in her limited state than at a former epoch, is infinitely more amiable and more witty than ever she was in Paris . . . the count de (*sic*) Neipperg, the favourite and husband of the archduchess, is at the head of all administrative services. He is a man of intellect and sound good sense. He runs the archduchess's court and the government of her little states brilliantly. Although a foreigner and a favourite, he is both esteemed and loved . . .' Even the caustic Chateaubriand judged Neipperg to be *Un homme de bon ton*.

In the summer of 1828, sad to leave their children if only for a few months, Neipperg and Marie Louise made another of their duty visits to Vienna. It was sad also, that owing to the secrecy surrounding their birth, the children should be obliged to refer to their father and mother as *Il Signore* and *La Signora*. A letter from Albertine written during the absence in Vienna – '*Mia cara Signora,* I'm very upset this morning because I have no news of the *Signore* . . .' – makes pathetic reading.

As usual all went smoothly in Vienna; affectionate reunion with Franz, with Francis, with the family, but for Marie Louise these festivities and quiet family gatherings were overshadowed by concern. Though at first she could not bring herself to admit it, Neipperg's health was becoming increasingly precarious. The least exertion exhausted him. He was being attacked continually by sudden bouts of violent fever and frightening spells of breathlessness.

On the way back to Parma, in the September, the journey was broken in the king of Sardinia's castle at Aglie. Neipperg's condition worsened. He was suffering from dropsy and an acute heart condition. He should not have moved, but, longing to see his children again, he insisted, finally reaching Parma on October 29th.

Marie Louise could no longer deceive herself; her adored husband had no chance of recovering. 'I feel myself dying with him,' she wrote miserably to Francis.

There was a slight rally in January, cruel in that it raised false hopes soon dissipated by a serious relapse quickly followed by the one-eyed general's death the night of February 21st/22nd 1829.

Marie Louise was completely unmoved by her first husband's passing, but her passionate grief at the loss of Neipperg inspired even her detractors with pity. The state funeral was grandiose though marred by a barbaric act; the shooting of Neipperg's favourite charger after his master's body had been lowered into his tomb. The sculptor Lorenzo Bartolini executed an impressive marble tombstone, strange mixture of the classical and modern style and on which the unfortunate charger figures prominently, today to be seen in Parma's Santa Maria della Steccata church. Yet despite the imperial court's acceptance of Neipperg during his lifetime, and this only added to the widow's grief, a strict injunction was received from Vienna that there was to be no *official* mourning.

The great turning-point in Marie Louise's life had been reached. It is possible, probable even, that she knew that with Neipperg's death happiness would for ever remain a memory. Yet cognizant of this sad verity, it is unlikely she was fully aware of the sorrows, troubles, and crises that were to assail her in the course of the next few years.

*   *   *

Fond father though he had become, Francis had no confidence in his daughter's capacities as a ruler while Metternich still looked upon her as scatterbrained and inept. Neipperg was therefore replaced in his capacity of ruler-de-factor by Baron Werklein. The baron was bigotted and suffered from a marked *bara sahib* complex *vis-à-vis* the Italians. The Italians he considered were 'natives' who should be 'kept in their place'. From the day of his arrival in Parma, he took it upon himself to undo all the good done by Neipperg and destroy that very genuine affection which, for twelve years, had existed between Marie Louise and her people.

Though Francis had gladly tolerated the fact that Neipperg was his daughter's lover – 'I will never have a more genuine friend than Neipperg' he was in the habit of saying – he had no idea, incomprehensible as this may seem, that the two Montenovos had been born before the morganatic marriage. Metternich on the other hand was perfectly *au courant*, and with a peculiarly refined cruelty, forced Marie Louise to reveal the truth. The pious Francis, who nevertheless had killed three wives in lawful wedlock as a result of his exaggerated sexual exigencies, was appalled.

My very dear Louise,
    I have received your letter of the 18th March and at the same time Prince Metternich has spoken to me. I cannot hide from you the profound distress which overwhelms me confronted with this situation about which nothing can be done and yet which, in the eyes of God and the world, cannot be excused . . . To conclude, I admit frankly that I am deeply distressed. But I am your father and my love for you entails my absolution. Try in the years to come to make some reparation for your sins by fulfilling your duties . . .

Marie Louise also dreaded the reactions of Franz whom she was now beginning to appreciate, a handsome eighteen-year-old youth already revealing flashes of his father's genius. 'He', (Franz) Francis had written in a second letter, 'has not asked me anything about the children (Montenovos) and if he does I will not mention their age. Unfortunately these details cannot be hidden from him permanently and you run the risk that when he does discover the truth, those tender and sacred sentiments which he cherishes for you will not be enhanced . . .'

We do not know what the young Reichstadt's 'sentiments' were. Already he had learnt something of diplomacy. If he was disgusted as, worshipping the memory of his father, he may well have been, he hid the fact, writing: '. . . my own sadness is doubled by the realisation of your sorrow. The memory of the defunct and of his kindness to me will always rest engraven on my heart . . .'

This letter was a balm to Marie Louise. She did not know that her son had remarked bitterly to his great friend Count Anton Prokesch von Osten: 'If Josephine had been my mother I should not be in the miserable situation in which I find myself today.'

It was not long, however, before fears of a more material nature began to assail the widowed duchess of Parma. Once again Italy was seething with Austrianophobia, but this time there was no Neipperg to act as an antidote to all but the most exacerbated nationalism. Werklein's tyranny and flagrant injustices had, on the contrary, nagged even the normally unpolitically minded citizens to make common cause with the insurgents.

Fighting broke out on February 10th 1831.

In the city of Parma itself there was a hint of comic opera about the revolution, for the mob seething round the palace was shouting '*Viva Maria Luigia*' at the same time as 'Death to Werklein'. The baron who was no hero fled at the first sign of trouble. The bewildered Marie Louise, bitterly hurt by this revolt on the part of her beloved Parmesans despite the fact that deputations from the mob begged her to stay, slipped away to Piacenza waiting there till an Austrian corps had restored order, not returning till August 8th.

Werklein had, in the meantime, been replaced by baron Marschall who, though as bigotted and anti-Italian as his predecessor, was a man of integrity. It was unfortunate that he cordially detested Marie Louise whom he looked upon as an incarnation of Messalina. Relying on Metternich's backing he treated her with the maximum of severity and the minimum of respect, going as far as to rebuke her to her face for not having a portrait of her husband Napoleon – he was not prepared to accept the marriage with Neipperg – in her private appartments.

As if these tribulations were not enough, letters from Vienna in the early months of 1832 brought news that her elder son was seriously, if not dangerously, ill. To begin with, these warnings made little impression. As a form of self-defence she had fallen back on the hypochondria of her years as France's empress, forgotten during her prolonged honeymoon with Neipperg. Letters to friends were filled with long dissertations on her own symptoms interspersed with such brief references to her son as 'God be praised he has recovered his appetite' and 'Thank heaven his chest is clear even though his liver does seem to be affected'.

It was only after the most urgent messages stressing that Franz had only a short time to live arrived in Parma that, accompanied by Marschall, she set out for Vienna via Trieste arriving at the Schoenbrunn palace the afternoon of June 24th. There she found her son lying on a camp bed in the same room that his father had occupied when, at the height of his glory, all Austria including Austria's emperor who, however, like the pliant bamboo had weathered the hurricane, had been at his feet.

The short life of the young Napoleon could be summed up as one of general sorrow, brief moments of exaltation, long periods of unrelieved frustration.

In spite of the furious Germanisation of his education directed by Count Maurice Dietrichstein, he had grown up in the aura of his father's glory. Threats and punishments, often corporal, had been unable to prevent him becoming steeped in the romance of Napoleon's meteoric career. Only the study of the art of war, military history, interested him. By the time he was fifteen he knew every detail of every intricate manoeuvre leading up to his father's great victories.

It is possible that if Franz of Reichstadt had been able to escape from Austria and not been marked by a fatal illness, he might have made his mark on the international scene. Even the most rabid anti-Bonapartists have admitted that his intelligence was remarkable. All his ambitions were concentrated on rising to the highest rank in the army, not through birth but, like his father, through personal genius. By the time he was eighteen he could inspire the admiration of men considerably older than himself and, at the same time, was attractive to women. From the age of sixteen – when he looked at least four years older – he had been accredited with a number of gallant liaisons, notably with countess Nadine Karolyi and the ballerina Fanny Elssler. One may have reason to treat these rumours with scepticism, but there is little doubt that, brief as was his life, it was brightened by a genuine love, eagerly reciprocated, for the Bavarian princess Sophie, the empress Caroline-Augusta's half sister and wife of the archduke Francis Charles, the emperor's second son.

Sophie at the time of her marriage was pretty and gay. She soon found that she and her husband had nothing in common. Starved of the love she longed for, she showered all her affection and repressed passion on Franz despite the fact that he was six years her junior. There is no reason to doubt that the father of her first son, Franz Josef who was to become emperor in 1848 and reign till 1916, was her husband, but there is perhaps more than a possibility that Corsican blood ran in the veins of her second son born only a few days before Reichstadt's death and whose life was to pursue a course almost as tragic as that of his putative father, ending before a firing squad at Queretaro in 1867.

Franz had been granted a commission in the Tyrolean *chasseurs* in 1828 at the time of Neipperg's last visit to Vienna; but, much to his disappointment, his doctor, Staudenheim, decided that he was not physically fit enough to stand up to the routine even of a garrison regimental life. He suffered from fits of giddiness, bouts of fever, a tendency to catch coughs and colds which Staudenheim diagnosed as the result of a precocious puberty.

In 1830, Staudenheim died and was replaced by Giovanni Malfatti di Monteregio who confirmed his predecessor's diagnosis, adding that 'the prince's principal weakness is his liver'. It was not in fact till 1831 that Franz was considered fit to assume his military duties and allotted a military household consisting of General Hartmann, Captain Standeiski, and Captain the baron Charles von Moll. The general and Standeiski were good soldiers but totally unsuited for such a position; von Moll, on the other hand, became a firm friend during the closing months of Reichstadt's life.

This much-longed-for military career was brutally cut short. The winter of 1831 Franz's health deteriorated rapidly till by the spring of 1832, even Malfatti was forced to admit that his patient was dying of tuberculosis.

Franz's death has been described graphically and in great detail in von Moll's diaries which at the same time throw considerable light – even though prejudiced – on Marie Louise's mentality at this tragic moment. Speaking of her arrival on June 24th, he says; 'He (Reichstadt) was sleeping when the archduchess made her entry into Schoenbrunn. Half past five was striking as we received her at the foot of the staircase . . . as the archduchess left the salon, General Hartmann introduced me to her. She said that her son had often mentioned me in his letters to which I replied that I was glad the prince had deigned to acknowledge my wish to be of service to him. As far as I could see the archduchess was trembling; she seemed to be feverish. With Countess Scarampi on her right and Marschall on her left she moved towards the prince's apartments and in the ante-room begged the general (Hartmann) to accompany her to the invalid's bedside. Malfatti was already there with the prince. As soon as he saw his mother the prince raised himself up, stretched out his arms towards her, and they embraced; the archduchess, her voice trembling with emotion said that she had come to look after him and that he must call her whenever he wanted her, whatever the hour of the day or the night, and that he must be quite frank also and tell her if he wanted to be left alone. The archduchess stayed for three quarters of an hour. When she left she did not seem to be worried any more, whereas the prince, to judge by his appearance and his pulse, was still deeply affected . . .'

The following day, after spending twenty minutes with her son during the course of the morning, Marie Louise drew von Moll aside: 'She said amongst other things that Malfatti was a danger-ous individual; she was resigned to the loss of her son and now he was trying to persuade her that this resignation was premature. As she said that "she was going to lose the prince" she burst into tears . . . He (Reichstadt) did not get up till four o'clock in the afternoon and then only for his bed to be made, and he remarked that bed was getting the better of him; three times during the day he'd tried to get up but hadn't the necessary will power to do so. He asked for a chicken wing then went back to bed after a few nibbles.'

The weakening Reichstadt became increasingly fretful. He complained to von Moll that he was being worn out by too many visits (including those of his mother) and that the only person he really wanted to see was the archduchess Sophie who was expecting her second child to be born any day.

On June 27th 'the archduchess' was distressed by 'the prince's taciturn mood' and two days later there is the entry – 'The prince slept well and did not cough much but for three days he has been terribly weak. His voice is hoarse and he has great difficulty both in walking and talking: this fact seems to presage the catastrophe for the very near future . . .'

For the rest of the month there are several further references to Franz's apparent unwillingness to see too much of his mother, and of Marie Louise's apparent satisfaction at not being called upon to perform the arduous and often unpleasant duties of nurse.

In July, succeeding entries in which details of the ravages the disease was causing to Reichstadt's frail body are not for the squeamish, there is only one bright moment, all too brief – 'At six o'clock this morning (July 6th) the archduchess Sophie gave birth to a boy.* The prince was very gay and in a happy mood. The weather was fine and he was able to spend several hours on the balcony . . .'

It was a short rally. When his mother came to see him at eleven o'clock the next morning – 'the prince began to complain again about the heat. He kept calling out "Air! I must have air!" Unable to stand the sight of his suffering, the archduchess left after staying only a quarter of an hour . . .'

Exceptionally hot weather set in, and Franz was able to be carried into the gardens for brief periods. Marie Louise was usually with him on these occasions but they seem to have had little to say to each other. Even this was beginning to be too much. By July 13th: 'He (Franz) was unable to keep his head upright on his shoulders, it shook like that of a paralytic (sic). Malfatti had the courage to say, "We're making no progress and the great heat is upsetting all my provisions." Towards one o'clock the heat was so great that he (Franz) had to leave the garden. Back in his room he said bitterly "I'm dying! Nothing now can give me any pleasure. You have no idea how exhausted I am." I did my best to comfort him by saying that to the best of my belief there was nothing really wrong either with his head or his stomach.'

The 19th, von Moll noted that it was unlikely 'the prince' would last till August 1st. There was also a caustic remark about Marie Louise's brief visit: 'Every three words she kept bringing the conversation round to the subject of one of her chamberlains whose name was on her lips every few seconds. Making enquiries later I found that she was talking about a certain Marquis Sanvitale, the favourite of the day and who is supposed to be

* Archduke Maximilian Ferdinand Joseph, future emperor of Mexico (see page 283).

marrying her daughter*. Oh! The amazing youthfulness of this woman's heart.'

Next day von Moll had an extraordinary conversation with Baron (whom he always calls 'General') Marschall which he recorded in full. To begin with, showing a total lack of sentiment, Marschall discussed with von Moll the list of gifts he proposed to offer – with Marie Louise's approval – to the members of Reichstadt's military household on the latter's inevitable approaching decease.† He then launched into a violent attack on Marie Louise herself after first slanging the late Adam von Neipperg whom he described as 'an immoral person delighted with himself who had encouraged the archduchess to act in a way that was beyond the bounds of human decency'. He then went on – 'The princess's lack of modesty was such that when her secretary Richter showed her police reports and indecent satires composed about her, instead of blushing she was amused by the vulgar expressions. As to her utter heartlessness, she was giving ample proof of this at the actual moment showing no interest whatsoever in her son; in Trieste where she had been accompanied by her lover, he had had to make a scene in order to oblige her to continue on the road to Vienna . . . No sooner had she arrived in Vienna than her one idea was to procure presents for her lovers, favourites, the nurses and midwives. . . By now through force of habit, the princess looked upon the carnal act as a natural function of the body to be satisfied with the same regularity as other natural functions . . .'.

There was, perhaps, a certain amount of truth in Marschall's accusations. Marie Louise had inherited her father's sexual appetite. Napoleon's latin ardour had in itself been enough to make her forget her fears and prejudices overnight. With Neipperg she had known perfect love, perfect harmony. His death plunged her into an abyss of grief from which it seemed there was no return to the light. She probably sought relief from her misery in indiscriminate sex as others might have sought precious mental oblivion through alcohol or drugs. At the same time Marschall was so prejudiced that he had no hesitation in making the wildest

* Albertine Montenovo married Count (not Marquis) Sanvitale in October, 1833.
† Von Moll was to receive 2,000 florins, a thoroughbred riding horse with saddlery, something (unspecified) chosen from Reichstadt's personal effects, and to be decorated with the Knight's Cross of the Order of Parma.

accusations. This is particularly evident in his remarks about Count Sanvitale. Marie Louise adored and was adored by both Albertine and William, and it is quite unthinkable that she would have had as a lover a man destined to be Albertine's husband. On the other hand there is no doubt that morally and to a certain extent physically, the sad years following immediately on von Neipperg's death were her darkest hour.

Two days later, Sunday July 22nd, the twenty-one-year-old duke of Reichstadt's life came, mercifully, to a close. 'At quarter to four (in the morning)' wrote von Moll 'the *valet de chambre* woke me to say that the prince's end was near. I rushed to his room. He was groaning "I'm dying. I'm dying." The assistant doctor Nickerl and Lambert the *valet de chambre* raised him on his pillows which seemed to calm him for a moment, but he was soon more agitated than ever and murmured "Fetch my mother" . . . I ran to wake up Countess Scarampi, the archduchess mother, Baron Marschall, Standeisky and the archduke Francis, and at the same time sent messages to General Hartmann and Doctor Malfatti. I went to meet H.H. the archduchess and accompanied her to the dying man's room, she was trembling convulsively and offered me her arm so that I could support her. When she reached the bedside she stayed staring fixedly at her son; she was incapable of saying a word. The prince looked at her and it seemed as if a silent message passed between them . . . I went to look for the archduke Francis then ushered in the priest. He was a young priest assisting at his first death bed. All through the ceremony (sic) he behaved calmly and tactfully. All those present fell on their knees, the archduchess leaning against an armchair . . . the archduchess looked as if she were going to faint and was helped onto a chair, but soon after went down again onto her knees. The death agony was calm and gentle; a few minutes after five o'clock the prince moved his head several times though without the usual contractions of a dying person; his breathing stopped; Malfatti got up, I followed his example and we leaned over the bed; the prince was dead. The archduchess raised her head after a few moments; she made an effort to get up but once more collapsed onto her knees. The generals Hartmann and Marschall led her out of the room . . .'

Even if hypochondriacal, Marie Louise was never hypocritical. Her subsequent letters afford further proof of Marschall's vicious exaggeration when he ranted about her 'heartlessness': 'My very dear papa' she wrote to Francis 'my poor son died at ten minutes past five. Heaven answered my prayers and granted him a peaceful death . . .' And to Albertine: 'God has destroyed much of the happiness that was mine; He alone knows why and I can but respect His will, but it is with you dear children that I will seek the only possible consolation still left for me . . .'

She was only forty-one years old, but in little more than three years sorrow has wrought such changes in her that the archduke Francis was heard to remark 'She's a toothless old hag, decrepit, a veritable ruin!'

Albertine's wedding took place on October 28th 1833 and her daughter's happiness, to which was added the pleasure of being a grandmother when the young Alberto di Sanvitale was born on November 25th 1834, seems to have restored a measure of sanity to Marie Louise's tortured mind. She was attempting also to find a place for her son William within the rigid circle of Viennese society. This was a far from easy task, but at last by pestering Metternich with an avalanche of letters at the same time needling her father, she managed to obtain for him a commission in the infantry. For William this marked the beginning of a brilliant career. Leaving the infantry, he rose like his father to be an outstanding cavalry general and colonel-in-chief of the Vienna Dragoons. On July 10th 1864, the emperor Franz-Josef conferred on him the dignity of prince of Montenovo. His son Alfred by his marriage with Countess Stephanie of Batthyani-Strattman, became grand master of ceremonies during the empire's final years.

With Albertine married and William in Vienna, Marie Louise was pathetically lonely in her palace. Though mellowed by years and a life overcrowded with emotion, she still longed for intimate male companionship. She was not hoping to re-discover the passion of her life with Neipperg, but merely somebody to share her loneliness.

Soon after Reichstadt's death, Baron Marschall had been replaced by Count Charles de Bombelles, younger son of the marquis de Bombelles, a widower with two children. The position of grand master of the court of Parma had been offered him by Metternich. Though not at all enthusiastic, he had accepted for the simple reason that he was exceedingly money-minded and the post carried with it a basic salary of 12,000 florins a year.

Bombelles arrived in Parma on August 8th 1833. Though he had none of Napoleon's ebullience or Neipperg's polished seduction, he had great distinction. Max Billard describes him as 'a noble figure of middle height, rather haughty and glacial giving the impression of being both serious minded and reserved. A remarkable rectitude, a careful manner of speech, rigidly self controlled, extreme prudence in the handling of his affairs and above all a great correctness of manner, made this gentleman of exalted birth a man well above the level of ordinary mortals . . .'*

Craving stability, thrown into his company all day and every day by the routine of government, it was almost inevitable that Marie Louise should begin to think of him as the person to fill the void in her life left by Neipperg's death. 'My health is greatly improved' she wrote to her father 'I haven't felt so well for four years as I do at the moment. Also I cannot thank you enough for your choice of Count de Bombelles. From every point of view it would be impossible to have a better majordomo . . .'

A letter to Victoria de Crenneville dated Christmas day 1833 went still further – 'I congratulate myself more and more each day on the acquisition (sic) we have made with M. de Bombelles; he is a real saint and is delightful in society . . .'

On February 17th 1834, Marie Louise – it is generally considered that the proposal came from her – and Count Charles de Bombelles were married secretly. Why secretly is a mystery. There was no legal obstacle to the marriage, and Francis having accepted one non-royal son-in-law was hardly likely to have objected to a second, especially as the count was one of Metternich's men. In spite of this the marriage was only revealed when Marie Louise was on her deathbed. De Bombelles never mentioned the fact as far as one can gather, and unlike most of the leading personalities of the day did not keep one of those revealing diaries, such a boon to future historians.

The true relationship existing between the duchess and her

* Bombelles' humourless pomposity was well illustrated by an anecdote current before his first marriage with an heiress, Mlle de Cavanagh. Not being well off the count did not allow sentiment to influence his business acumen. 'An income of 20,000 "*livres*" or no Bombelles' he is supposed to have said to his future mother-in-law. When the latter pointed out that this was quite a considerable sum especially as he was making no contribution, he replied in a voice of thunder, 'What do you mean? AND MY NAME!'

principal adviser soon becoming obvious caused a certain measure of severe criticism, in turn repeated in Vienna, but though well aware of this Marie Louise and her third husband continued, obstinately, to guard their secret, and the only person in whom she might have confided, her father, died the following year.

The emperor Francis's death was the last great sorrow in Marie Louise's life. Her love for him was sincere and had never faltered even at the moment when for the sake of political expediency he had thrown her into 'the Ogre's' arms. Strangely enough this love was shared by the Austrians despite the fact that the early years of his reign were associated with humiliating defeats, loss of territory and foreign occupation, and the tears shed by so many of the vast silent crowd the day of his funeral were heartfelt. 'He, (Francis), was the person I cherished most in this world' was Marie Louise's tribute. 'He was everything to me, father, friend and counsellor in all my difficulties . . .'

The daughter survived the father by only twelve years; twelve years which compared with the previous storms that had swept her existence were comparatively uneventful. In fact it would be difficult to imagine a more staid couple than the duchess of Parma and Count Charles de Bombelles.

Rather than wildly happy, Marie Louise was contented; contented to let the days slip past at a placid rhythm. Mentally she had reached the corner of the fire, carpet slipper, stage. She rose at nine, attended to her correspondence at eleven, then dressed. There was a formal *déjeuner* at midday to which guests were invariably invited. It was a brief meal for at one o'clock the duchess liked to return to her apartments either to play the piano or paint. At three o'clock, a walk, a quiet hack, or a drive in her carriage returning, according to the season, at five or six. Dinner* at nine o'clock, afterwards a game of billiards, chess or back-gammon; bed punctually at midnight.

It was a pity that these last years were marred by a last scandal,

* Her appetite was distinctly robust as shown by the following menu of a typical family dinner served by her staff of French and Austrian chefs.

Le potage Semel – Knödeln
Le boeuf sauce raifort au bouillon
Les cervelles frites aux choux–raves
La grive aux petits croutons
Le poulet roti
Croquettes du Roy.

one which in all probability was completely unjustified and set in motion by the bragging of an unscrupulous adventurer whose 'indiscretions' were seized upon eagerly by the press, and especially by the French press.

All her life Marie Louise had been a music lover and an accomplished musician. In Parma it delighted her to play the role of patron of the arts. Nicolo Pagannini was a great favourite at her court and in 1844 received the Order of San Ludovico de Parma. The young Giuseppe Verdi was also encouraged and offered the duchess the score of an opera he had written based on the story of Falstaff, but evidently not that of his last great masterpiece composed over forty years later.

It was natural, therefore, that when one evening a young tenor, a Frenchman Jules Lecomte, sang magnificently at the opera, he should be invited to the palace on several occasions. Lecomte, however, was not only a singer but a writer with an exaggerated sense of fiction and publicity. Well aware of the duchess's past reputation, he decided that he would make out that he had been the lover of the ex-empress of France. 'Yes, my dear friend' he wrote to his publisher 'I am Napoleon's successor; this may not be realised in the Tuileries, but I have realised it here in Parma. I sang for Marie Louise; she asked me to stay for supper; the supper lasted all night. When I woke in the morning I could imagine myself to be the emperor!'

In view of Marie Louise's age, Bombelles's moral fibre and the evolution in her character, Lecomte's boast was almost certainly the child of his calculating, not over honest, mind. Yet it was, and still is, widely believed, particularly in France. So much so that one can read '. . . *Si Bombelles était mort, nul doute que ce confrère* (Lecomte) *ne fût devenu le quatrieme mari de l'ex-impératrice; il fut, du moins passagèrement, le successeur de Napoleon . . .*'

Armed rebellion broke out again in Italy in 1847, and this time Parma was not spared as it had been during Neipperg's lifetime. Bombelles, however, whose 'reign' can be said to have steered a midway course between Neipperg's liberal principles and Werklein's blind tyranny, was equal to the situation. The troubles were suppressed quickly and harshly, restoring an uneasy peace.

Marie Louise was in Bad Ischl. Bombelles assured her that there was no need for her to come back and that everything was well in hand. Thankfully she carried on to Vienna where she spent a few days with William, happily embarked on his military career, visiting also the Habsburg family vault in the Capucin church to say a prayer beside the coffins of her father and her son.

Late November she returned to Parma, and almost immediately was confined to her bed with a feverish cold accompanied by all the signs of pleurisy. However, on December 9th she felt well enough to go for an afternoon drive; but the same evening after dinner began to shiver and complain of severe chest pains. The doctor (Fritsch) was called immediately and prescribed bleeding. Marie Louise listened patiently then said calmly – 'You will see. I shall never get up again. Within eight days I will be carried away.'

The 12th, her birthday, she sent for the bishop of Parma to hear her confession and give her communion. After this she devoted her time to drawing up the final details of her Will. She was sinking fast and on the 16th, in the presence of her family – with the exception of William somewhere en route between Vienna and Rome – received extreme unction. While the prayers for the dying were being read she retained an extraordinary serenity as though death, far from being an enemy, were a friend whose coming she welcomed.

In the meantime William, hearing that his mother was *in extremis*, left Vienna at the gallop accomplishing the journey to Parma in record time. Setting off from the Austrian capital on the 15th, he was in Parma on the 18th. He was just too late. Napoleon's second empress, von Neipperg's widow, wife of Count Charles de Bombelles had breathed her last at ten minutes past five the evening of the 17th.

Marie Louise had lived long enough to atone for her errors, frailties and lapses from the 'straight and narrow' paths of duty and morality. Even the most indulgent could not pretend that she had not, despite the circumstances, been guilty of the most callous betrayal of Napoleon or that as a mother she had not failed her first child as dismally as she had failed her first husband.

Yet – if one may exclude the comparatively brief period when sheer grief drove her into the mire of a numbed nymphomania – from the moment she set foot in Parma, she was a changed character. To Neipperg she was a devoted wife after being an equally adoring and faithful mistress. She was an exemplary and loving mother to their children. Her loyalty to Bombelles, despite the Lecomte scandal, cannot really be doubted. Had she lavished one iota of the care, compassion and interest that she bestowed on the people of Parma on her French subjects, popular opinion in France might well have raised an unsurmountable barrier to the Bourbon restoration. For though she was a foreign ruler, representative of a generally hated foreign occupying power, the sense of personal loss penetrating the hearts of most Parmesans exists after the lapse of one hundred and twenty-three years.

It would be difficult to imagine a more touching individual tribute than Parma's Glauco Lombardi museum containing a unique collection of Marie Louise's personal belongings, jewels, dresses, portraits, letters, canvases painted by her own hand, souvenirs of every stage of her life. But still more moving is the fact that the kindly memory of this Austrian, by the hazards of history automatically the enemy, has survived wars, factional strife and blind idealogical fanaticism.

As recently as 1969 in the preface to his book *Maria Luigia*, the author Ferrucio Botti speaks of the '*riconoscenza che ogni parmigiano deve alla sovrana incomparabile che fu gioia e vanto dei padri nostri*,*making it clear that in his opinion and in that of most of his fellow citizens of Parma, the mortal remains of the *sovrana incomparabile* should be brought back to the land where she not only loved but was loved.

* ... recognition that every citizen of Parma owes to his incomparable sovereign who was the joy and boast of our fathers.

Bibliography

Principal works consulted:

Aubry, Octave	*Le Roi de Rome.* Plon 1937.
Aubry, Octave	*Napoleon.* Flammarion 1936.
Bainville, Jacques	*Napoleon.* Fayard. 1931.
Bessard, Raymonde	*La vie privée de Marie Louise.* Hachette 1951.
Billard, Max	*The marriage ventures of Marie Louise.* Nash 1910.
	The private diaries of Marie Louise. Murray 1922.
Botti, Ferrucio	*Maria Luigia, Duchessa di Parma Piacenza Guastalla.* Casa editrici Luigi Battei (Parma) 1969.
Castelot, André	*L'Aiglon.* Le livre contemporain. 1959.
Cecil, Algernon	*Metternich.* Eyre and Spottiswoode 1933.
Delderfield, R. F.	*Napoleon in love.* Hodder and Stoughton 1959.
De Marcelay, Jean	*Le meurtre de Schoenbrunn.* Correa 1953.
Dixon, Pierson	*Pauline.* Collins. 1964.
Dupont, Marcel	*Napoleon en campagne de Wagram à Waterloo.* Hachette 1955.
Lacroix, Désiré	*Le Roi de Rome.* Garnier Frères (undated).
Lenotre, G.	*Croquis de l'épopée* (La Petite Histoire). Bernard Grasset. 1932.
Ludwig, Emil	*Napoleon.* Modern Library (New York) 1924.
Madelin, Louis	*Lettrés inédites de Napoleon à Marie Louise* (1810 – 1814). Editions des bibliothèques nationales de France. 1935.

Masson, Frédéric	*Marie Louise, Impératrice de France.* Société d'Editions Littéraires et Artistiques (Paris) 1910.
Oddie, E. M.	*Marie Louise, Empress of France, Duchess of Parma.* Matthews, 1931.
Pedrotti, Pietro	*La fin du Roi de Rome* (diaries of Baron von Moll). Editions du milieu du monde 1947.
Robiquet, Jean	*La vie quotidienne au temps de Napoléon.* Hachette 1943.
de Saint Amand, Imbère	*Marie Louise and the invasion of* 1814. *Elba, and the hundred days.* *Happy days of Marie Louise.* (the three volumes published by Hutchinson 1891.)

Memoirs of:
Baron de Menéval
Caulaincourt, Duke of
 Vicenze
Captain Coignet   Bibliothèque nationale (Paris).
Constant
Hortense, Queen of
 Holland
Savary

Index